Doing Time

Prison Experience and Identity
Among First-Time Inmates

Contemporary Ethnographic Studies

Jaber F. Gubrium, *Series Editor*

Doing Time
Prison Experience and Identity
Among First-Time Inmates

by RICHARD S. JONES
Department of Social and Cultural Sciences
Marquette University

and

THOMAS J. SCHMID
Department of Sociology
Minnesota State University-Mankato

JAI PRESS INC.
Stamford, Connecticut

Library of Congress Cataloging-in-Publication Data

Jones, Richard S. (Richard Statler), 1953-
    Doing time : prison experience and identity among first-time inmates / Richard S. Jones and Thomas J. Schmid.
        p.   cm. — (Contemporary ethnographic studies ; vol. 9)
        Includes bibliographical references and index.
        ISBN 0-7623-0543-6 (alk. paper)
            1. Prisoners—United States—Attitudes. 2. Prison psychology—United States. 3. Imprisonment—United States. I. Schmid, Thomas J. II. Title. III. Series.

    HV6089.J66 2000
    365'.6'0973—dc21   00-035606

CONTENTS

LIST OF FIGURES

LIST OF TABLES

Preface

This book is a case study of people in exile. The specific group of people we studied were inmates in a maximum security prison and, in this sense, our work also can be accurately classified as a "prison study." Most of our analysis is about how inmates experience prison, and our final chapter both contextualizes our research within the prison literature and examines the implications of our work for correctional policy. The experience of being exiled, however, is phenemonologically grounded in where one is "exiled from" more than in where one is exiled to. Much of our analytic focus and theoretical interest, accordingly, lies beyond the prison world. We address this point in our final chapter, where we discuss what inmates' experiences suggest about larger questions of cultural adaptation and identity transformation.

This book is also the product of an extended and rewarding collaboration between the authors that covered a number of years. As we describe in a methodological appendix, our relationship began as professor and student and evolved rather suddenly into an ethnographic research team of "outside" and "inside" observers of the prison world. This collaboration resulted in a number of articles, three of which have been incorporated into this monograph. Chapter 3, which presents our analytic model, is a somewhat abbreviated version of an article that originally appeared in Volume 2 (1990) of *Perspectives on Social Problems*, edited by Gale Miller and Jim Holstein. We are grateful to Gale and Jim for both their editorial assistance and their critical comments on this paper. Chapter 7, on inmates' adaptation strategies, is a modification of an article originally published as "Ambivalent Actions: Adaptation Strategies of First-Time, Short-Term Inmates" in Volume 21 (1993) of the *Journal of Contemporary Ethnography*. Patricia and Peter Adler, who edited the journal during that time, were wonderfully helpful and supportive of this work. Chapter 8, on inmates' identity work, is a revision of "Suspended Identity: Identity

Transformation in a Maximum Security Prison," which originally appeared in Volume 14 (1991) of *Symbolic Interaction*. This article, which was subsequently reprinted in a number of anthologies, was greatly assisted by the editorial guidance of David Maines.

With these three articles serving as rather expansive windows on our analysis, we were generally satisfied that our research had been suitably presented to the sociological community, and we moved on to other interests and projects, including a few that we conducted together. Periodically, however, we would find ourselves discussing this prison study as unfinished business. We did so in part out of a growing appreciation that the view of prison life presented in our analysis—and made possible by the combination of our methodology, our research questions, and the particular circumstances that initiated our study—was indeed a distinctive one. We understood that there were not only descriptive details but also analytic elements of prison as lived experience that we had not yet developed. Our view of the project as unfinished business was reinforced by the encouragement (and sometimes gentle cajoling) of others who insisted that there was more of this story to be told. Chief among these was Jim Thomas, whose support and assistance over the years we gratefully acknowledge. We also wish to express our appreciation to Jim Holstein and Jay Gubrium, whose sociological work and editorial advice helped us to reexamine our ethnographic data through a broader experiential framework.

Recognizing that there was a larger story to be told and actually telling it, of course, were quite different matters, and we found that task of expanding our analysis into a full monograph did not mesh easily with our other commitments. The opportunity to tell this story arose through a sabbatical that Tom received from Minnesota State University, Mankato—a good portion of which was devoted to the preparation of this manuscript. It is probable that *Doing Time* would never have been completed without the writing time provided by this sabbatical, and we are grateful for it. Our writing process during this period, ironically, became a mirror image of our earlier fieldwork process: just as Rick had once prepared fieldnotes and sent them off to Tom for review and suggestions, now Tom was mailing manuscript chapters to Rick for his comments. Through numerous mailings, telephone calls, e-mails, and revisions, we were eventually able to put together this "full version" of our prison research.

Throughout this process, we were inspired, supported, encouraged, and tolerated by those who count the most. For all of these things and more, Tom would like to thank Sharon, Caitlin, and Jake. Rick would like to thank Kathy, Zachary, Jonah, and Adnita.

Although we cannot acknowledge them personally, we would nonetheless like to thank the Warden and Associate Warden of "Midwestern" prison, for their no-strings-attached approval of our research interviews. At the top of our list of acknowledgements are the men who shared their prison experiences with us during the fieldwork and interview phases of our research. In this study, as in most sociological research, there are no immediate benefits from research participation, except for whatever intrinsic value might be found in an opportunity to tell one's story. We are grateful to these men for their acts of sharing, and we have tried to honor our ethnographic commitment to render their words and experiences accurately in our analysis.

Chapter I

Introduction

It looked nasty. But I didn't want to go inside. It was scary; it is ... you come inside, all of a sudden the light ... the sun, was gone. The door shuts, and all you got around you is concrete and metal. I mean it was ... scary. It was like, well you know this is going to be my world for a while.... It's an awesome feeling.... It was a nightmare come true.

These words describe a border crossing. They are the words of a maximum security inmate, recalling his arrival at prison on the first day of his sentence. Once this man walked into the prison, and the gate shut behind him, he left behind his familiar social world and entered a new and unfamiliar one, with its own social organization and culture. And, at least for a time, his experience was "a nightmare come true."

The man who uttered these words, in a research interview, had never before viewed a prison "up close," but he had already devoted considerable time to building an image of what a maximum security prison was like. He had a far more personal reason for doing so than most of us do, but his initial conceptualization of the prison world was not really very different from that held by most people in our culture, and it was based on more or less the same cultural resources.

Prisons are part of our shared social landscape. The idea of prison is in our vocabulary and, therefore, in our lives. We know that prisons exist and we know why they exist. Most of us know where a prison is located, and we have probably driven by a prison wall. We use "prison" as a metaphor for our lives or those of other people. We have viewed films or television shows about prisons. We undoubtedly have glanced at a newspaper article about correctional policies or prison incidents, and we may be aware that our country is in the midst of a historically unprecedented era of prison-building. We know about prisons as part of our general cultural awareness of our own society.

Our knowledge of prisons, to be sure, is not very detailed. We cannot really know what it means to be confined in a prison for months or years.

1

And even if we have toured a prison or know someone who works in a prison or has served a prison sentence, we cannot really know what kind of people prisoners are. But we nonetheless do have some ideas of what prisons are like, and these ideas—these *images*—enable us to talk about prisons with others—to argue that modern prisons are too soft on criminals or that inmates become hardened criminals within our prisons; to assert that existing prisons should be improved, that new prisons should be constructed or that too much money is already being spent on prisons; to bemoan that judges are becoming too lenient with convicted felons or to protest unreasonably long sentences.

How do we derive these prison images? They are not derived from any single source, but we have only a limited number of sources on which to base them. One of these is fictional accounts: novels, films, and television entertainment programs that unquestionably color our ideas about prison. We know that the events depicted in fictional accounts may not be entirely accurate representations of what takes place in real prisons, yet we do not know precisely how they differ. This distinction becomes further clouded in films or television programs that are "dramatizations" of actual events. We do not try to evaluate the accuracy of every film we see, of course; nor do we derive our imagery from any single representation. Nevertheless, it is possible to formulate images of prisons and prisoners on the basis of fictional accounts alone.

Journalistic accounts are another, more direct, source of our prison images. Many of these are prosaic (and often ignored) reports on political appointments, correctional spending, prison overcrowding, the construction of new facilities, or policy analyses. Periodically, we encounter (and pay greater attention to) more sensational stories on prison disturbances or incidents, which typically present prison life as an anarchical world of random violence and heinous atrocities. Prisoners, by extension, are portrayed as violent people who are capable of enormous cruelty to their fellow inmates and to the world at large. In these written or broadcast accounts, riots and other forms of prison violence may be attributed to the kind of people who are sent to prison or to substandard conditions, poor management, or other factors. Regardless of how these things are explained to us, however, the underlying image is usually the same: a prison is a separate world, segregated from the larger society, for the confinement of violent criminals; violence is constantly just beneath the surface of the prison world, and it can erupt at any time.

It is from these kinds of fictional and journalistic sources that we create our cultural imagery of prison as a distant world of random violence. This imagery is at once both disturbing in its inhumanity and reassuring in that it locates this inhumanity elsewhere, outside the boundaries of our own social world. We may be horrified by some of the stories we see about prison life, but we are rarely surprised by them, because they fit our imagery. Nor are we particularly intimidated by them, because they occur in a separate world, far removed from our everyday lives. And while we understand that our actual knowledge of the prison world may be highly limited, it is nonetheless adequate for our needs, which are also quite limited.

We would expect this same level of knowledge to be inadequate for someone who must directly participate in the prison world—for example, for the man we quoted at the beginning of this chapter. And yet, because he had never been to prison before (and perhaps also because he had never associated with people who had been to prison), he initially crossed the border between the outside world and the prison world with a personalized and intensified version of the same prison imagery that most of us hold. This level of knowledge *was* inadequate for his needs, which is why he pronounced his border crossing as "a nightmare come true."

Doing Time describes life in a maximum security prison as experienced by first-time prisoners. It is an examination of how participants in the prison world arrive at a fuller understanding of this world through direct experience. Three interdependent research questions guide this study. Our first question is: how do first-time, short-term inmates *orient* themselves to the prison experience, and how do their orientations change during their prison careers? This question involves a consideration of the prison images that these individuals bring with them as they begin their sentences and the changes in imagery that take place as a result of their actual experience in prison. We expect that the inmates' imagery will influence how they respond to the prison environment. Our second question is, therefore: how do these inmates *adapt* to the prison world, and how do their adaptation strategies change throughout their prison careers? Our third question is: how does prison *induce changes in inmates' self-definitions* throughout their prison careers? This question is also concerned with imagery, including the relationship between prison images and self-images.

PRISON AS A SOCIAL WORLD

A person who begins a prison sentence does in fact enter a "social world" (Unruh 1980; Strauss 1978; Shibutani 1955) that is organized differently and centered around a different culture than the everyday world left behind—a passage that is acknowledged by the prison culture distinction between the world of "the joint" and the outside "free world." Vague cultural images of prison are an insufficient basis for participation because they are stereotypic. They may contain some truth but they also obscure truth; they are imprecise, emotionally laden, and therefore flawed guidelines for action. In this respect, the experience of going to prison can be compared to other cultural border crossings, such as a refugee's sudden and involuntary immersion into another society—a point of comparison we will return to later.

There is, to be sure, more enlightening information available on the prison world. Sociology has produced an extensive literature on the social organization and culture of prisons and on the processes through which inmates become socialized to prison life; we refer to this literature regularly in subsequent chapters and return to it directly in our final chapter. Undoubtedly, the most often-cited concept within this literature is that of "prisonization," which Donald Clemmer (1958, p. 299) defined, in *The Prison Community*, as "the taking on in greater or less degree of the folkways, customs, and general culture of the penitentiary." This socialization process, according to Clemmer, operates over time, first initiating the inmate into, and then making him or her part of, the inmate social and cultural system. Clemmer further noted that no inmate could remain completely unprisonized; merely being an incarcerated offender exposed one to certain "universal features" of imprisonment, which include assuming a subordinate status, learning prison argot, taking on a prison style of eating habits, engaging in various forms of deviant behavior, and developing negative attitudes towards guards. Prisoners are thus assimilated into an inmate society which places considerable importance on antisocial attitudes and behavior; within this society, prisoners show solidarity and gain status by adhering to the "inmate code." Moreover, according to Clemmer, the longer the prisoner's stay, the greater the immersion into the inmate subculture.

Following Clemmer, two general theoretical models were developed to account for inmates' adaptations to imprisonment: the "deprivation model" and the "importation model." The deprivation model essentially suggests that inmate culture is a collective response to the numerous deprivations or pains associated with imprisonment (see Sykes 1958; Goffman 1961; Sykes and Messinger 1960). Proponents of the importation model argue that the problems associated with confinement do not solely determine the extent to which inmates respond to the dictates of the inmate subculture; rather, a pre-incarceration socialization process begins to influence inmates' receptiveness to the prison social system. In more general terms, the importation model focuses on how factors external to the prison situation affect patterns of adjustment within the prison (see C.W. Thomas 1977; Irwin 1970).

Doing Time offers an alternative perspective on the prison experience. Our fieldwork corroborates much of what the traditional research on prisons has documented, but our analysis suggests a different way of understanding changes in inmates' outlooks and behavior. Rather than focusing on internal and external determinants of prison adaptation patterns, our analysis focuses instead on inmates' experiential realities and their orientations to the practical problems of everyday prison life to explain these changes. In contrast to most of the contemporary literature on prisons, consequently, we see inmates as more actively engaged in social life and social action as interpretive processes.

THE PHENOMENOLOGY OF PRISON EXPERIENCE

Our analysis of the experiences of new prison inmates draws upon a long tradition of interpretive sociological theory and ethnographic research that connects human action and intersubjective meanings (Prus 1996). The theoretical contributions of George Herbert Mead (1934) and, in particular, Herbert Blumer (1969) emphasize the centrality of meaning as a basis for human action and the need for social scientists to decipher these meanings through appropriate methods. Working within this same intellectual tradition, W.I. Thomas (1931, p. 42) introduced the concept of "the definition of the situation" to express the idea that social action is not simply a response to the environment but rather an active effort to define and interpret the context in which we find ourselves, assess our interests, and then select appropriate attitudes and behaviors:

> Preliminary to any self determined act of behavior there is always a stage of examination and deliberation which we may call the definition of the situation.... Facts do not have a uniform existence apart from the persons who observe and interpret them. Rather, the "real" facts are the ways in which people come into and define situations.... If men define situations as real, they are real in their consequences.

Situations are not inherently meaningful; rather, meaning is problematic and people create it, largely through interaction with others (Blumer 1969). Therefore, defining any situation is a process of "reality construction" through which human actors make their experiences of the world around them orderly and understandable (Berger and Luckmann 1966). Our analytic concern, stated in these terms, is with how new prison inmates define their situations, including their prison imagery, the problems they see as resulting from their imprisonment, and the activities they engage in to address these problems.

Someone who is sentenced to prison begins to prepare for the ordeal that awaits. As Alfred Schutz (1962) has noted, people experience a situation as something they are doing, as a project they are working toward in that world. Preparing for prison and then living through a prison sentence are, therefore, human activities that must be *accomplished* (Garfinkel 1967). While defining their situations and working on the practical problems of their imprisonment, however, inmates are also necessarily engaged in acts of self-definition. As Blumer (1969, pp. 536-537) notes, any extended line of human action takes place through a process of self-indications. Moreover, as Schutz has argued, a person's sense of self as working toward a goal is experienced as his or her total self (Schutz 1962; Collins 1988, p. 275). As we analyze how inmates experience and adapt to the prison world, therefore, we are also concerned with the implications of their experiences for their self-definitions.

In order to analyze and present the phenomenology of prison life, it is necessary to employ a methodology that will provide first-hand knowledge of how inmates conceptualize their experiences and extended first-hand observation of how they live their lives in prison. Our study is based on an ethnographic approach that we describe in greater detail in a methodological appendix. Briefly, we were able to achieve extraordinary access to inmates' day-to-day lives while one of the authors (R. Jones) was serving a year-and-a-day sentence in a maximum security prison for men in the upper midwestern region of the United States. With the cooperation of prison officials, we were able to capitalize on these circumstances for our research. Our initial research model was derived primarily from 10 months of participant observation data, based on a research collaboration between an "inside" and an "outside" observer of the prison world. These data were supplemented and to some extent guided by a prison journal kept by one of the authors. We subsequently extended this analysis by returning to the prison for focused interviews with an additional sample of first-time inmates serving sentences of two years or less.

PLAN OF THE BOOK

Doing Time presents an analysis of the phenomenological experience of the prison world and the consequent adaptations and transformations that it evokes. We begin, in Chapter 2, with a description of our research setting, Midwestern Prison, and of what happens to a new inmate when he first arrives at this prison. Chapter 3 introduces the basic theoretical model for this study, outlining how new inmates' experiential orientations to the prison change as they move through their prison experience. These orientations, as we demonstrate, entail something more than the beginning and ending of their prison sentences or their gradual socialization into the prison world; they are better viewed in terms of inmates' efforts to address their practical problems of imprisonment, as these problems are defined during a particular phase of their prison experience.

The next three chapters explicate the experiential orientations. Chapter 4 focuses specifically on the preprison orientation that new inmates bring with them to the institution and examines what happens to this orientation as inmates acquire direct prison experience. Chapter 5 presents an analysis of inmates' midcareer "prison orientation," which is comprised of a substantially changed conceptualization of the prison world, a redefinition of the problems imposed by imprisonment and, consequently, an altered strategy for responding to their problems. Chapter 6 examines how inmates again modify their definition of their situation and, therefore, their behavior as they begin to develop a "postprison orientation" at the end of their sentences.

In Chapter 7, we return to the fundamental question of how inmates adapt to the prison social world, while in Chapter 8 we examine the "identity work" that inmates perform throughout their prison experience. Both chapters demonstrate how changes in experiential orientation lead to changes in adaptation and identity work. Finally, in Chapter 9, we discuss the implications of our research for the social science literature on prisons, for correctional policy, and for larger theoretical issues of cultural adaptation and identity. A detailed description of our research methodology is presented in the appendix.

Chapter II

Midwestern State Prison

Midwestern prison matches the cultural image of what a prison should look like. It is an old-style "big house" maximum security institution for men (see Irwin 1980). Located about 30 miles outside of a metropolitan area, its 22–acre compound is surrounded by a massive stone wall, capped with razor wire and interspersed with seven guard towers. It stands as an architectural symbol of the idea that prison is a separate world for the incarceration of violence-prone criminals. As such, this looming structure unquestionably intimidates new inmates who are sentenced here. In the words of the inmate we quoted in Chapter 1, it is an "awesome," "nasty," and "scary" institution.

Belying its menacing architecture, Midwestern prison has a reputation among both correctional practitioners and experienced inmates as a secure and generally humane facility, with a relatively low incidence of violence. It is one of three maximum security correctional institutions for male felons in a state that consistently ranks at or near the bottom of the 50 states in terms of its rate of incarceration. During our research, Midwestern had an average daily population of 1,400 inmates, with an average sentence of 46 months. The average age during the period of our research was 32 (except in unusual circumstances, only inmates over the age of 25 are sentenced to Midwestern). Seventy percent of these inmates were white, 19 percent were African-American, 8 percent were Native American, and 2 percent were Hispanic (with 1 percent from "other" racial or ethnic groups). Sixty-four percent were incarcerated for crimes against a person, 22 percent for property crimes, and 11 percent for drug offenses.

In the first part of this chapter, we present a brief description of the facilities, programs, and services available at Midwestern prison; in the second part, we describe the procedures that are followed when inmates arrive at the institution. In both of these discussions, we emphasize those programs and activities that are most relevant to first-time and short-term inmates.

9

FACILITIES, PROGRAMS, AND SERVICES

Midwestern was built in 1914 as an industrial prison. Except for alterations necessitated by technological advances and additional programming, its physical plant has remained unchanged since that time. Figure II.1 provides a map of the principal buildings and open spaces within the prison walls. The main structure is constructed in a telephone pole design, with a central corridor extending from the administrative offices, and wings extending at right angles from this corridor. The wings closest to the administrative offices are the main cell halls (A and B), each of which contains 512 individual cells. Further along the corridor are two smaller cell halls (C and D), a recreation area, laundry area, auditorium, dining hall, and kitchen. The health services and mental health units are in a separate building. Across a roadway from these structures are five industries program buildings and the facilities maintenance buildings. Outside the prison wall, there is also a separate Minimum Security Unit for selected inmates who are close to the completion dates of their sentences.

The internal prison buildings are based on traditional maximum security architecture, featuring concrete walls and floors, iron bars, and very few windows. These characteristics result in an austere, institutional atmosphere, which becomes charged with an undercurrent of ambient noise as the cacophony of sounds from cellblock and work activities echoes off the hard surfaces of these buildings. The cell halls are constructed on an "inside cell" design, in which cellblocks are located back-to-back in the center of the hall, and there is a open corridor (or "flag") between the cellblocks and the outside wall of the cell hall. Each cellblock has four tiers of cells, and a narrow walkway runs the length of each tier. In the cellblocks and other facilities, there are prominent observation posts for security staff. Inmates are subjected to continual surveillance by correctional officers at these posts, by officers who circulate throughout the population, and by others who monitor inmates with closed-circuit television equipment. Inmates are counted several times each day and are frequently subjected to personal searches as they circulate within the institution.

Programming Operations

Cell Hall A has been divided into three sections. One-half of the hall (256 cells) is devoted primarily to the Reception and Orientation Unit (R & O), to which all incoming inmates are initially assigned. In addition to inmates assigned to R & O, this half of the cell hall also houses inmates who are assigned to one of the institution's vocational training programs and a few inmates who are employed in the kitchen and dining hall. The other half of Cell Hall A is subdivided into two separate units. The "A Aca-

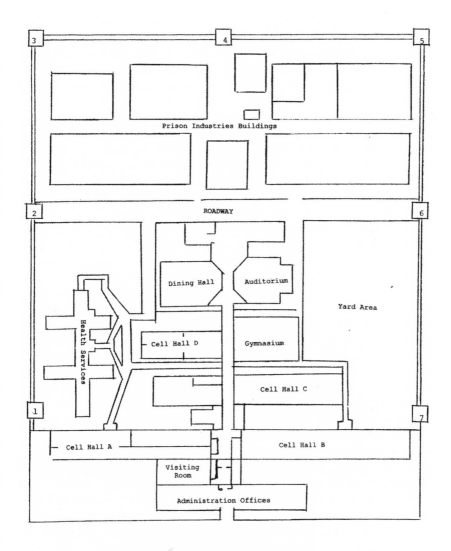

Figure II.1. Midwestern Prison

demic" Unit, which contains a quarter of the hall's cells (128), houses inmates assigned to the Heart of the Earth Education Classes, an educational program for Native Americans. Also residing in this unit are parole violators and other inmates who are on "temporarily unassigned" status, inmates on "unassigned idle" status (i.e., those who choose not to work or participate in a prison program), and a number of inmates who are classified as having a high escape risk. The remaining quarter of Cell Hall A (128 cells) is the "A Segregation" Unit. Inmates convicted of, sentenced for, or being detained for violating institutional rules are housed here, as are a small number of inmates on "administrative segregation" status.

Cell Hall B, which remains as it was originally constructed in 1914, houses inmates of various description and institutional status. Its principal occupants are inmates assigned to work in the institution's industry programs, laundry workers, commissary workers, inmates assigned to the clerical and janitorial work in Cell Hall B, and inmates who have been given "permanent idle" status by the prison's Chief Medical Officer because of medical or physical conditions that do not allow work assignments.

Cell Hall C, which was originally built to house 36 segregation inmates, is the base for Atlantis, Midwestern's chemical dependency treatment program. Included in this program is a therapeutic community made up of approximately 30 inmates. In addition, unit staff provide overall supervision to various groups and programs concerned with chemical dependency, including Narcotics Anonymous and Alcoholics Anonymous groups and treatment groups conducted twice weekly at the Minimum Security Unit. They also provide intake orientation and diagnostic services for inmates entering the institution, and coordinate a university course on chemical dependency education.

Like Cell Hall A, Cell Hall D has been divided into three sections to accommodate various programs. One of these is Insight, an educationally oriented program that includes up to 26 inmate students and five inmate staff in its academic division and up to 10 inmate students and one inmate staff in its vocational division. The academic division is for inmates who are both working and pursuing a Bachelor's degree on a full-time basis. Inmates in the vocational division participate in a six-month, full-time training program in computer programming.

The Skills Development Unit in Cell Hall D is a work and treatment program that includes up to 60 inmates who have voluntarily or involuntarily entered protective custody status. The objective of this program is to return inmates to the open population, based upon specific and individually negotiated treatment goals. The third program in Cell Hall D is the facility's sexual education and evaluation center, a 36-bed residential unit that provides a six-month psycho-educational program for sex offenders. This program offers group therapy, self-help support groups, and classes designed to assist sex offenders in stopping future violent or sexually abusive behavior.

Employment

Midwestern prison maintains a "full employment" policy, which means that any inmate who wants to work has a job. This policy is feasible because of the extensive industries program that Midwestern has operated since its inception in 1914. This program, which is housed in five buildings within the prison compound and additional facilities outside of the wall, is designed to provide inmates with a close approximation of employment in the outside world. There are a variety of jobs available, the majority of which are related to the manufacture of agricultural equipment in the metal products factory. Inmates work seven-hour days, in such job classifications as welder, machinist, metal fabricator, or assembler. Other industries operations include a foundry, sheet-metal shops, machine shops, wood shop, welding shops, furniture assembly shops, paint shops, an auto and truck body shop, and an engineering and design division.

There are also a limited number of jobs in private industry programs located within the prison; these jobs often pay higher wages (which can equal the federal minimum wage) but generally stipulate specific qualifications, including job skills brought into prison or gained through a prison training program, or other restrictions. Other jobs, mainly maintenance or clerical positions, involve working directly for the prison. These positions have lower wages, usually paid as a flat daily rate, but they are also less time-consuming, typically requiring two to seven hours a day.

The money that inmates earn from their jobs is managed for them through a system of inmate accounts. Each inmate has two accounts, a spending account and a savings account. The first three paychecks that an inmate receives are put into his spending account. After that, his paychecks are split, with half going into spending and half into savings until the inmate has $100 in his savings account. This sum constitutes the inmate's "gate money," which will be given to him on his release from prison. Once he has achieved this amount, all of his wages go into his spending account unless he stipulates that he wishes to continue depositing half of them into his savings account. Inmates may draw upon their spending accounts through a voucher system, for purchases made in the prison canteen or ordered through the prison commissary.

Special Services phone call

In addition to its academic, vocational, treatment, and work programs, Midwestern offers a range of social services and related programs to its inmates. Special services include an assessment committee, a due process unit, and a variety of specialized programs. The casework staff both inside the institution and on the Minimum Security Unit are considered brokers of available services.

The Health Services staff includes one full-time physician, three registered nurses, two dentists, and one dental assistant. Health Services is responsible for maintaining inmates' medical records and providing 24-hour health care coverage. Psychological Services offers mental health and emotional assessments of all inmates when they arrive and subsequently at the request of staff. Staff in this unit also provide short-term therapy during emergency or crisis situations, and referrals to other treatment facilities.

The Recreation Department provides recreation and leisure programs and activities for the entire inmate population, sometimes bringing in outside volunteers to provide expertise in recreational activities. There is a large two-story gymnasium, with a main floor court large enough for three cross-court games of basketball to be played simultaneously; at the rear of this court is a station at which inmates can check out basketballs, footballs, frisbees, and other recreational equipment. The basement of the gymnasium, which is accessed by stairs located outside the main court, contains three specialized locations that are often intimidating to (and avoided by) new inmates: the weight room, a boxing ring, and a music room. The prison yard, which is about the size of two football fields, can be entered directly from the gymnasium or from a separate entrance on the central corridor. Included in this area are a softball diamond with bleachers along both base lines, a tennis court, handball courts, and a walking track around the perimeter. In the winter, a skating rink is created for broomball. Organized recreation activities include intramural teams in softball and broomball, exhibition softball games between outside and inside teams, and a club football team that plays (and regularly loses to) small college junior varsity teams. The recreation department also sponsors movies, music, and similar activities in the prison's theatre-auditorium.

The Education Department is designed to serve the educational needs of the inmate population. It offers vocational and academic testing and counseling services, vocational and academic study programs, college courses, creative arts courses, library services, and on-the-job training. It also helps to enroll qualified students in out-of-institution programs.

The Religious Services Program has a resident Chaplain Director for all religious programs in the institution. The chaplaincy role is adapted to the skills, interests. and discipline of the individual chaplains. The chaplains also serve as religious brokers for civilian groups of various denominations. There are 17 different religious groups active at Midwestern prison.

Outside Contacts

Contact with the outside world is possible through three different avenues: letters, telephone calls, and visits. The prison has a relatively liberal policy regarding mail privileges: an inmate may send or receive as many letters as he chooses. Mail that is sent into or out of the prison is examined by prison officials for contraband but is not censored or read for content. Mail is distributed to inmates in their cells Monday through Friday, following the afternoon cell count and prior to their evening meal.

Inmates may also make, but not receive, telephone calls. A limited number of telephones are available in the cell halls for local calls, and each cell hall has one telephone designated for long distance calls (which must be collect calls, placed by the desk sergeant). There are usually long lines of inmates waiting to use the telephones, and time limits, which are enforced by the inmates themselves, are placed on the length of phone calls.

An inmate is allowed to have 12 visitors on his visiting list and is allowed 12 hours of visiting per month. To place someone on his visiting list, the inmate must first send that person a visitor's clearance form (which asks for the name of the prospective visitor, and his or her address, relationship to the inmate, and prior criminal record). After this form is completed and returned to the prison, it is reviewed by prison officials. Once a visitor is cleared, prison officials notify the inmate, who then notifies the visitor. The inmate is allowed to add or remove persons from his visiting list whenever he desires.

The institutional visiting procedures sometimes present difficulties for inmates. When visitors arrive at the prison (an inmate may have up to four visitors at one time), they have to register at the information desk at the main entrance to the prison, specifying the name of the inmate to be visited. Visitors are then asked to take everything out of their pockets and walk through a metal detector. After this has been done, the inmate is informed of his visit over a loudspeaker (e.g., "Jones, 109908, you have a visit"); when he hears his name called, he reports to the visiting room. Visiting hours are from 1:00 pm to 9:00 pm Tuesday through Sunday, so an inmate might be in the cell hall, at a work station, in a recreation area, or at any number of other locations when he is called for a visit. At some of these locations, the noise level can be too high for an inmate to hear his name being called, so he cannot report for his visit; although such incidents are infrequent, they are a source of great frustration for both inmates and visitors when they do occur. Once an inmate does hear the announcement, he reports to the visiting room, where he removes his rings, wallet, and identification card. He is then frisked, a procedure intended to prevent him from passing contraband, especially cash, to his visitor. After a visit has ended, visitors leave by one door and the inmate by another. The inmate is then strip-searched for contraband, after which he returns to his cell block, work station, or activity.

Visits typically last an hour but can be as long as two hours unless the visiting room is too crowded. The prison's visiting room has a number of features that are designed to create a pleasant atmosphere, including brightly painted walls, a carpeted floor, and a play area with toys and games for children. These features are offset, however, by other factors that are designed to enable the security staff to maintain control of this space. Thus, chairs are formally arranged in straight rows, and the room is usually so crowded that it is impossible to avoid hearing other inmates' conversations. Privacy is further curtailed by a visiting room guard stationed on a raised platform and additional guards stationed behind a two-way mirror. Visiting is regularly disturbed when guards rush over to an inmate, to enforce visiting room rules or to terminate an inmate's visit because they suspect that contraband has been passed between visitor and inmate.

Minimum Security Unit

The Minimum Security Unit (MSU) is available to 94 inmates who have good work and behavior records and who are nearing their release dates. This program is intended to prepare inmates for their returns to the outside world by providing them with a nonsecure residential environment and gradually introducing them to greater contacts with the outside world. We describe the application process for MSU and the MSU environment in a later chapter; in this section, we outline the increased outside contacts made available through this program.

Inmates who are approved for transfer to MSU are transferred to a nonsecure residential building located outside the prison wall and are subsequently referred to as "residents" rather than "inmates." Most MSU residents must work, and most are assigned to shipping and receiving positions at the nearby prison industries warehouse (also located outside the prison wall). During nonwork hours, residents are free to enter and leave the residence at will, within certain geographic boundaries.

In contrast to maximum security inmates, MSU residents are granted an unlimited number of visitors and unlimited visiting hours. There is also greater access to telephones. Family counseling is available for both inmates and spouses, and married residents are eventually allowed to spend 48 hours together in a private residence on the prison grounds. Residents who make satisfactory progress through the MSU "step" program (based on 30-day intervals without violations of house or work rules) are eligible for temporary leaves from the institution, in the form of "special duties," and eventually, "furloughs."

Special duties are escorted outside trips that can last up to four hours. Inmates are accompanied on these trips by a guard, staff member, or volunteer (who can be anyone not on the inmate's visiting list) who has undergone Midwestern's escort training. Residents are allowed one special duty per week when they have reached Step II of the program; a Step II inmate is allowed to go on special duties devoted to shopping or church, while Step III residents are given the added privilege of going to dinner, movies, or sporting events.

A resident who has been in Step III for at least 30 days is eligible for a furlough, a three- or five-day pass away from the institution. For these leaves, the resident notifies his caseworker where he will be staying during his furlough; this information will be verified by the staff. The inmate is expected to obey all laws and the regulations of the Minimum Security Unit (primarily, no use of alcohol or drugs), and to return to the unit by a designated time. The intended purpose of these trips is to provide the inmate with a gradual reintroduction to the outside world, to give him an opportunity to reaffirm ties with family and friends, and to enable him to apply for jobs or otherwise make plans for his future.

ARRIVAL, PROCESSING, AND ORIENTATION

At the beginning of his sentence, a new inmate is typically transported to Midwestern prison by a deputy sheriff from the county in which he was convicted. What happens upon the inmate's immediate arrival at the prison depends on the time of day at which he arrives. When he first enters the prison, he is placed in a holding cell to await in-processing. If he arrives early in the day, he will have only a brief wait. If he arrives later, he may remain in the holding cell for several hours. If he arrives at night, he will stay in the holding cell only until he is strip-searched; all other processing activities will be postponed until the following day.

Processing introduces a new inmate to some of the institutional degradations that go along with any prison sentence. The first of these is a strip search, during which the inmate's clothing and body cavities are thoroughly scrutinized for contraband. He also has a mug shot taken, is fingerprinted, has a medical examination, receives an identification card, is issued prison clothing, and is asked to give additional information for his prison file.

After he has been processed in, an inmate is given his initial cell assignment, which he will retain for about a week (although the timing and length of all orientation activities is subject to some variation). All arriving inmates are housed on a ground-level cell within the Receiving and Orientation Unit of Cell Hall A. The R & O assignment enables new inmates to be segregated from the rest of the prison population, in order to protect them from exploitation from other inmates. A ground-level cell allows correctional officers to monitor the behavior of the new inmate closely.

Except for parole violators, each entering inmate (whether or not he is a first-time inmate) participates in a 28-day period of orientation to the institution and its programs. During his first week, he is allowed out of his cell only for brief periods and only for specific reasons: to shower, use the telephone, report for an orientation activity, or keep scheduled appointments with prison staff. He eats his meals with other R & O inmates at picnic tables located on the "flag" just outside of ground level cells, rather than in the prison dining hall. He is required, during this week, to participate in a battery of medical, psychological, and educational testing.

During his first two weeks, an inmate must also attend a series of 31 orientation classes, together with other arriving inmates. These classes, which range from 10 to 45 minutes in length and are held on the R & O flag, are conducted by prison staff and inmates from various departments and programs. Classes can be completed in any sequence, so an incoming inmate can begin attending classes immediately. One class focuses entirely on discipline. Inmates are given a copy of the Inmate Discipline Regulations, along with a brief lecture on several chronic problem areas that frequently result in trouble for inmates, including disobeying orders, disrupting head counts, entering unauthorized areas, interfering with staff, engaging in verbal abuse, possessing contraband, and dealing drugs.

Another class is devoted to sentence reduction possibilities, including "good time" and the "MAP contract." At Midwestern, a prisoner's sentence is reduced by five days for every month of "good time"—that is, time during which no serious infraction of prison rules occurs. The Mutual Agreement Pact (MAP) is a sentence reduction procedure through which the program review committee agrees to release a prisoner at a specified date if the prisoner successfully completes a behavior contract agreed upon by the prisoner and a prison caseworker, and approved by the program review committee. The contract may include such activities as the completion of rehabilitation programs, educational advancement, or vocational performance. The extent to which a sentence can be reduced by such a contract is defined through an established matrix, based on the severity of the prisoner's offense and a scale of demographic variables that are statistically correlated with release success. Other classes are devoted to such topics as laundry procedures, mail distribution, available educational and vocational programs, recreational opportunities, employment possibilities, and rehabilitation programs.

A new inmate will remain assigned to the R & O cellblock, and therefore separated from the general inmate population, through the first month of his sentence. After his first week, however, he is likely to be reassigned to a cell on a higher tier in the R & O Unit, leaving the first floor cells available for newly arriving inmates. This move is accompanied by greater mobility, which also means that the inmate will now be under less constant observation by guards. Following reassignment, an increasing amount of the inmate's time is spent outside of his cell, eating meals in the prison cafeteria, exercising in the gym, visiting the library, or attending weekend movies in the auditorium. Sometime during the orientation period, the inmate meets with his caseworker and begins to make decisions about participation in educational or rehabilitation programs or possible areas of employment. At the end of his orientation, he is reassigned again, to the designated cell hall for his work or program status.

The orientation program at the beginning of inmates' sentences, like the minimum security program at the conclusion of their sentences, is a well-reasoned and well-intentioned institutional effort to provide inmates with a structured transition between the outside and prison worlds. Any such program, however, can only be of limited assistance to a new inmate who views his sentence as a "nightmare come true." That inmate's early prison experience will be shaped more by the violent imagery he carries with him than by the presentations and advice he is given through an orientation program. The understanding of the prison world he derives from this imagery, the resulting problems he believes he must face, and his personal efforts to address these problems constitute an experiential transition between the outside and prison worlds. It is this transition with which our analysis is directly concerned.

Chapter III

Experiential Orientations to Prison

Chapter 2 provided an overview of the prison itself and an outline of what happens to new inmates when they enter prison and begin their sentences. The question that we begin to address in this chapter is: how do new inmates *experience* prison? As we undertake this analysis, two provisos become clear.

First, not all inmates—not even all first-time inmates—experience prison in the same way. Every inmate will approach his sentence with his own fears and expectations, emotions and preparations, problems and solutions. We cannot rely on social science research to discover or document all of the idiosyncratic variations of the prison experience. By observing a group of inmates as they progress through their sentences, however, and by talking with these and other inmates, we can begin to decipher commonalities and shared understandings in how inmates view imprisonment, in the practical problems they feel compelled to resolve, and in their attempted solutions to these problems. Second, the traditional concept of "prisonization," despite the elemental truth it contains, is an inadequate framework for understanding how inmates experience prison.

The research on prisonization, including both the deprivation and importation models derived from it, begins with the premise of a rather monolithic "prison culture" (or "prisoner culture;" see Hayner and Ash 1939) to which inmates are exposed by virtue of their imprisonment and into which they are gradually but inevitably socialized as they progress through their prison careers. We want to offer a new way of viewing the prison experience by asking the question of what happens to the concept of "prisonization" if we think about it experientially rather than as a matter of organizationally given steps or stages. We do this by focusing on the process through which inmates who have no prior direct knowledge of prison come to know the prison world.

THE SOCIAL MARGINALITY OF NEW INMATES

When new inmates are sentenced to prison, they have already lost their status as free adults but have not yet achieved any meaningful status within the prison world; they are, to older inmates, "fish" (see Cardozo-Freeman 1984; Irwin 1980). They can shed this label through their increasing participation in prison life, but a short-term inmate is unlikely ever to achieve a significant prison status. The new inmates' participation in the prison world will continue to be inhibited by their ties to, and identification with, the outside world. This *social marginality* is the overriding sociological characteristic of new inmates' prison experiences. In some respects, these inmates' situation is parallel to that experienced by immigrants who expect to return to their country of origin within a few years' time (see Shokeid 1988; Morawska 1987) or who otherwise manage to maintain a "sojourner orientation" (Gibson 1988). Immigrant sojourners, however, can typically draw on shared symbols or institutions in their transient adaptations to a new culture. New inmates, in contrast, have little in common with one another except their conventionality (Schmid and Jones 1991) and, consequently, have fewer collective resources to draw upon as they confront the problems presented by their sudden immersion into a new and different culture.

Our question, then, is how new inmates, initially as discrete individuals, orient themselves to the prison experience and how their orientations change as they progress through their sentences. Our primary focus in this chapter is with inmates' shifting images of the prison world and the corresponding changes in the problems presented by their prison sentences. In subsequent chapters, we will expand our consideration of their prison orientations to include their changing adaptation strategies and identity work.

PRISON ORIENTATIONS: IMAGES AND PROBLEMS

The principal change in inmates' prison imagery is easily stated: inmates progress from a view of the prison world that is dominated by the themes of violence and uncertainty to a view that is dominated by the themes of boredom and predictability to a view in which the prison is seen primarily as an obstacle to continued participation in the outside world. Throughout their entire prison careers, the overriding problem faced by all new

Table III.1. Orientation and Prison Imagery

	Preprison	*Prison*	*Postprison*
Inmate perspective	Outside looking in	Inside looking in	Inside looking out
Central concerns	Violence/Uncertainty	Boredom	Uncertainty
Specific problems	Survival	Endurance	Reintegration
Orientation to space	Prison as separate world	Prison as familiar territory	Prison as separate world
Orientation to time	Sentence as lost time	Killing time/time as measure of success	Sentence as lost time/using time
Supportive others	Family and friends	Partners	"Real" family and friends
Perception of sentence	Justified and unfortunate	Arbitrary and unjust	Arbitrary and unjust (intensified)
Predominant emotion	Fear	Detachment	Apprehension (about outside)

inmates is that of surviving the ordeal of a prison sentence. As outlined in Table III.1, however, the specific meanings of this problem depend on the inmates' changing orientations to the prison world. Thus, at the time of entry to the prison world, an inmate addresses the problem of survival quite literally: he is concerned with avoiding, or protecting himself from, injury, rape, or death. At a later point in his sentence, survival becomes a matter of enduring the unchanging, regimented routine of the prison world. As the inmate prepares for exit from the prison world, his concern gradually shifts to the question of how he will survive in the outside world after having served a prison sentence.

PREPRISON ORIENTATION

The "preprison orientation" is one of an outsider looking in. A first-time inmate, by definition, arrives at prison without an experiential understanding of the prison world. He has to construct an image of this world based on whatever resources are available to him. He begins to do so well before the beginning of his sentence. In this sense, a newly sentenced felon's cognitive entry into the prison world begins not with his arrival at the institution but rather at the moment he attempts to *envision* himself in the prison environment. His preprison imagery will guide both his preparation for his sentence and his initial behavior in prison, until he is able to revise his imagery on the basis of actual prison experience.

The inmate's preprison imagery reflects the perspective of someone who lives in the outside world. Its principal source is the *shared public meanings*, or cultural stereotypes, that exist in our society about prisons. These shared meanings, in turn, are heavily influenced by fictional or journalistic accounts that emphasize the violence of prison life. As the following excerpts from our interviews illustrate, new inmates readily acknowledge the effect of media depictions on their imagery:

> Oh, you can watch it on T.V. ... the news. They'll come out on the news and say there's a stabbing or a drug-related mishap in [Midwestern] prison.... That's the only thing a person's got to go by, is what they watch on T.V. or what they hear.

> * * *

> Well, I was scared to come here because ... I figured that people would be bothering you, you know—probably playing games, doing stuff to you. Probably something like you see on T.V., on the documentaries, like Stateville. After seeing that documentary, it really changed my idea of the inmates.

It is not that inmates accept journalistic and fictional accounts unequivocally; it is simply that they have no direct experience with the prison world, so they have no way of knowing how accurate or inaccurate these accounts are.

Shared public meanings are supplemented by at least three other sources of "information" about prison. First, any *personal experience* that felons have with the criminal justice system, especially with jails or juvenile correctional institutions, shapes their anticipatory image. Second, felons attempt to concretize their prison images with *information provided by others* who are presumed to be more knowledgeable, especially jail cellmates, jailers, and, in a few instances, former prison inmates. Finally, each felon, while attempting to project himself into the prison world, draws upon his own *imagination* about what prison will be like. Violence and uncertainty are shared public meanings about the prison that lead to specific fears for the felon; the felon's fears, in turn, personalize and intensify these meanings.

Preprison imagery is necessarily *abstract*. Lacking direct prison experience, a felon who is anticipating his prison sentence is able to construct only a vague picture of what to expect. The abstract form of the image does not in any way diminish its potency; if anything, the emotional and behavioral implications of the image are intensified. For many felons, the preprison image also seems to be, in some respects, *illusory*—a quality that is undoubtedly related to both the intangibility of the image and the emotional impact of arrest, court appearances, and sentencing. The preprison image conflicts so sharply with the individual's assumptions about reality and about his own identity—and in this sense violates what Schutz (1962, p. 11) called the reciprocity of perspectives—that it appears to be dreamlike. This sense of unreality is experienced not only during a felon's anticipation of his prison sentence but often, intermittently, for weeks or even months after his sentence begins.

The dominant theme of the preprison image, again, is *violence*, a view that is sustained by both popular and social science accounts of the prison world (Silberman 1995). Every inmate we talked with, in both the field-work and interview phases of our research, arrived at the institution with an intense fear of prison violence. A 32-year-old inmate, asked what he had expected prison to be like, replied:

> Sleeping in a cell; getting up; guys walking around with knives, killing you for no rea-son at all; guards standing over you with a club. If you get out of here alive, you're lucky.

Many inmates expressed specific concerns as well—particularly a fear of homosexual rape—but this picture of prison as a place of diffuse violence was repeated by inmate after inmate.

Closely related to the theme of violence is that of *uncertainty*, not only in the sense that new inmates know very little about prison but in the sense that prison is defined as an inherently unpredictable place. When one is sent to prison, one no longer controls any part of one's life. Worst of all, violence is believed to occur on a random, and therefore unpredictable, basis: new inmates believe that at any time, without reason, they might be beaten, raped or murdered.

The themes of violence and uncertainty affect the preprison image that felons hold of both guards and prison inmates. Not all newly sentenced felons formulate a preprison image of prison guards but those who do typ-ically see them as hostile, possibly brutal, and in any case powerless to pre-vent the random acts of violence committed by inmates. All newly sentenced felons construct an image of prisoners. Like guards, prisoners are viewed as being antagonistic, but they are also viewed as being *alien*—as somehow different from the rest of us. The most important difference, however, is that they are seen as violent people who compulsively prey on others.

When speaking of inmates' "preprison image," we do not mean to sug-gest that all new inmates begin their sentences with identical mental pic-tures of the prison world. Nonetheless, the ideas of prison as a violent place and prisoners as violent human beings were expressed by every inmate with whom we talked. Beyond these universal features of the pre-prison imagery, there are certain other features that also are common to the preprison images of virtually all new inmates. Our analysis of how these inmates define the prison world therefore begins with an examination of these common features.[1]

A felon awaiting the beginning of his sentence clearly defines prison in both spatial and temporal terms. Prison is a place, physically separate and hidden from his own world, to which he will be exiled for a certain (although not precisely specified) length of time. Furthermore, prison is viewed as punishment in large part because it *removes* the individual from his own world and because it *disrupts* the normal flow of time that exists in his world. A prison sentence is *time that is taken away* from the individual's life.

But the significance of a prison sentence extends beyond its disruption of an individual's normal world of space and time. Prison also disrupts an individual's participation in a social network of friends, relatives, and associates. This meaning of a prison sentence accounts for the felon's concern, in a self-dialogue he conducts before and immediately after his arrival at prison, about the effects of his sentence on his family and friends. Because of this meaning, some felons terminate intimate relationships, sometimes even before the beginning of their sentences. While prison necessarily disrupts an inmate's relationships, what a felon does not know, and what causes his concern, is how much damage his relationships will incur and how irreversible this damage will be.

A central theme of the preprison image, then, is the idea of *loss*—of place, time, and social network, but also of *self-determination*. New inmates understand that they will no longer have control over most aspects of their everyday lives. Imprisonment means relinquishing this control to prison administrators, guards, regimented schedules, and perhaps other prisoners; thus, another integral component of a felon's self-dialogue is how to survive this loss of self-determination.

Most inmates admit responsibility for their crimes, and most view prison as a logical consequence of law violation. They may not believe that their own sentences were appropriate for the crimes they committed, and they unequivocally do not see themselves as being anything like the "criminals" who are in prison. Nevertheless, when a new inmate enters prison, he sees his own difficulties with the criminal justice system as a *personal misfortune* rather than as an outcome of a corrupt system.

The emotional dimension of the preprison image follows directly from the themes of violence and uncertainty: it is extreme *fear*. Newly sentenced felons are completely and overwhelmingly intimidated by the prison—or, more precisely, by the image that they hold of the prison world. They are able to articulate a number of specific "pains of imprisonment" (Sykes 1958), including loss of intimate relationships, loss of contact with family and friends, loss of identity, and so on. What they fear most, however, is the physical and sexual violence that they believe will result from their contact with prison inmates. Table III.1 summarizes the prison imagery held by inmates during their preprison (and subsequent) orientations.

The immediate problem presented by this imagery is, as we have noted, physical survival. An intimately associated problem is that of *identity preservation*. Put another way, new inmates preparing for their imprisonment must devise some way of protecting themselves from the annihilative dangers of their preprison imagery. In Chapter 4, we describe the inmates' preprison experiences and take a closer look at the preprison imagery they construct. We also examine how inmates translate this imagery into "entry tactics" that express the violence of their imagery and are intended to address their primary concerns of survival. Finally, we consider what happens when inmates actually arrive at prison—how well their entry tactics work for them, how they modify both their imagery and their tactics in conjunction with their early experiences in prison, and the "identity work" they engage in as part of this experiential process.

PRISON ORIENTATION

The "prison orientation" focuses on the present-time experience of prison life as an inmate's day-to-day reality. As an inmate acquires actual experience within the prison world, his orientation to prison, including both his image of the prison and his behavior within prison, changes substantially. Although his transitional status may inhibit him from ever completely understanding all dimensions of the prison social world, his imagery becomes more concrete, because it is based on first-hand experiences, and more complex, as it is expanded by his knowledge of prison programs and services, his increasing differentiation of guards and inmates, and his familiarity (and perhaps limited involvement) with the illegal economy and other aspects of prisoner social organization. Because this imagery is more concrete and complex, his imagery also becomes more definitive; it is the outside world that now begins to seem illusory.

The most profound definitional change that occurs is a change from the belief that prison is a violent world to the belief that prison is a fundamentally *boring* world. This change is not a simple recognition that prison is less violent than anticipated, for a good deal of violence does in fact take place. Nor is it a simple response to the unchanging daily routine faced by inmates after the first two months of their sentences. Rather, the change is the net result of many smaller definitional changes, including changes in the images of other inmates and guards, that reduce the inmates' preoccupation with prison violence. Prison can be boring only when violence is no longer an intense, ubiquitous fear.

The change in a new inmate's definition of other inmates is particularly striking. Before he enters the prison, as we have described, most propsective inmates see all other prison inmates as hostile, violent, and alien. As a new inmate forms tentative friendships and nodding acquaintanceships with others in his cellblock, he gradually modifies his definition of other inmates: *most* inmates are violent and alien but at least a few other inmates are more or less like himself. As he becomes able to interact with an increasing number of inmates—on the cellblock, at work, and in recreational settings—his definition is further modified: there are *some* inmates, including a number of identifiable individuals and groups of inmates, who are hostile and potentially violent and who should therefore be avoided. Most inmates, however, are not nearly as abnormal as had been anticipated. Although he will continue to make some distinctions between himself and other inmates (for example, that others are less mature or less intelligent), his image of them undergoes considerable change within a few months time. Within a few months, he has progressed from viewing all inmates as abnormal to a more discerning and differentiated view of the inmate population, which allows that most inmates are "normal."

A new inmate's image of prison guards undergoes a similar, though less extensive, modification. His stereotypic view of guards becomes differentiated on the bases of friendliness, flexibility, and consistency. He becomes able to identify which guards will engage in casual conversation and which should be avoided at all times. Because of the institutionalized animosity between them, most new inmates continue to view all guards in primarily negative terms, but their image of the guards becomes multidimensional.

A differentiated image of guards and other inmates helps to reduce a new inmate's obsession with prison violence because it reduces the number of presumed sources of violence. If all guards are not antagonistic, then all guards need not be feared. If most inmates are basically normal, then most inmates are not a constant threat. These changes in imagery, however, can only have a limited effect on the inmate's fear of violence. In his preprison image, an inmate's fear stemmed primarily from the uncertainty of *random* violence. Even if an inmate believes that there are relatively few "abnormal" individuals in prison, he can still believe that he will be subject to random acts of violence by these individuals.

In order for a new inmate to change his definitions of prison from a violent world to a boring world, his uncertainty about prison must be reduced. This reduction does, in fact, happen. A new inmate's entire prison career can be conceptualized as a process of decreasing apprehension and uncertainty about the prison world. This statement must be qualified, however, in two respects. First, a new inmate's uncertainty and apprehension about prison are substantially reduced during his prison career, but they are never eliminated. The prison world never becomes as certain or predictable as the outside world, and the inmate never feels completely secure within his prison world. Second, the reduction in uncertainty and apprehension experienced by a new inmate does not occur in a linear fashion; rather, the pattern is one of an *erratic reduction in uncertainty and apprehension.*

The process is erratic because of dramatic events—assaults, rapes, homicides, and suicides. As a new inmate becomes familiar with the prison world and his uncertainty and apprehension begin to decline, a dramatic event shocks the inmate back to the "reality" of his preprison image. Following dramatic events during the first weeks of his sentence, his uncertainty and apprehension become as intense, or more intense, than when he first walked into prison. With lessening effect, this pattern repeats itself during the first several months of his sentence, each dramatic event providing a significant setback to the general definitional changes of declining uncertainty and apprehension.

As the inmate's sentence progresses, these incidents have declining shock value because dramatic events are themselves subject to definitional change. By listening to prison gossip about the incidents and talking with others about them, new inmates *actively seek* to "make sense" out of prison violence, so that they can learn how to avoid it. As dramatic events become defined as the consequences of violating prison norms, they become "explained" acts of violence rather than random acts of violence. Accordingly, violent incidents that occur at the middle of an inmate's prison career clearly have less shock value than those that occur near the beginning of his sentence. Within two or three months of his arrival at prison, a new inmate is able to "explain" most dramatic events and to rationalize those that he cannot specifically explain. The more that dramatic events can be explained away or rationalized, the less effect they have on the inmate's uncertainty and apprehension about prison life.

The evolving image of prison as a boring world is actually the product of two definitional processes. First, the dominant theme of the preprison image—prison as a world of random violence—is weakened, in the manner we have described. The second definitional process is much simpler: it is the increasing realization of the unchanging daily routine in prison. The early weeks of an inmate's sentence were filled with stimuli: in-processing, orientation classes, interviews, cell transfers, the exploration of new territory, meeting other inmates, a job assignment, and other events. After two or three months, however, his world becomes highly structured and repetitive. By the middle of his career, his daily life is overwhelmingly controlled by a regimented schedule of work, meals, and evening diversionary activities.

Just as his preprison image was dominated by the theme of violence, the prison image that an inmate holds during his prison orientation is dominated by the theme of boredom, but it encompasses other definitional changes as well. Some of these are subtle, especially those involving the dimensions of space and time. The prison walls that were formerly perceived as enclosing a distant, spatially separate world to which criminals were exiled have now become the outer boundaries of the inmate's day-to-day world. Prison is no longer quite as strange or as frightening. Although a first-time, short-term inmate never considers prison to be his "home," it does become his primary world of reference at the middle of his prison career.

An inmate continues to view his sentence as a disruption of his personal life and, hence, as time that has been taken away from him. By the middle of his prison career, however, time begins to have special meanings *within* the prison world as well as in relation to the outside world. Time becomes a measure of his *success* at survival. At the beginning of his sentence, his intense levels of uncertainty and apprehension were related to his recognition that most prison experiences, possibly including his worst fears, still lay ahead. By midcareer, prison life has become routine and dramatic events have lost much of their shock value. From this perspective, the inmate's concern becomes one of killing time within an unchanging and boring daily routine. And killing time is useful; the more time that an inmate has served and, especially, the greater *proportion* of his sentence that he has served, the more confident he becomes in his abilities to complete his entire sentence. Moreover, time becomes a measure of an inmate's *status* in prison. In a general sense, he gains in status simply by serving time, because he becomes a more "experienced" prisoner. But it is not only the actual time he has served that affects his status; the length of his sentence is also significant. It is for this reason that inmates typically describe their sentences in terms of the maximum amount of time they could serve rather than the actual amount of time they expect to serve.

An inmate's initial view of his sentence as a disruption of his social network of family and friends is altered by a prison perspective on relationships. When he has served several months, the inmate has been able to interact with a variety of other prisoners. He has made a number of casual acquaintances and has probably established at least one solid friendship or partnership. This new network does not replace his old one, but it reduces the amount of time he spends thinking about his outside associates, and perhaps reduces his involvement with them as well. For the inmate, maintaining outside relationships is very stressful, primarily because of a lack of control over those contacts and over events that take place outside the prison walls. Because of this, many inmates maintain that doing time would be much easier without outside contacts. For reasons that we will examine in more detail later, this idea of terminating outside contacts because they are too stressful is undoubtedly a protective rationalization. Outside contacts continue to be important to inmates at midcareer: thus, although many inmates contemplate terminating their outside contacts at this time, few inmates actually do.

By the middle of their sentences, most new inmates have changed their assessment of the criminal justice system and their relationship to it. They have heard about, witnessed, or experienced a host of inequities in prison. Some of these are minor: approved transfers not being implemented on time, visitors being stranded because of prison lockups, or staff members failing to follow through on a promised course of action. Others are more serious, such as disciplinary actions taken against inmates because of staff errors. Of more consequence still are the inequities stemming from actions of the judiciary or parole authorities. New inmates learn that other inmates, convicted of more serious crimes, are serving sentences that are not appreciably longer, and in some cases even shorter, than their own. As the prison and the entire criminal justice system come to be perceived as unfair, an inmate redefines his own sentence as a *personal injustice* rather than a personal misfortune. This is not a matter of the inmate denying responsibility for his own criminal behavior. It is a matter of relative deprivation; when a new inmate sees the sentences that other prisoners are "getting away with," he begins to define the system itself as unjust.

These various definitional changes are accompanied by a change in the inmate's emotional response to his imprisonment. His apprehension about the prison diminishes. As the outside world becomes less salient and the prison world becomes defined as boring rather than violent, he begins to take on what Clemmer (1958) has called the "universal features of prisonization," becoming physically lethargic and emotionally apathetic. Intermittently, he also experiences varying levels of tension resulting from the monotony of his everyday life within an environment that remains basically uncertain and potentially dangerous.

The changes that take place in an inmate's imagery occur because of the knowledge he gains through direct *participation* in the prison social world. While his preprison imagery was principally based on shared public meanings about prison, much of his subsequent imagery is based on first-hand experience and shared subcultural meanings within the prison world, which emphasize the interminable boredom of prison life. First-time inmates may still possess only incomplete knowledge of the prison social organization and they may be only minor participants in that organization, but their participation is sufficient to enable them to view prison from the perspective of organizational insiders.

As the prison imagery held by first-time, short-term inmates during their mid-sentence prison orientation (summarized in Table III.1) comes to approximate that held by long-term inmates, the problem posed by their imprisonment shifts from an outsider's fixation on physical survival to an insider's focus on enduring prison boredom. This problem requires both different adaptation tactics and a different form of identity work. In Chapter 5, we document how changes in inmates' prison imagery come about and how inmates continue to draw upon their evolving understanding of the prison world to confront the problems of their imprisonment.

POSTPRISON ORIENTATION

The "postprison orientation" offers an inside-looking-out perspective on prison life. As they prepare for their exit from the prison world and anticipate their return to the outside world, inmates gradually move away from their prison orientation toward a "postprison" orientation, again bringing an outsider's perspective into their view of the prison world. At the prison we studied, this change is facilitated by a Minimum Security Unit, located on the prison grounds but outside the maximum security walls and available to many inmates for the final months of their sentences. Not all prisoners participate in this unit; inmates must apply for a transfer, and acceptance depends both on the crimes for which they were sentenced and on staff evaluation of their potential for success in the unit. There are three features of the minimum security unit that facilitate change in inmates' imagery: a more open physical and social environment, the fact that the unit lies just outside the prison wall (so that an inmate who is transferred is also physically removed from the maximum security prison), and greater opportunity for direct contact with the outside world.

The prison image associated with this postprison orientation directly reflects the inmates' continuing marginal status. It is essentially a synthesis of their earlier images, combining the insider's view of prison as a world of boredom with the outsider's view of prison as a fundamentally alien world. An inmate's boredom, for example, is temporarily interrupted by a transfer to minimum security. Yet, despite the considerable physical and social differences between maximum and minimum security, inmates' lives again become dominated by a standardized routine within a relatively brief period of time following their transfer. Minimum security residents do have greater freedom of mobility, fewer restrictions regarding visits, a somewhat less regimented life-style, and eventual eligibility for home furloughs, but these privileges are tempered by the hardships of living in "half freedom" and under program regulations that are viewed as petty.

The imagery of the postprison orientation also retains other features of the insiders' prison image, including a view of their sentences as a personal injustice. Although minimum security residents no longer experience uncertainty about the possibility of violence, they continue to view their prison world with some degree of uncertainty, just as they did at mid-career, because of their lack of control over their own lives.

Elements of the preprison, public image are also present in the release image, albeit in modified form. This is particularly evident when minimum security residents look back at the maximum security prison. This institution again comes to be viewed as a spatially separate world that is quite distant from the residents' own world. In contrast to the beginning of their sentences, residents now know what life is like within the prison walls, but even with this knowledge, prison again starts to appear as an alien world as the inmate turns his attention to the outside world.

As they look forward to their return to the outside world, inmates tend to think about their sentences in much the same manner as they did in the earliest stage of their careers. Prison is viewed as time that has been taken away from them—as a disruption of the normal flow-of-time that exists in the real world. In *Asylums*, Goffman (1961, p. 168) observed that one of the dominant themes of inmate culture is "a strong feeling that time spent in the establishment is time wasted or destroyed or taken from one's life." In contrast, we found this feeling to be strongest at the beginning and end of the inmate's prison career, when he is least influenced by the shared meanings of the inmate culture. The other meanings of time that were accepted at midcareer—for example, time as an indicator of status—become unimportant. In the postprison orientation, inmates become increasingly concerned with marking time, or using time, until their release dates arrive.

Prison is again defined as a disruption of an inmate's prior network of social relationships. The prison social network that had been established during the middle months of his sentence withers, because a minimum security resident is isolated from his prison social network, and the network itself now appears artificial. In the final weeks of his sentence, an inmate is more interested in reestablishing ties with relatives and friends on the outside. The more successful he is at reestablishing these ties, of course, the less important his prison friendships become.

Perhaps the most important similarity between the preprison image and the release image is in the resident's definition of other inmates, especially maximum security inmates. In his preprison image, he saw prison inmates as violent, hostile, and entirely unlike himself. Within a few months, he had developed a differentiated image of other inmates, and he now saw most inmates as normal. In his release image, he again sees maximum security inmates as essentially abnormal and alien human beings, who are quite different from himself. His release image of other inmates remains much more differentiated than his preprison image and he no longer fears maximum security inmates as he did at the beginning of his sentence. Nonetheless, there is a clear reversal in his differentiation of other inmates and his identification with them.

An inmate's emotional response to prison involves appreciably less fear at the middle of his sentence than it did at the beginning. This trend continues; he experiences virtually no fear about his life in prison following his transfer to minimum security, although he gradually becomes more apprehensive about his return to the outside world. The lethargy and apathy that characterized the middle of his sentence also diminish at the end of his sentence because of his growing orientation toward the outside world.

Just as increasing participation in the prison social world enabled an inmate to modify his preprison imagery, his simultaneous decreasing participation in the prison world and increasing participation in the outside world provide the basis for his release image. Transfer to minimum security removes the inmate from most of the dangers of maximum security, provides him an opportunity to look back on the maximum security institution from a vantage point of physical and social distance, and affords him more contact with the outside world, through greater visiting privileges, outside activities, and furloughs. As his orientation returns to the outside world, his image of the prison becomes closer to that held in the outside world. At the beginning of his career, a new inmate looks at prison entirely from an outsider's perspective. During the middle of his career, this perspective has not disappeared completely but it has receded, and the inmate looks at prison largely in terms of the meanings that he shares with his fellow prisoners. As he anticipates his return to the free social world, he begins to adopt an outsider's perspective once again. He cannot return completely to the public stereotype with which he entered prison, because he has become a part of the prison world and he knows the stereotype to be inaccurate. As his own involvement in the maximum security prison seems more and more distant, however, his concluding image (summarized in Table III.1) again becomes clouded by the public stereotype.

As inmates develop a "postprison orientation," the problem presented by their imprisonment changes from simple endurance of the prison world to a concern with how this world has and will affect their lives on the outside. Their adaptation tactics and identity work change accordingly. We examine these experiential processes in Chapter 6.

SUMMARY AND DISCUSSION

Clearly, prison images held by new inmates cannot be understood solely in terms of what goes on inside prison walls. Rather, this imagery derives from inmates' social marginality and their orientation to both inside and outside concerns. The images themselves draw upon subjective meanings associated with both the outside world and inmates' direct experience in prison. Prison images, then, depend on inmates' shifting orientations between the prison and the outside worlds, and on the effort required to address the practical concerns of doing time.

New inmates, at the time of their entry to the prison world, recognize that they face a fundamental transformation of their social worlds. Based on the violence of their outsiders' imagery, their earliest survival tactics are protective and defensive in nature. But they also recognize that their outsiders' understanding of the prison world is both abstract and incomplete. Their driving motivation at the time of entry to the prison world is to make sense of this world by acquiring more, and more precise, information. As we will demonstrate, virtually all of their early survival tactics operate as *information-seeking* tactics as well as protective measures. The tactics they adopt enable new inmates to interact more with other inmates, to gain direct experience in prison, to acquire an insider's perspective on the prison world, to contrast this perspective with their outsider's stereotypic view, and to adjust their own imagery accordingly. In this sense, it can be argued that the inmates' survival tactics not only result from their prison imagery but also allow the revision of this imagery.

As new inmates reshape their image of the prison world to one that more closely approximates the perspective of long-term inmates—that is, as their imagery shifts from violence to boredom—there is also a shift in what they believe to be the immediate problems of their imprisonment, from physical *survival* to *endurance* of a boring prison world. As this happens, new inmates are in the least marginal phase of their prison careers. They share with long-term inmates a common imagery of the prison world, a common set of problems presented by their prison sentences, and not surprisingly, common tactics for addressing these problems. By midcareer, new inmates are using an insider's perspective to address insiders' problems.

This relative integration into the prison world is short-lived, however, and inmates' marginality within the prison world again becomes evident as they prepare for their exit from prison. As they begin to focus on the impending problems of "getting out"—where to live, how to earn a living, how to deal with the effects of their prison sentence on their relationships with others—it becomes increasingly apparent that their prison orientation is inadequate for dealing with the outside world. They find themselves contrasting their own (insiders') perspective with that of the world they are about to enter. Thus, the prison image held at the time of release is a product of inmates' experience and contrastive work.

The next three chapters provide a close-up view of new inmates' prison experiences and their interpretive work within prison. In the final three chapters, we return to the larger issues of prison adaptation, identity work, and the theoretical and correctional implications of our analysis.

NOTE

1. Boulding (1961) has suggested five basic dimensions of an individual's subjective knowledge: space, time, personal relations, the world of nature (relational imagery), and emotion. Our analysis borrows from Boulding's discussion.

Chapter IV

Preprison Orientation: From the Outside Looking In

A first-time inmate's preprison orientation, as we have noted, is developed prior to his arrival in the prison world and refined during the early weeks of his sentence. Beginning with no experiential knowledge of prison, he begins to construct an image of the prison world from the moment he imaginatively projects himself into prison. Based on this imagery, he also identifies specific problems of his impending imprisonment and devises a general strategy for addressing these problems. The first part of this chapter examines how a first-time inmate constructs his preprison imagery as he prepares himself for his sentence. Later in the chapter, we look at what happens to his imagery and strategy once his sentence actually begins.

PREPARING FOR PRISON

The essential problem confronted by a felon facing a first prison sentence is this: he is about to be forcibly removed from the social world he knows and involuntarily placed into a world about which he knows little, but fears greatly. The minimal knowledge he does possess is based primarily on shared public meanings, largely derived from fictional and journalistic media depictions. His most pressing need is to "fill in" his vague picture of the prison world, and he has few resources available to help him do this. We outlined the general process through which he assembles this image in the previous chapter; we now explicate this process, drawing upon our interview and fieldwork data.

IMAGE CONSTRUCTION

A felon's adaptation to prison life begins well before his arrival at the prison institution: it begins as soon as he seriously attempts to envision himself in prison. Anyone who knowingly participates in illegal behavior may speculate from time to time about what life in prison might be like, but this speculation typically involves fanciful, and sometimes even glamorous, images of prison life. More serious conceptualizations of the prison world, and his participation in it, take place following the felon's arrest, and these projections become more frequent as the likelihood of conviction and sentencing increases. This *anticipation* of the prison world is especially significant for men who are being sentenced to prison for the first time, because the prison imagery they formulate will affect not only their preparations for their sentences but their initial behavior inside the prison walls.

In addition to media portrayals, first-time inmates have three general resources for building their prison imagery: information accrued through their own criminal justice experiences, prior to and during their present difficulties; information provided by others; and their own imaginative projections of what prison will be like. Working from these limited resources, future inmates assemble vague but functional understandings of the experiences that lay ahead of them. Despite considerable differences in the amount of information available to the inmates we studied, we found remarkable similarities in the prison imagery they created.

Lacking firsthand experience as a prison inmate, a newly sentenced felon looks to any related experiences that might approximate the prison world. If he has served time in a juvenile correctional facility, his experience there will certainly influence his view of the adult prison. If he has been in jail before, he will extrapolate from that experience to visualize what longer-term imprisonment will be like. His treatment by police, county jailers and others throughout his current legal difficulties provide small clues about how he might be treated in prison, and felons with no prior criminal justice history will place even greater weight on these experiences.

Most first-time inmates spend some time in county jails, following their arrest or prior to their transfer to prison. (Some have spent time in jail for earlier offenses that did not lead to a prison sentence.) For many, the county jail provides their *only* direct contact with men who have served time in prison. Jail cellmates thus become an especially important, although not necessarily accurate, source of information. Some felons find these contacts helpful, in that they serve to temper the harsh prison images they have been constructing on their own. As illustrated by the following interview excerpt, from a 37-year-old inmate convicted of theft, others find that discussions with jail cellmates exasperate their prison images:

> It made me fearful because of the type of people I was talking to. I felt, oh my God, is this the type of person, with this intellectual level, I am going to be dealing with for I don't know how long? I knew I was capable of probably handling it, mentally, but I know it's a great big mental adjustment because you don't know to what extent that people are going to fly off the lid, that they are mentally stable or how much importance that male ego or machoism or whatever—that's a real big thing to them.

Virtually all newly sentenced felons actively cultivate jail cellmates as sources of information, asking them questions about prison life. Of course, if they personally know other people who have served prison time, their imagery will also be affected by the stories these people tell.

While awaiting the beginning of their sentences, felons grapple with the information they receive from these various sources and try to apply it to their own situations. Because the information tends to be incomplete and conflicting, most of these men do not develop unified conceptions of the prison prior to their arrival at the institution. Even personal reports from ex-prisoners and direct experience in juvenile institutions or county jails yield, at best, only a partial and biased picture of prison life. Nonetheless, felons do *construct* an image, using their various sources of information along with media depictions and their own imaginations as raw materials. As one of the men we interviewed succinctly stated:

> I had an uncle sent to prison once. I suppose T.V., books, imagination. You kinda imagine what it would be like to be in that situation.

Components of this image include both general expectations about institutional life and specific fears that felons hold about the prison world.

The specific institutional features that felons try to anticipate depend on the informational resources available to them, but they are also influenced by felons' emotional states. It is not surprising, then, that the dominant feature in every felon's preprison imagery is his conceptualization of prison inmates. In keeping with his violent image of the prison world as a whole and his fear of going to prison, every first-time inmate with whom we talked reported a preprison visualization of other inmates as brutal, inhuman creatures. We will cite two interview excerpts, both from men convicted of sexual misconduct, to illustrate this imagery:

I thought the inmates would be—like you wouldn't be able to talk to them. It was hard time they were doing here ... and I thought you wouldn't be able to talk to them. If you said something to them, I thought they would try to hurt you.

* * *

I thought they'd be more or less like, you know, the animals that you run into on the street ... and ghetto types and that type of thing—rather rough, trying to beat you out of something continually.

Many new inmates also embellish this conception, incorporating speculations about inmate gangs or a prison underworld and wondering whether they will have to confront such larger dimensions of inmate culture.

Apart from this violent view of other inmates, there are no other universal features in a felon's preprison imagery. Many of the men we talked with did indicate that they had speculated about what guards might be like, and most versions of this speculation saw guards as impersonal, mean, hypocritical, corrupt, and either hostile to new inmates or powerless to protect them from older inmates. Similarly, those who speculated about what their days would be like in prison tended to build upon the violence and hostility they associated with inmates and guards. Although specific expectations ranged from the belief that inmates would be locked in their cells most of the time to the notion that their days would be given to enforced menial labor, most felt that their days would be dominated by the avoidance or confrontation of physical dangers.

Depending on their experiences in county jails and the information they have received from various sources, newly sentenced felons may also formulate other conceptions about institutional life, ranging from mundane details to matters of social organization. Based primarily on their limited confinement in county jails, for example, most expect that their prison cells, food, and general living conditions will be spartan. A number of first-time inmates also reported that they had tried to collect advance knowledge about correspondence and visiting privileges, recreational facilities, early release decisions, contraband, and illegal activities by inmates.

A convicted felon's fears about prison both contribute to and result from the construction of his preprison imagery. Like anyone who watches television or reads a newspaper, he has seen stories about prison riots, murders, stabbings, and beatings. Like most people in our society, he believes that the prison world is fundamentally a violent one. Unlike most people, however, he is about to enter this world, so this general cultural image becomes greatly amplified and personalized in his own mind. His principal fears about prison accordingly center around his concerns for safety. He is afraid of what might happen to him in prison. He is afraid of being injured. He is afraid of dying. And perhaps more than anything else, as illustrated by the following interview excerpts, he is afraid of being sexually assaulted.

> I was worried about being raped for the most part, that's about it. You know, I had a good friend at [a community treatment program] who was raped in [another prison in the state] and he's having a lot of problems because of it.
>
> * * *
>
> Dying. Getting sex from the rear entry. Being knifed or maimed so when I get out I will get out in two pieces. Being exploited.

Most first-time inmates approach their sentences with great trepidation about both their physical survival and their sexual integrity.

Many felons also fear losing contact with the outside world, particularly with their wives or lovers, family members, and close friends. Two interview excerpts illustrate the specific and the general versions of this fear:

> Well, I was mainly worried about my girl. I was worried about losing her. And I think that is one of the hardest things to take, is losing someone you love while you're in there.... You know that at even a year, that's a long way off for someone on the street waiting for you.
>
> * * *
>
> I did have a concern over the people that I am really close with. A lot. I was afraid that I wouldn't have the relationships that I had before I went in.

At Midwestern Prison, even the minimum possible sentence of a year and a day means that, with the "good time" provision, the inmate may be apart from his family and friends for nine or ten months. The stress which an absence of this length can place on personal relationships is not lost on new inmates, who know that they are powerless to prevent change in their relationships. Even before they arrive at prison, many felons begin to experience a fear that letters and visits from the outside will decrease or cease entirely after the first few months of their sentences.

Still another fear held by newly sentenced felons is that *they* will be changed as a result of their imprisonment. The issues here range from a fear of "going crazy" to a more generalized concern that the inmate will somehow not be the same person when he comes out of prison. We again refer to our interviews to illustrate both the specific and general versions of this fear:

I had a great deal of fear.... I don't like to be in closed places, small quarters. I am a little claustrophobic.

* * *

Oh, I kind of had an idea, and I still do, if I had to spend a significant period of time in prison, I would quite naturally internalize a lot of really shitty behavior. Who knows? A survival type of—a bunch of really sick games, you know. I know I would. A guy just doesn't make it unless he does.

As we discuss further below, the importance of these expressions of concern over personal change is that they initiate a self-conscious questioning of a new inmate's identity, even before the inmate begins his prison sentence.

To summarize our analysis thus far: felons who are confronting a first prison sentence do not simply and passively wait for their sentences to begin. Once they begin to consider imprisonment as a real possibility in their lives, they actively construct an image of the prison world, based on the limited resources they have available. Their image construction activities focus on the violence and uncertainty of prison life, and define the inmates' problem as one of survival. But they also do more than simply conceptualize prison. Even before their arrival at the institution, they initiate two tentative and overlapping responses to this problem. First, as part of their imagery construction process, they engage in an ongoing self-dialogue which constitutes an incipient form of *identity work*. Second, they formulate an *anticipatory survival strategy* for their imminent imprisonment.

IDENTITY WORK

A felon's anticipation of his prison sentence invariably results in a self-assessment, in the form of a running self-dialogue. This assessment essentially begins at the point that he first imagines himself in prison, but it escalates as the probability of imprisonment increases, particularly during his trial or sentencing. Typically, this self-dialogue involves reviewing the events leading to his arrest and trial, questioning his motivation for his crime, analyzing the implications of his sentence for his family and friends, and above all, attempting to figure out what all of this means to himself, to his life. A 42-year-old inmate, convicted of first degree sexual misconduct, expresses the frenetic nature of this analysis:

How did I get into this spot?... How did I—how did my lifestyle get me to this point and—you know, 'cuz I had to own the responsibility on it for being involved. I didn't agree with their [the officials'] opinions, but you start taking a review—it's almost like your life is passing before your eyes. You wonder how in the heck you got to this point

and, you know, what are—what's your family gonna think about it—your friends, all
the talk, and how are you going to deal with that—and the kids, you know, how are
they gonna react to it?... All those things run through your head.... The total loss of
control—the first time in my life that some other people were controlling my life at
that point.

Clearly, a new inmate's fears about his impending sentence provide fuel to
his self-dialogue, as voiced here by a 41-year-old inmate sentenced to
prison for a probation violation.

Just broke down and cried for hours. The thought of even coming here was just so
remote. I couldn't conceive of them sending me here.... I didn't really entertain the
thought of coming down too much. I thought about it, you know, only as, if I ever got
to prison, that would be the last stop. I really didn't pursue it any more than that. I
guess I just couldn't really imagine being sent up.

Among his major fears, as we have seen, was that he would be changed in
prison. A 26-year-old inmate expressed this fear:

I was wondering what type of person I was going to become if I went there. What
would I turn into and what would I be like when I got out? Would I like myself anymore? Would I be compatible with society? That type of thing.

Self-consciously reflecting upon or questioning one's identity is an integral part of most identity transformation processes. That this occurs during new inmates' *anticipation* of prison suggests that the prison world
begins to have an effect on their identities *prior to* their actual participation
in that world. It also means that new inmates begin to work on problems
concerning their identities before their sentences begin.

The intensity and sophistication of such self-analyses vary considerably,
but all new inmates seem to experience some identity questioning at the
time of their arrest, trial, and sentencing. The men we interviewed
reported that their self-dialogues became especially intense as the beginning of their sentences approached. An examination of the extended
self-dialogues that take place at the time of entry to the prison world
therefore is particularly revealing about how new inmates experience
imprisonment.

Whether a convicted felon is bound over at the time of his conviction
or allowed to report for sentencing at a later date, the first day of his
sentence usually begins at a county jail or detention facility, where he
awaits official transfer to the state prison. In some counties, this waiting period can extend to several hours or the entire day. Regardless of
what prior experience felons have had with jails, this final day in jail is
different, in that it is all but impossible for a felon to think about anything other than his imminent prison sentence and the events that led

him to his sentence. Questions that he may have previously considered only lightly now demand serious attention. He again reviews his illegal behavior and his motivations for that behavior, and wonders how he ever allowed himself to get involved in these activities. He may also wonder how he allowed himself to be caught, and question his earlier complacency or analyze the mistakes he made. The impact of his incarceration on his family and friends also is likely to be a part of this renewed self-dialogue, along with feelings of remorse or grief about having caused these troubles. This is one inmate's description of his final day in jail:

> It was a weird day. I thought I would go crazy. My emotions ran wild. One minute I would be on the verge of tears, the next minute I would be laughing it off. I kept thinking they [jailers] forgot about me. The afternoon dragged on and on. It sure gave me time to think, especially about how I was such a dumb ass to put myself in this position. I also thought about how good my family and friends had been to me through this whole ordeal. I also thought that they would forget me once at [Midwestern]—only time will tell.

Above all, the prison itself dominates the felon's thoughts. He cannot really see himself as being similar to other prison inmates—even though he does not have a clear conception of what other prisoners are like. He dreads the idea of going to prison but may also be impatient with this final day of waiting for his sentence to begin. Any conversations he has with jailers or jail inmates center primarily on prison, in a last-minute attempt to compose a clearer picture of what his life in prison will be like. Both his fears about prison and his resolve to survive the prison are strengthened through his self-reflective process.

A new inmate's self-dialogue, on the day his sentence begins and in the days and weeks before that, takes place in a rambling, chaotic fashion rather than an orderly one. None of the questions he raises receives an entirely satisfactory answer. Rather, the same questions, analyses, fears, and survival plans keep recurring in random order: each concern is dealt with until another issue asserts itself, and that issue dominates his musings until another topic arises, and so on. The net effect of this self-dialogue undoubtedly varies from individual to individual, but for all new inmates, it is a primary means of anticipating and "working through" the problems of their imprisonment—constructing an image of the prison world, identifying the problems facing them, engaging in identity work in response to their feelings of fear, vulnerability, and isolation, and devising a preprison survival strategy.

ANTICIPATORY SURVIVAL STRATEGY

While he is engaged in this running self-dialogue, ruminating over prison dangers and his fears of physical and social survival, a convicted felon also creates what can be called an "anticipatory survival strategy" for dealing with prison life. In his study of the prison world, Irwin (1970, pp. 67-79) discusses three general modes of adaptation: *jailing*, which involves an accommodation to the prison world; *gleaning*, which involves self-improvement through participation in prison programs; and *doing time*, which consists of maintaining a general orientation toward the outside world and avoiding active participation in the prison world. New inmates generally come to prison armed with an isolationist strategy that could be described as an extreme version of "doing time."

Elements of this strategy include firm vows to avoid all hostilities with other inmates (to the extent that this is viewed as possible), to keep unnecessary contacts with other inmates to a minimum, and to ignore all questionable information received from other inmates. Because most of a felon's fears focus on the violence of prison life, he also mentally prepares to defend himself in any way possible if hostilities cannot be avoided. Some felons said that they began weight-training programs or otherwise sought to change their appearances, in order to embody these resolutions. A 27-year-old inmate, convicted of the unauthorized use of a motor vehicle, summarizes this tactic:

> Eat a lot; put on weight; try to look as sloppy as I could. Be rude to people; try not to appear as a pleasant person; try to make myself appear disgusting.... I'd say I was going to be less sociable, that's about it. I was going to mind my own business, and have as little to do with other people as possible.

Most presume that prison guards offer no real protection against violence and that interaction with guards may well provoke hostilities with other inmates; consequently, they also expect to have minimal contact with guards and other prison staff.

As part of their "identity work," many felons also reported a resolve not to let themselves be changed by their imprisonment, as described by this 26-year-old inmate convicted of selling marijuana:

> My strategy was not to become a cold, heartless person, if I could help it at all. Not to join in the mentality of irrational behavior.... For example, I was told in county [jail] that people are divided into groups, and if you're not prejudiced [when you enter prison] you will be when you get out. I consider myself more humanitarian—all people are equal. Those types of things.

Similarly, felons may prepare for their first prison sentences by devising ways of keeping their minds occupied—to keep themselves from stagnating—during their year or so of incarceration. These plans may include activities such as reading, correspondence courses, or other forms of self-improvement, but they are more likely to be in the form of general goals than specific activities. By pursuing these goals and adhering to the protective resolutions of their anticipatory survival strategies, many of these men expect to complete their entire sentences in virtual isolation from other inmates and prison staff.

Before his sentence actually begins, then, a first-time inmate has created an imagery of the prison world, identified his fears about physical and social survival, and articulated a rudimentary anticipatory survival strategy. But he also recognizes that his conceptualization of prison life is incomplete and that he has a great deal to learn about prison, especially during the initial weeks and months of his sentence. He will enter prison in an acute state of wariness, expecting that his fears will materialize at any time and yet not really knowing what to expect. Nonetheless, this violent image, these survival fears, and this anticipatory survival strategy are what he carries with him when he walks into the prison institution— and they remain central elements of his ongoing self-dialogue after he arrives at prison.

ARRIVAL AND EARLY EXPERIENCES

Once a felon arrives at prison, he will begin to learn how accurate his prison imagery is, filling in vague speculations with direct observations, reinforcing some of his understandings, revising others. His arrival at prison also serves as a test of his anticipatory survival strategy, although it is by no means a precise test, as he is likely to alter both his imagery and his strategy almost immediately. His first days and weeks in prison are best viewed as a barrage of sensory impressions and conflicting information, from which he reshapes his prison imagery to match his experiential reality. He must do this by himself, at least initially, rather than through conversations with others. He proceeds in the only way possible, by observing and listening to everything and everyone he encounters, and by continuing to engage in an intermittent self-dialogue about his situation. In this part of the chapter, we examine how the imagery which a new inmate brings into prison becomes modified by his early prison experiences. We will also examine the changes that take place in his survival strategy during the initial weeks of his sentence, and the identity work he continues to perform.

ARRIVAL

A felon's self-dialogue will almost certainly continue during the transfer itself, although the ride to the prison may also offer some relief from this introspection if he is able to converse with the driver or other prisoners during the trip. Confined by handcuffs and leg irons, however, it is difficult to escape a self-acknowledgment that this drive is giving him his last view of the outside world—of cities, towns, and countryside—for an extended period of time. In this passage, a 42-year-old inmate recounts his thoughts during his ride to prison:

> You're trying to think like, really, what am I heading into here? It was at night, it's in winter, and you're wondering that I've been down this particular road so many times in my life and here I am going to the penitentiary and I'll be there for a long time and what am I going to do there? What do they want from me, you know? Am I going to be locked up all the time?... How am I going to get on in there and, you know, make friends and that type of thing? All these things were running through.

Prisoners who arrive at night see very little of the prison's exterior, and those who arrive during the day later remember little about the exterior or the prison grounds, except for the massive wall that surrounds the institution. Still, as is clear from the following interview excerpts, new inmates find that their first glimpse of the prison is intimidating:

> I saw this big, ugly building and I saw a couple of guys walking in. Then I thought, my god, people live here! In cages!

> * * *

> I saw an old place; it looked real old. By just looking at it, it looked pretty scary. It looked like hard-core time, my first opinion of it. It looked like a pretty rugged place, put it that way.... It made me nervous. It made me think that you are really going to have to be sharp—to be on your toes when you go in there.

Whether a new inmate has been transferred alone or with others, he feels completely isolated as he is led, still bound hand and foot, through the front door of the central prison building. As the first iron gate slams shut behind him, its sound echoing down the cellblock halls, he is overcome by the emotion of being separated from his own world and exiled into a new, dangerous, and unknown world.

In the following passages from our interview transcripts, a 41-year-old inmate and a 30-year-old inmate recall their first reactions during their arrival at prison:

Just the thought of everybody—you know, I'll be an "ex-" when that thing opens up—for a long time and it's just ... it's, you know, you're locked up and you feel like an animal.

* * *

I think the first thing that came into my head was, well, you did it this time.... It was just like my whole world really crumbled. I says, well, the outside world does not exist anymore, that's all. I kept saying that to myself over and over again. You get there—when that door closes—even though you know how much you got to do, it feels like, well, this is it, you know, this is the rest of my life.... It's like being branded right in the middle of your back.

This initial sense of confinement, like every other experience at the beginning of a new inmate's sentence, is given profound symbolic importance in his continuing self-dialogue.

After the new inmate is led into the prison, he is placed initially in a holding cell. If he is placed in this cell by himself, the self-dialogue that he began earlier in the day in jail will continue, focusing especially on his fears. A 42-year-old inmate convicted of criminal sexual misconduct recounts his impressions and thoughts in the holding cell:

I'm sitting there watching what was going on. They're processing a few guys in and out, and everybody seems to be sort of friendly and normal—not real, you know, "I'm the guard, you're the inmate" type of thing. They're not pushing anybody around or anything like that. They're observant and all that. Then they brought in two guys from someplace else. And one of these guys was about 6' 6", and he must have weighed almost three hundred pounds, and he had—was the biggest thing I'd ever seen. It was unreal. He had this black overcoat on him and I thought, oh god.... I suppose this place is just full of these guys.... At the time, that fear, that fear just got you all the time.

If there are others in the cell, he may engage in his first tentative interaction with fellow prisoners, usually on such topics as inmates' offenses, their sentences, and their expectations or past experiences of prison life. Most important, and contrary to his preprison beliefs, these conversations demonstrate that a new inmate can communicate with other prisoners, at least to a limited degree. Holding cell conversations do not lead to any essential modification of a new inmate's image of other prisoners, but they do constitute an initial, modest departure from his plan of complete isolationism.

We itemized in an earlier chapter the "in-processing" procedures that new inmates experience when they are transported to the prison. These activities are the first real contacts that new inmates have with guards and other prison staff. Although an everyday routine for the staff, these procedures are anything but routine for new inmates, many of whom are intimidated by virtually every step in the chain of processing activities. From the inmates' emotionally charged vantage point, any act or any comment will be interpreted as either an affirmation or a refutation of their violent prison imagery, and inmates will respond accordingly. In this interview excerpt, for example, an inmate expresses his gratitude at being treated civilly:

> They took me to the control center [security center] and they made me sit there. And there was a lady in there, behind the cage, and she gave me a sandwich and a thing of milk. And they called my name and I went behind another locked gate, and I went downstairs where they photographed me and made me sign a thing where I would have visitors and fill out some papers and stuff. That guy was really nice, he really eased me a lot. He told me what it would be like. He told me there is really not much violence here; he told me about where these Indians jumped a guard—that's the only thing that has happened here recently. He said that basically there wasn't a whole lot of violence here. He eased my mind a whole lot; he was a real nice guard. I don't know his name or anything, and I never saw him again, but he eased me a lot. He told me what it was sort of going to be like.

Another inmate describes both a benign processing experience and a disturbing one:

> They took me to the security center—took me downstairs. There was a very nice young man … he was the guard who took the pictures. Very nice person. He laughed and said, "What are you doing here?"—thought it was a joke. Said you'd do all right here, and went through my clothes. He was very gentle about it. Took my picture and told me to relax…. Before they took me into there, the goon squad undressed me. They were nasty…. They told me to take my clothes off, and they looked up my ass with a proctoscope, thinking that I had drugs on me. They were a little bit disappointed; they didn't find anything. Went though me quite thoroughly, as a matter of fact.

Obviously, anything that directly reinforces an inmate's prior fears will have an especially powerful effect on his sense of well-being:

> They brought me into a room and strip-searched me. One guard commented on how pretty I was, and suggested I grow a beard, while the other guard said I didn't have to worry because of my size. Needless to say, I didn't really need to hear that conversation.

We found no consistent positive or negative pattern of guard–inmate interaction during processing, but offhand remarks—such as this suggestion to grow a beard—are not unusual. Whether offered maliciously, jokingly, or as a sincere attempt to be helpful, such comments underscore the prisoner's fears about violence and sexual abuse. And when remarks of this kind are combined with "helpful" suggestions—for example, that correctional officers are available for assistance if the inmates should hear about trouble in the prison—new inmates typically view such encouragement with suspicion and renew their resolve to avoid nonessential contacts with guards.

After he has completed the preliminary in-processing procedures, an inmate is placed in his initial cell assignment, on the ground level of the Reception and Orientation (R & O) cellblock. This enables the R & O desk sergeant to "check out" a new arrival, by observing him closely and asking him questions. The sergeant may use this opportunity to ascertain how an inmate will react to certain situations, as described here:

> I was then brought to my cellblock.... When I was turned over to the desk sergeant, he proceeded to jump on my ass. I was sure I was back in boot camp. As scared as I was, I didn't need this. He was telling me how he was glad to have me here, and that I would enjoy the place. He asked me if I was glad to be here, and I said no. He kept asking it over and over until I said yes. Just to shut the guy up, I agreed with everything he had to say.

From the guard's point of view, such an interaction can be used to establish an understanding of the guard's control over a powerless inmate (Fleisher 1989). From the perspective of the inmate's preprison orientation, an exchange of this kind can serve only to fortify his prior fears about prison.

Although the inmate himself is locked inside his cell, other inmates in R & O have the run of the "flag" area outside of his cell. This puts the new arrival in the awkward position of being "on display" for other prisoners—a frightening experience for someone who is looking at prison through the lens of his preprison imagery. A 26-year-old inmate recounts this experience:

> On my first night here, I really felt that I was on display. I wanted to sit in the back corner of the cell so no one could see me. I'm not sure whether I felt embarrassed about being in the joint, or maybe embarrassed about not being one of the other inmates ... or quite possibly it was fear of the unknown. I did not like people coming by and just gawking at me like some freak. Only one person who came by stopped and said something. He asked who I was, what I was here for, where I was from—just checking me out. Lots of things were going through my mind when these people were passing by. Some of these guys were just curious—they were seeing if old friends were arriving ... or people from the same county jail they were in. But the most prevalent idea was that these guys were checking to see how big I was, how tough I was.

In this exposed and highly vulnerable situation, a new inmate calls into play all of his prior fears and violent imagery, and attributes nefarious motives to other inmates' curiosity, as depicted in these passages from our interviews and fieldnotes:

Oh yeah, people walk by and say, "Are you so and so? Are you from this place? First time here?"... I wanted to be left alone. I thought they were asking a lot of questions that weren't any of their business. Trying to get friendly with me, and I wasn't sure why.

* * *

One other inmate told me that outside his cell that first night was a card table with four blacks sitting at it. [He said] "They were constantly staring at me. They would look at me, then look at each other, and start laughing. I knew what they had in mind."

The accuracy of a new inmate's interpretation is again beside the point: from his preprison orientation, the experience of being "checked out" by other inmates clearly sustains both his sense of vulnerability and his image of other inmates as hostile and violent.

While he is being observed by others, a new inmate also watches the activities taking place outside his cell, examining everything he sees through the interpretive frame of his preprison orientation. This description, from a 26-year-old convicted of selling marijuana, illustrates how an inmate's observations are colored by his preprison fears:

A bunch of people staring. Yeah, everybody stops; seems like everybody holds their breath when you walk in. They're all looking at you.... They were out loose! Looking. Talking. You could hear people. See 'em talking as you're walking down the hallway—then there'd be talking, and all of a sudden everybody would look—here comes a new guy.... They kinda look you over, check you out, see what kind of person you look like—if you're a goon, a snitch, a baby raper.... It's like walking into a neighborhood where you don't know anybody. This neighborhood is all killers, murders, car thieves....

Most new inmates, when asked about their first night in prison, reported their surprise that other prisoners were "out loose"—walking around, playing cards, even smoking marijuana in open view. Although the idea of prisoners milling about the cellblock may be contrary to a newcomer's prior expectations of the prison world, it is perfectly compatible with his prior fears, as suggested in this interview passage from a 42-year-old inmate:

Total fear. Really just a—you know, I sell for a living ... so I deal with ... that going out and bring your best foot forward everyday, but just the fear of the unknown is totally—totally did a mind trip on me. It really did.

It is in this emotional state that a new inmate faces the solitude of his first night in a prison cell.

After the cellblock has been cleared for the evening head count, a new inmate feels relieved that his first day in prison is finally over. But he immediately discovers a central fact of prison life: he is never really alone, not even when locked in his cell for the night. Besides the guards who pass by his cell on their rounds, he is surrounded by a tremendous cacophony—television sets and stereos blaring, prisoners yelling back and forth between cells, and other, indistinguishable sounds—until the 10:00 lockdown. Some new inmates try to block out this noise, and the day's events, by reading or sleeping. A more common response is to return to the self-dialogue that the inmate initiated that morning at the county jail, and extended during the drive to the prison and then in the holding cell when he first arrived. The same thoughts and concerns return:

> I had done a lot of thinking during the stay about my situation, wondering why I let myself get into this position. I kept going over and over again in my mind all the good-byes. I knew it would be a long time before I'd see these people again. I was absolutely terrified. I couldn't sleep very well that [first] night [because of the] combination of uncomfortable bed, being scared, and all the noise.

With less than a day of prison experience, his fear and uncertainty about his immediate future are also incorporated into his self-dialogue. Two excerpts from our interviews illustrate this:

> Oh, like God, how am I going to put up with all this, you know, all this noise and all the, you know, just being locked up with like three or four hundred people—and that you probably wouldn't pick as your neighbors, you know, and so just the very idea—alone ... that you're in a—you're being forced into a group that you don't want to be in.... How the hell are you going to deal with that without being, you know, constantly pissed off or bummed out?

* * *

> Well, it's a shock because you're in there and it's your first day and you look at how long you got, an ungodly amount of time. Right then, you don't know that you can have a radio or T.V.—I didn't. I didn't know anything about it, and part of their game—I found that they played with you—is that they won't tell you anything. They won't tell you a damn thing. The staff won't tell you nothing—half the time they tell you something, they are lying to you. 'Cause they're here just to get their paycheck.

On balance, a new inmate's experiences during the first day—from his arrival at prison through in-processing, his initial cell assignment, and evening lockup—have served more to confirm than to refute his fears about prison. As he looks ahead to his second and subsequent days, moreover, he knows that he still understands almost nothing about the prison world into which he has been unwillingly placed.

THE FIRST WEEK

The questions and concerns that dominate a new inmate's first night continue through his first week in prison. He returns to his self-dialogue every evening after lockup, and whenever else he has the time to do so. As explained by one inmate:

> We have so much time to ourselves that we can't help but spend a lot of time contemplating our situations. Your thoughts run the gamut from what it is like on the outside; what it will be like on the outside; what's happening to you in here; is anyone thinking about me?

This introspection is facilitated by the newcomer's marginal status during his first week: he is no longer an active member of the outside world but not yet an active member of the prison world. The reality of his sentence is now unequivocal: not only is he behind bars, but he has been virtually cut off from all contact with the outside world.

Although there is no rule that prohibits him from receiving visitors during his first week, only his parents and wife, if he has one, are automatically placed on his visiting list. Visiting forms must be mailed to all others; by the time these forms have been completed and returned, and official clearance granted, the inmate is usually into the second or third week of his sentence. Inmates can receive mail during the first week, but few do. If a new inmate has any outside contact, it is likely to come through a telephone call that he initiates himself, but long lines and strict time limits inhibit him from exercising this privilege often. Many of the inmates with whom we talked said that they had no outside contact at all during their first week in prison.

New inmates understand that they remain isolated from most of the prison world, as well as separated from the outside world. Their first week is filled with numerous activities, but most of these are confined to the R & O cellblock. The newcomers are required to participate in a battery of medical, psychological, and educational tests. They attend orientation classes together, and they eat their meals together, as even meals are taken not in the prison cafeteria but at tables outside their cells. They may cautiously talk with other incoming prisoners during meals or classes, but they know that they have not yet experienced "what prison is really like." Whenever they are not attending scheduled activities or appointments, moreover, they remain locked in their cells and therefore isolated even from other R & O inmates. From a preprison orientation based on a violent imagery of prison and an isolationist survival strategy, this period of separation is welcomed by new inmates. They fully appreciate, however, that it provides them with only a temporary postponement of their inevitable encounters with prisoners from the general population.

The first week in prison can result in some positive modifications of a new inmate's prison image. Prison food, for example, is better than the meals served in most county jails and, therefore, better than new inmates had expected. Most new inmates can also take some comfort from the fact that they have completed a week of their sentences without major confrontations. Because they have had the opportunity for at least minimal interaction with other incoming inmates, they discover that they *can* talk with others and that at least some other inmates do not possess the "hardened" characteristics that they had attributed to all prisoners.

For a number of reasons, however, these discoveries provide only small comfort. A new inmate knows that he has yet to encounter prisoners from the general population. He recognizes that he has yet to experience "normal" prison life, and he may even desire to "get on" with the next phase of his sentence. The information he has received from other R & O inmates—about prison activities, programs, guards, or prisoners in the general population—is contradictory and difficult to interpret. Thus, at the conclusion of his first week, a new inmate still possesses only a vague, uncertain conceptualization of prison life, and one that is still dominated by the idea of violence.

IMAGERY MODIFICATION

The preprison orientation remains essentially intact through the early weeks of a new inmate's sentence. He continues to view the prison as violent and uncertain; he continues to view other inmates as dangerous and alien; he continues to see his paramount problem as one of survival. Nonetheless, he acquires enough new information during these weeks, from official sources and his own observations, to modify his preprison imagery in several respects.

We described, in Chapter 2, the orientation classes that all arriving inmates are required to attend. On the surface, these classes appear to be precisely what new prisoners need: a structured presentation of information about prison life, which could reduce the overwhelming uncertainty they have about their immediate futures. These classes do succeed to some extent, in that they do provide a crude outline of the rules and activities of the prison. This success is severely limited, however, for a number of reasons. First, orientation classes are understood to present only an *official* view of the prison world. Even first-time inmates know that the prison does not operate exactly as described by the prison staff and that this official view needs to be contrasted with the "inside information" they can receive from other sources, including jail cellmates, guards, and other prisoners. Some of the advice they receive through these informal channels is even prefaced with the admonition to disregard information received from official sources. A second limitation stems from the time at which orientation classes are offered, immediately after the new inmate arrives at prison. Although this is precisely when new inmates have the greatest need for information, it is also a time during which they are particularly ill-prepared to assimilate this information accurately, because of their vulnerability and their apprehension about prison. Finally, the most important limitation of the orientation program is simply that it does not address the predominant concerns of new prisoners, especially their fears of sexual or violent assault. Although new inmates are allowed a gradually increasing amount of independence and mobility during the program, they still have had only the most restricted contact with inmates from the general population. Orientation classes do not address these central fears, and would probably be ineffective if they did. Official prison policies, information about available educational or rehabilitation programs, and recreational opportunities are all irrelevant to these fears. Information about regulations regarding outside telephone calls, correspondence, and visits is useful, but it does not speak to concerns about how many visits or letters a prisoner will receive, or how long they will continue. Assessing the validity of their prior fears and expectations, testing the utility of their anticipatory survival strategies, and developing a more consistent image of the prison world are all activities that inmates must accomplish outside of formal classes.

If orientation classes contribute relatively little to a new inmate's prison socialization, other experiences during the first weeks of his sentence have a greater impact on his understanding of the prison world. His early weeks in prison are marked by expanding opportunities, and obligations, for interaction with staff and inmates. These interactions affect his image of the prison world and, ultimately, his survival strategy and his identity work as well.

It is during the orientation phase that a new inmate has the greatest amount of interaction with prison guards. His early "drill sergeant" image becomes modulated by his discovery that there is considerable variation within the security force: some guards are friendly, while others are indifferent or hostile; some are able to overlook minor rules infractions, while others are "hard-nosed;" some behave consistently, others capriciously. This revelation, like most discoveries in prison, is based in part on direct experience and in part on information received from others. Some degree of mistrust remains, and most inmates continue to avoid contact with guards unless absolutely necessary, but this discovery of differences among prison guards results in at least a minor alteration of an inmate's preprison imagery and, thus, edges him closer to a more realistic comprehension of prison life.

A parallel change in definition takes place concerning other prisoners. Although a new inmate continues to view the general population as consisting of violence-prone human beings with whom he has nothing in common, he does begin to interact with specific other inmates in the R & O cellblock, including both other new inmates and more experienced prisoners. Interaction is initiated in a number of ways. If a new inmate is a member of an ethnic minority group, members of the group will approach him soon after his arrival on the cellblock. In fact, *any* evidence of special group affiliation or common interest can facilitate interaction, as suggested by this excerpt from an interview with a 26-year-old inmate convicted of a drug offense:

> Well, I'm a motorcyclist and when I first came in here, them were the first people to talk to me.... They approached me. I was wearing a Harley-Davidson t-shirt. They seen me and they come to my cell and they approached me, and they told me what was going on in the prison with the blacks, the whites, the niggers, the Mexicans. They told me about it, you know, and they told me if anything ever comes down—any riots or anything like that, you know–that you always have a lot of people backing ya up. I was just kind of initiated in the biker group.

Even when obvious connections to an established group are lacking, interaction emerges from practical needs or sociability. A 30-year-old inmate convicted of criminal sexual misconduct expounds:

> Everybody in R & O especially, everybody's always borrowing from everybody else, you know, so you're going to have people come up, sitting there watching T.V. and somebody'll come up and say, "You got some coffee?" "Yeah." So they sit down and start talking, talking a little bit. Pretty soon, little by little, you get to know a little bit about everybody around your immediate area and what not. I think it's a gradual change. I think it's an almost natural change, because it's really not that drastic. It's just the right—I mean you pick up—it's just kind of like being born. First you're crawling around and then all of a sudden you get up and take a few steps and you sit down, then a few more, and pretty soon you find yourself walking, and the time is going by fast.

Initial conversations usually center on the crimes for which inmates were convicted, the lengths of their sentences, and various aspects of the prison world, as these are the experiences that new inmates have in common. Within these conversations, however, inmates often find other points of common interest, including the discovery of a *shared uncertainty* about prison life. Although they do not immediately alter their views of the general population, the tentative friendships that can arise through these commonalities are the first significant fissures in the anticipatory imagery that new inmates carried into the prison from the outside world.

An inmate's contacts with other prisoners increase considerably after he has been reassigned to another cell within the R & O cellblock. Reassignment, which usually occurs after the first week, entails a move to a cell on a higher tier, leaving first floor cells available for newly arriving prisoners. The move is significant in two respects. First, the physical move is accompanied by greater mobility, which also means that the inmate will now be under less constant observation by guards. Second, even though the inmate has only moved a short distance, his change of cells requires him to adjust to a new group of inmates, in what is essentially a new environment. The satisfaction of increased mobility is thus tempered by his apprehension over increased contact with other inmates. It is largely in response to this apprehension that a new inmate forges the basic elements of his prison survival strategy.

SURVIVAL STRATEGY

Most new inmates bring to the prison an anticipatory survival strategy that consists of little more than a series of protective resolutions to stay out of trouble by avoiding unnecessary contacts with both inmates and guards. Although the spirit of this isolationist strategy continues to guide new inmates for some time, its literal application becomes tempered by the experience-guided modifications that inmates make to their prison imagery. As their view of the prison world becomes more concrete, their guidelines for surviving this world become more specific as well. Within a few weeks of their arrival, most new inmates have forged a more sophisticated survival strategy that includes four basic elements: territorial caution, impression management, selective interaction with other inmates, and a partnership with one other inmate. We will describe each of these briefly.

Territorial Caution

Following reassignment, an increasing amount of the inmate's time is spent outside his cell, eating meals in the prison cafeteria, exercising in the gym, visiting the library, or attending weekend movies in the auditorium. Each of these locations adds another dimension to his prison life, but each must be approached cautiously because each involves being in contact with the general inmate population. A new inmate is not aware of territorial norms or other informal rules that might exist and, consequently, approaches each new location warily, as if he were entering enemy territory. A 25-year-old inmate convicted of burglary depicts both the positive and negative aspects of new territory:

> I was scared having to go down to that big chow hall. That big chow hall where you see all the inmates, you know, it seemed like a lot of people…. I was looking forward to getting out, so I could move around … but I was scared of the people.

Every new location requires an inmate to search for clues about how he should act. If he misses these clues, he can suddenly find himself in a difficult situation. For example, one of the men we interviewed recalls an altercation that followed a violation of telephone norms:

> I got into a big … thing with one of the black guys, because there's a specific time [limit on the telephone], 10 minutes or something like that. If you go longer they get on your case, and … [he] was trying to make an issue out of it, just to throw his weight around a little bit—'cuz I'd seen him in action a little bit.

Other inmates described similar exchanges in the cafetaria and recreational areas. Because behavioral guidelines are not provided by prison staff, a new inmate is often forced simply to "follow the crowd" to discover appropriate behaviors. By thus engaging in *territorial caution*—observing others, looking for behavioral clues, and then deciding on the safest course of action—he gradually learns how he should act in various locations within the prison.

As he is exploring his expanded physical environment, the inmate also gains insight into the social world of the prison. For example, as he observes others smoking marijuana or gambling, he learns that the prison world of the cellblock is quite different from that described in orientation classes. Although most new prisoners have generally been aware of this discrepancy all along, many are nonetheless surprised by the openness with which illegal activities occur.

It also becomes apparent that illegal activities are *optional* features of prison life. With this recognition comes a more realistic understanding of "doing your own time." It is both unnecessary and impractical to avoid all contact with other inmates. In addition to the tentative friendships that are formed among new inmates during orientation, superficial contact with other inmates is also possible. Illegal activities observed among the general population should be ignored, however, and invitations to participate should be declined. "Doing your own time" becomes a matter of noninvolvement in these activities, as suggested in this fieldnote excerpt:

> In walking around the yard and the cellblock or going to the movie, [the new inmate] notices other inmates smoking marijuana or participating in drug deals. He also may be hit on by a hustler, offered gifts and such from complete strangers. All this tells the inmate that he sees, hears and speaks no evil. These are important words to live by. The hope is that if you don't bother anyone else, they won't bother you. For your own good, don't get involved. Those individuals who get into trouble bring it on themselves.

This insight, made possible by the knowledge gained through territorial caution, is an important step in the evolution of a new inmate's survival strategy. But the inmate requires something more than precautionary behavioral guidelines; he also needs some means to confront the prison world directly. Impression management skills, a second component of his emerging survival strategy, provide these means.

Impression Management

A new inmate enters prison, as we have seen, with an overwhelming fear of physical or sexual assault from other inmates. During his early weeks in prison, one his foremost concerns is to hide his fear of other inmates, as noted in this interview excerpt:

> I just kept walking fast, you know, moving with the crowd. And I kept my eyes open.... People would eyeball me, you know. I could just tell by the way they were looking at me. They've been here too long, or else they were gay before they got here.

At the same time, although he does not consider himself to be like other prisoners, he does not want to appear too different from them. It is primarily for this reason that new inmates elect to wear prison-issue uniforms, even though they have the option of wearing their own clothes. Beyond matters of outward appearances, however, the inmate also tries to cultivate a nondistinctive presentation of self. In this interview passage, a 32-year-old inmate convicted of medical fraud outlines the desired presentation:

> Well, I learned that you can't act like—you can't get the attitude where you are better than they are. Even where you might be better than them, you can't strut around like you are. Basically, you can't stick out. You don't stare at people and things like that. I knew a lot of these things from talking to people, and I figured them out by myself. I sat down and figured out just what kind of attitude I'm going to have to take.

The first-time inmate's problem, then, is to learn how to look and act like other prisoners so that he can blend into the inmate population.

The immensity of this problem can be seen in a new inmate's early explorations of prison territory. Observing others from a distance may provide general interactional clues to the situation, but the very act of entering a new territory is a highly self-conscious endeavor, especially if the inmate is alone. He does not know where, nor precisely how, to walk. He is uncertain how he should carry himself, or where to focus his eyes. To walk rapidly through the cellblock or yard with downcast eyes is a clear sign of intimidation, and yet there is a concern that direct eye contact with other prisoners might lead to confrontation. A typical compromise is to walk with a self-imposed slowness, with eyes focused directly ahead. A 23-year-old inmate recalls his early ventures into new territory:

> I finally got out of orientation. I was going out with the main population, going down to get my meals and things. The main thing is not to stare at a bunch of people, you know. I tried to just look ahead, you know, not to stare at people. 'Cause I didn't know, you know. Basically, I just didn't really know; I just had to learn a little at a time.

At this point in his prison career, a new inmate possesses only the most elementary *impression management* skills, but he clearly recognizes their importance.[1] His skills continue to develop throughout much of his career and, as we discuss in subsequent chapters, they ultimately become the foundation for his participation in the prison world.

Selective Interaction

As he is given greater mobility within the prison, a new inmate finds that it is possible, and at times necessary, to interact with other prisoners, outside the confines of the R & O cellblock. If he is to partake in any group recreational activities, from athletics to card playing, he must communicate and cooperate with others. Even if he avoids these activities, he soon learns that he will be approached by other inmates, for one reason or another, in the cafeteria, on the yard, or during any of his other explorations. He may also find it useful to approach others. But his preprison image of inmates prevents him from engaging in the kind of casual, everyday interactions that are commonplace in the outside world. Instead, he learns to engage in *selective interaction*, always preferring the company of acquaintances to that of strangers, and striving to minimize interaction with anyone who might pose danger.

To engage in selective interaction is to make decisions about which prisoners should be avoided entirely. Sometimes, this means avoiding entire groups of inmates:

> I stayed away from the blacks and the Indians [and the] Mexicans. I let everyone sit where they wanted to [in the theater] and I sat in the balcony.... I didn't want to get involved.

Others make this identification on an individual basis, systematically observing others to determine who should be avoided. In the following interview passages, two inmates convey the guidelines they followed in this regard:

I found that on my own, I guess ... I just watched, listened, stayed away from the people that were loud. Stayed away from the people who talked a lot of shit.

* * *

I used my own senses about who to stay away from.... Pick up vibes—watch other people's actions.... I look for people to hook up with. People showing them respect without them having to come overly violent, without them having to go out of their way to get this respect from other people. They usually are [the] more stable people you run into in here. People that I stay away from are people that are shooting off their mouths, people who are acting like a tough. People who are basically trying to gain that respect that I was talking about.

It is ironic that in their evaluation of prisoners who should be avoided, new inmates rely on the same behavioral clues that they are consciously incorporating into their own attempts at impression management.

New inmates use a similar method to identify inmates with whom they might associate, because they offer the possibility of nonthreatening interaction or because they might provide some measure of protection. A 41 year-old-inmate in prison on a probation violation details his decision-making criteria:

I pretty well picked and choosed who I wanted to be seen with.... I just watch people. If I don't like what they're doing, how they walk, how they talk—get a lot of feedback from other people too, you know—within a week or two you can ... pretty well tell who you want to associate with. There's just a handful of people that I associate with and that's it. I keep my distance all the way around.

As this statement illustrates, behavioral clues are supplemented by information provided by others. Thus, the more that new inmates establish relationships with some prisoners, the more they can draw upon these relationships to help evaluate other prisoners.

Although inmates differ in how selective they are, all new inmates engage in selective interaction as part of their survival strategy. The significance of their early associations, however, extends beyond inmates' attempts to avoid violent confrontations. If friendly relations can be established with some prisoners, then a correction is needed to the new inmate's preprison imagery: the majority of the inmate population may still be viewed as hostile and violent, but the prison includes "normal" men as well. This revision provides grounds for optimism regarding the new inmate's chances for survival.

Partnerships

In the early weeks of their sentences, most new inmates have contact with a number of other prisoners but primarily associate with one or two others, with whom they feel most comfortable. These tentative friend-ships, which are usually formed with other new inmates, become gradually elevated to the status of "partnerships," through a process that involves both an interactional development of the friendship bond and institutional recognition of that bond.

The interactional process has already been outlined: these friendships are generally based on common backgrounds or interests, including a shared uncertainty about prison life. They become strengthened because they exist within the hostile world of the prison and because they enable a mutual exploration of this world. These friendships take on added impor-tance through the recognition given them by both prison staff and other inmates. The term "partner"—which is simply the prison term for such a friendship—is used very casually within the prison, so it has little effect on a new prisoner when he first hears it. Both guards and other inmates refer to partnerships, however, and both make the assumption that an inmate's partner will help him survive in prison.[2] This passage from our fieldnotes indicates how these assumptions are conveyed to new inmates:

> The first time I heard the term used in the prison was during Phase I and one of the sergeants used it. He said that if one of us was being brought to segregation, it would be better if our partner kept his cool, avoiding going to segregation, so he could be out working to get things straightened out. Your partner is of no use to you if he is in segregation also.

> The second time that I can remember hearing the term was during Phase II. A lifer came up to me and asked if my partner had been shot before—I guess he had a scar on his back that looked similar to a bullet wound. At first, I didn't know quite who or what he was talking about. He had to describe him (my friend) to me. From that point on, I have heard and used the term frequently.

By presuming the significance of partnerships, guards and inmates provide both a label and a definition for the friendship bond.

As we discuss in the next chapter, partnerships have multiple adaptive functions for new inmates at various stages in their prison careers. During the early weeks of his sentence, a new inmate's driving motivation is to understand the prison world so that he can survive within it; accordingly, the primary value of a partnership at this stage is as a means of "making sense" out of prison life. This function includes the mutual exploration of prison territory, but it also includes a comparison of prior expectations about prison, the exchange of prison information, and, most important, the *mutual interpretation* of information received from orientation classes, prison officials, inmates, and other sources.

The interpretive function of partnerships can be illustrated by looking at one form of prison information, such as the role of racial and ethnic groups in the social organization of the prison. At Midwestern, the major prison groups are whites, blacks, and American Indians. Simply by observing other prisoners, a new inmate can discern that most interaction takes place within these groups rather than across groups. But when he can discuss his observations with his partner, he becomes able to derive more precise ideas about both the prison stratification system and its implications for his own behavior. By trading and analyzing the information they have, partners can share the established interactional rules they have learned or formulate their own. Partners come to recognize, for example, that the numerical majority held by whites does not translate into power within the prison social structure.[3] They may decide that it is acceptable to talk with someone from another racial group in some situations but not in others. They begin to make finer distinctions within ethnic groups; at Midwestern, for example, both black and white inmates distinguish between young Indians, who essentially constitute a prison gang, and older Indians, with whom communication is much easier.[4]

Information about the racial stratification system, the prison economy, the distribution of prison jobs, the availability of contraband, and other aspects of the informal social structure can be acquired from several sources. All of this information, however, requires sorting out and evaluating before it can be used as a basis for action. A partnership provides a social relationship through which this interpretive process can take place. Because it provides a foundation for a interactional rather than an individual interpretation of the prison world, a new inmate's partnership gradually evolves into the single most important element in his prison survival strategy.

INTERPRETING PRISON: THE INTERPLAY OF IMAGERY AND STRATEGY

The survival tactics that new inmates develop in the early weeks of their sentences are all designed to protect inmates from the dangers of the prison world. But each of these tactics also enables inmates to *acquire* more knowledge about the prison world, by allowing them to explore and interpret that world. In this sense, inmates' survival tactics both reflect their prison imagery and contribute to its revision. This interplay of imagery and strategy can now be summarized.

A new inmate enters prison with an imprecise but violent prison image and an anticipatory survival strategy based on this image. In the early weeks of his sentence, he remains highly apprehensive and uncertain about the prison world. Through orientation classes and his own explorations, both his understanding of prison life and his survival strategy become more sophisticated. This increased sophistication is not something that simply results from a week or two of prison experiences; it is, rather, the product of the inmate's *active* attempts to "make sense" of his prison experience. He knows that his survival requires a more comprehensive understanding of the prison, and he works to achieve this understanding.

Orientation classes give a new inmate only a limited knowledge of the prison, and he finds it necessary to supplement what he learns in these classes with other types of information. He does this initially by observing other inmates—watching their actions, following them to the cafeteria and other locations and, from the time of his arrival, eavesdropping on their conversations. A 26-year-old inmate describes these first steps:

> I kept pretty much to myself [during] those early parts [of the sentence]. Well, I definitely had an open ear for the inside scoops.... Like overhearing conversations. How things work—kinda get a feel of what I'm up against.

He also talks with other inmates, beginning with other incoming inmates in the R & O cellblock, and questions them about the prison. A 37-year-old inmate explains:

> Well, eventually I asked people questions but then, you know, people come up to you and start talking, whether you want to listen to them or not.

Guided by territorial caution, impression management and selective interaction, he gradually extends his contacts to a wider range of inmates, as described here by a 23-year-old inmate:

> I would hear stuff from the guys, the group I was talking with. We would be talking to other people. Like there's this one Indian that was there that the guy I knew got to know, and he had been in here before. He let us in on a lot of stuff.

He then combines the information from his observations and inmate conversations with the information he receives from guards, other prison staff, and orientation classes, and deliberately reconstructs his image of the prison world.

Inmates vary in the sophistication with which they approach this experiential "data collection and analysis" but, as the following interview excerpt illustrates, some inmates become remarkably systematic in this endeavor:

> I talked to prisoners for the most part. I observed and I talked to some guards.... Sort of played it by ear, I guess, and if someone appears to be friendly, I might have a couple of words with them. That would be up to the day—maybe a few more words the next day. Just sort of feel people out ... I got myself a little notebook pad and I took a lot of notes, asked the guards a lot of questions. Tried to find different ways that a

person can get out or cut their time short or transfer to a less secure area—what would be a good cell hall to be in, which one was quiet, which one was safe—find out, you know, things about the prison and about people.

Many inmates, of course, use a more casual interpretive approach than suggested by this excerpt. Nonetheless, our data clearly demonstrate that new inmates are actively engaged in making sense out of the prison world rather than passively absorbing the institutional routines of this world.

Constructing and then revising a working conceptualization of the prison world is difficult, because of the contradictory information an inmate receives about official and unofficial prison policy, parole or program review procedures, and other aspects of prison life. A 24-year-old inmate summarizes:

> There was a lot of differences from what I had heard. Everybody comes up to you and tells you something different. The person in education told us something different. We come back, the guards tell us something different when we ask them. You ask the inmates, they'll tell you something different.

Faced with such conflicting information, an inmate is unable to resolve completely his uncertainty about prison. He is able to reduce it, however, by following two interpretive caveats. The first is simply to adopt a practice of never fully accepting information received from any single source. Advice about the parole/program review process, for example, whether it is received from a caseworker or another inmate, is considered to be at best a *possible* indication of future events. The second practice that a new inmate follows is to rely on his partner to help him interpret any information about the prison. This does not mean that he will accept all of his partner's advice without question (although he is likely to give it greater credence than advice from other sources). Rather, it means that information he receives from various sources will be discussed, evaluated, and acted upon in conjunction with his partner.

As an inmate's uncertainty about the prison world diminishes, he finds himself *disseminating* as well as soliciting information about survival in prison. A 27-year-old inmate explains:

> In general, I saw two different groups—the groups that had been here for a while and the groups that just got here, and I'd say I talked—I probably had as much communication—you know, both groups about the same amount. I'd get information from the groups that had been here a while and—someone who was new, you know, I'd pass it on to them.

A new inmate's role as "carrier" of prison information certifies his genuine participation in the prison world. In contrast to the anticipatory image and survival strategy constructed independently by each new inmate, the image and strategy that an inmate formulates during his early weeks in prison are products of a specific socialization process, in which an inmate acquires information about the prison from older inmates, interprets it with his partner and perhaps one or two others, and then transmits this information to still newer inmates.

A new inmate's survival strategy is intended to enhance his understanding of the prison social world and to enable him to act upon this understanding. He requires a survival strategy because be believes the prison to be a strange, unpredictable, and violent world, to which he does not really belong. Throughout the initial weeks of his sentence, in other words, he continues to view the prison world from the perspective of the outside world. In the next section, we reexamine a new inmate's social marginality at this point in his prison career.

SOCIAL MARGINALITY

In a number of respects, the transformation that takes place among first-time inmates just a few weeks into their sentences is remarkable. They have modified and reconstructed their preprison imagery to incorporate everything they have learned through their initial experiences in prison. They have broken through their anticipated extreme social isolation and developed a survival strategy that enables them to engage in cautious interaction with some other inmates. But even as they are accomplishing all of this, they continue to hold only a marginal status in the prison social world. They are, in fact, prison inmates, but they remain "outsiders" in the prison world. Their social marginality is sustained by the identity work they continue to perform, acutely reinforced both by contacts they have with the outside world and by events that take place within the prison world.

IDENTITY WORK

Throughout his first weeks of prison life, a new inmate's primary need, as we have seen, is to make sense of his new social world, in order to survive. His crowded schedule of processing activities and orientation classes diminishes his capacity to engage in the kind of self-dialogue that characterized his jail stay prior to prison and the first few days of his prison sentence. Nevertheless, he regularly returns to this self-dialogue, especially at night, in his cell. The same concerns—questioning his past behavior and motives, reliving the events leading to his prison sentence, worrying about the effects of his sentence on family and friends—are still present. Added to these concerns is the need to assimilate and interpret all of the information he has acquired through his various efforts to understand the prison world and his place in it. His apprehension about prison is directly connected to his uncertainty: until he can make sense out of the behavior of guards and other inmates—so that he can predict, at least in a general sense, what will happen next—he will continue to see himself as highly vulnerable and essentially defenseless.

An inmate's self-dialogue, then, becomes an integral part of the process through which he actively revises his conceptualization of the prison world, including his image of other inmates. At the same time, a new inmate makes use of his self-dialogue to *differentiate* himself from other prisoners. He entered prison, as we have seen, with the belief that prison inmates were an alien and hostile breed of men, with whom he had nothing in common. His early experiences in prison allow him to make some exceptions to this image but he continues to see himself as different from other inmates. The following interview passage, from a 37-year-old inmate convicted of theft, illustrates this:

> Of course I saw myself as different. I feel that there are some people here who are basically good people. I didn't find anyone who I would go out of my way to get to know, or to have anything to do with. I felt that I was here because I did something wrong, just like everyone else that was here. I felt that maybe I was a lot more educated than some people, and maybe less educated than a few. I was definitely more mature than most of the people.

It is through his nightly self-dialogue that a new inmate continues to assert these distinctions—that he is different from other prisoners and that he does not belong in their world.

The differentiation he maintains through his self-dialogue gets directly translated into his behavior in prison. His earliest interactions with other prisoners express the self-insulation of the anticipatory survival strategy that he brought into the prison. As stated by one of the inmates we interviewed:

> [I was] reserved ... I wouldn't be very [communicative], you know. I'd try to keep conversation to a minimum.... I wasn't interested in getting close to anybody ... or answering a lot of questions. You know, try to cut the conversation short ... go my own way back to my cell or go to the library or something.

Even as he expands his exploration of the prison world, using territorial caution, selective interaction and impression management techniques, he holds onto his policy of self-insulation. These guarded interactions allow a new inmate to maintain some version of his preprison image of other inmates, while excluding himself from this social category. An inmate's partnership is the most significant exception to his differentiation process, but it also contributes to it. An inmate's ability to converse freely and more authentically with his partner enables both partners to draw a protective line of demarcation around their friendship, thus distinguishing themselves from other prisoners.

OUTSIDE CONTACTS

An inmate's socially marginal position in the prison world is reinforced by his contacts with family and friends. After the first week or so of his sentence, the necessary forms to enable the prisoner to receive visitors have been completed. By this time, he also has had opportunities for telephone calls with outsiders, and he may have received letters from them. These initial contacts are particularly meaningful for a first-time inmate because they can provide him with a reaffirmation of his ties to the outside world and fortify his belief that he does not really belong in the prison world.

An inmate's first contact with the outside world is ordinarily by a telephone call—which must be initiated by the inmate himself—within a day or two of his arrival at the prison. This is usually a highly emotional experience, as this excerpt from Jones' prison journal suggests:

> Called Tom Schmid on the phone. You don't know the nice feeling it is to talk to someone you know from the outside. I had a smile on my face for the next half-hour. After hearing that familiar voice, I kind of got a little choked up. It was hard to talk. I had so many things to say but couldn't think of one while I was on the phone. Fortunately, Tom did all the talking.

While almost all new inmates report that their first telephone calls were gratifying, a few noted that this effect is very short-lived and that these calls also contributed to their loneliness or depression about being in prison.

Letters are less predictable than telephone calls because the inmate has no direct control over them. Nonetheless, receiving a letter from a friend or family member has similar impact, as illustrated by these passages:

> Mail is passed out right before supper. We sit in our cells and wait for them to come around. The first week … there was no way I was going to get any mail. Even though I knew that, it was still a letdown when the guard passed my cell. Butterflies go

through your stomach while you're waiting. It took 10 days for my first letter to arrive, and then I got three. I didn't know which one to open first. I kept reading them over and over again.

* * *

No one will ever know what it means to get letters from friends or hear their voices. They don't really have to say anything. Just taking the time to write shows they care and they haven't forgotten you. That is one of the big concerns.

Face-to-face visits elicit an even more intense reaction:

Before entering prison, I don't think I ever got natural highs—probably was too loaded to notice. But when you are sitting in your cell bummed out and you hear your name called—it's a definite rush, equal to any I had on the streets. Your body begins to tremble; the excitement in you increases; breathing is faster; you sit in the visiting room waiting for the visitor; you see them and all of a sudden everything is fine. It's like you're not even here.

* * *

I was actually shaking when I went to the visiting room. The time went by so fast [one hour]. Boy it feels good to get a visit.

Despite some social awkwardness inherent in the situation, initial visits seem to pass quickly for most inmates. Outsiders want to know how the inmate is doing, and the inmate is able to describe his early prison experiences, point out that he has had no real difficulties so far, and comfort his visitors with his assessment that many aspects of prison life are less severe than he had anticipated. Visitors, in turn, provide the inmate with news of the outside world, thereby confirming his relationship to that world.

At the beginning of their sentences, then, most new inmates find their telephone calls, letters, and visits to be highly emotional experiences, which provide welcome relief from the danger and uncertainty of the prison. These contacts reassure inmates that they are still socially connected to the outside world, and concomitantly reinforce their belief that they do not belong in the prison world. But outside contacts also underscore a new inmate's social marginality in another respect, by emphasizing his lack of control over events in either the outside or prison worlds. That is, because outside contacts are themselves unpredictable, inmates recognize the dangers of granting them too much importance. If receiving a letter or visit can produce euphoria within the restricted and intimidating world of the prison, *not* receiving an expected communication can be devastating, as indicated in this fieldnote excerpt:

Inmates in here are on this emotional tightrope. This institutional living kind of distorts your thinking.... Any little thing can upset your balance—a Dear John letter, no visits when you expect them, a missed appointment.

The sudden mood shifts that can arise from inmates' lack of control over outside communications collide with the inmates' growing recognition that emotional survival in prison requires them to "do their own time."

Dramatic Events

Just as outside contacts reinforce an inmate's marginality, so do *dramatic events* within the prison world. A new inmate, as we have described, is gradually able to reduce his uncertainty about prison life during his initial days or weeks in prison. His developing survival strategy makes his uncertainty, and the accompanying apprehension, more manageable. He does not feel secure in prison, but he does achieve a somewhat more realistic understanding of the prison world, and he has increased confidence that he will survive his sentence. He takes comfort in minor victories; a night, a week, two weeks, or a month in prison are recognized as milestones, not so much because they represent the partial completion of his sentence as because they represent periods of time that have passed *without incident*. Whenever a new inmate reflects on the fortune that his worst fears have not materialized, he feels slightly less apprehensive about his situation.

Invariably, this emerging sense of security is abruptly shattered, when one of the new inmate's prior fears about imprisonment does occur. We will use several data excerpts from our interviews and fieldnotes to illustrate the effects of violent incidents on new inmates' interpretation of prison life, beginning with these reports of inmates' "first" dramatic events:

> Just when you get a grip on things and start to feel somewhat comfortable, something happens to upset things—a rape.... There is no way that anyone is safe in this place. You really have no protection at all. The only time you are safe is after 10 p.m. lockup. I don't know any of the details and don't care to know them. It just makes me sick to think about it.

* * *

> The [second] day that I was here was when _____ was killed. That, that comforting feeling that I had left me. I was scared again. I thought, damn, somebody got killed—like that.... Yeah, I was going to be more careful, to watch what the heck was going on.

The critical incident need not, and generally does not, involve the new inmate himself; the fact that he hears about or witnesses it is sufficient to decimate his feelings of relative security. Assaults, homicides, suicides, rapes, or similar dramatic events violently underscore a new inmate's outsider status in the prison world. The shock value of a dramatic event is evident in the inmate's prison image, his adaptation strategy, and his identity work.

The immediate effect is on his conceptualization of the prison world. If a dramatic event occurs during the first few days of his sentence, it instantly validates and intensifies his prior fears about prison life. If he has managed to serve several days or weeks of his sentence without major problems, a dramatic event annihilates his sense of relative security and his guarded optimism that he will be able to survive the prison ordeal. Concomitantly, it restores the intimidating, terrifying image of prison life that he brought to the prison, as this inmate explains:

> Just a couple of weeks after I got here, a dude over in A-Hall jumped, I guess—at least, they call it suicide—and hit his chest on the floor and picnic tables. I was down getting my basic—you know, state clothes, shoes and [they] brought him out and it just bummed me out. They were trying to make him breathe. He wasn't breathing and, shit, he was dead. Kind of, ah, wow, you know....

> * * *

> I heard about a guy getting his head crushed down in the weight room.... Well, when I heard the part where they took a barbell and hit him over the head and the fluid that surrounds the brain was spilling on the floor, ah, that really got cruel, so I was thinking, how can someone actually do that? Why not just beat a guy up? Why do they have to try to kill him, and get more time?

This effect is so powerful that a temptation often exists—a few days after a dramatic event—to "write off" the incident as an isolated occurrence, and to struggle to regain the sense of well-being that had been gradually developing. Although some inmates are successful in recapturing a feeling of security, it is again sabotaged by another dramatic event, a few days or weeks later.

> I would say after two weeks I felt really calm about being here.... After about the third week, there was another rape. This really shocked me. It upset this comfortable, safe world I had imagined I was living in. I realized that the first rape wasn't an isolated event. It also made me paranoid all over again. I had to reshape my whole outlook on this place.

An inmate's "outsider's" view of the prison world is thus strengthened through these violent reassertions of his preprison imagery.

Dramatic events have an equally powerful effect on a new inmate's adaptation strategy. Depending on how long his sentence has been incident-free, his initial, extreme "do your own time" strategy will have been modified to accommodate meaningful interaction with one or a few inmates, superficial contact with a larger number of inmates, exploration of the cellblock and prison yard (with impression management techniques), and possibly even minimal participation in illegal activities, such as drug use or gambling. While a dramatic event is not likely to nullify these modifications entirely, it will increase the inmate's caution when exploring new territory and fortify his resolve to avoid any persons, behaviors, or situations that hold a potential for confrontation.

> I've seen a total of four blood pools that were obvious.... Every time I see it, I just keep thinking of what was the mechanics of the situation. How did it happen?... I've learned to treat situations extremely delicate. For the most part, you can't trust anyone. You've got to be very extremely cautious with your relationships with other people.

In this way, dramatic events encourage at least a partial return to the self-insulation of the inmate's anticipatory survival strategy.

Finally, dramatic events also promote a renewed self-dialogue. As the new inmate has been adjusting to the prison world, his periods of introspection have focused less on the behavior and motives leading to his incarceration and more on making sense out of the prison world and his position in it. Throughout this time, he has been unable to resolve his identity concerns or overcome completely his initial feelings of helplessness, and a dramatic event, above all else, heightens his sense of vulnerability.

> Probably the biggest fear that a new inmate has is that of sexual assault. The reason ... is that it is not only a physical attack, but it also brings in a question of masculinity. In a place where "macho" is very important, this type of attack is difficult for the inmate to handle. It is considered very disgusting and demeaning.

Following a dramatic event, his self-dialogue is also likely to include a self-analysis of his ability to protect himself. In contrast to the pre-prison self-dialogue through which he initially formulated his resolve to defend himself as necessary, the inmate now has some direct experience in the prison world, and self-defense is no longer an abstraction. He now knows what other prisoners look like and has a better idea of what self-defense would entail. Nonetheless, through both his self-dialogue and his conversations with other new inmates, he reaffirms his resolution:

> I was scared as hell, as [were] the others, no matter how brave they sounded. But I told myself that I would fight, even if they did have a knife. I figured I would rather be stuck than have to live with the rape. I couldn't just let someone get away with it. I would have to fight.

Beyond this analysis of how he would respond to an assault, dramatic events also lead to renewed introspection about all of the inmate's earlier identity concerns, including the fundamental distinction he makes between himself and other inmates.

SUMMARY AND DISCUSSION

A first-time inmate develops an orientation toward the prison world prior to his arrival at the prison institution. Drawing upon media portrayals, his own criminal justice experience, information provided by others, and his own imagination, he constructs a vague but nonetheless useful image of prison life. Working from this imagery, which emphasizes the violence of the prison world, he identifies the problems he expects to encounter, formulates a strategy for addressing these problems, and initiates a form of identity work through a recurrent self-dialogue. He carries this preprison orientation with him to the prison, where it will serve as his interpretive framework during the initial days and weeks of his imprisonment.

Following his arrival, a new inmate is experientially introduced to prison life through formal orientation classes and his own explorations. Through these resources and his own interpretive work, he gradually expands his understanding of the prison world and accomplishes some reduction in the uncertainty with which he initially faced this world. During this time, he learns about prison programs and procedures, achieves some familiarity with guards and other prison staff, and establishes some contacts with other prisoners. His early experiences in prison enable him to reformulate his prison imagery, alleviate some of his anxieties, and gradually increase his confidence in his ability to survive. His tenuous feeling of security is shattered, however, when he hears about such dramatic events as rape, murder, assault, or suicide—and his continuing interpretive work must take these events into account.

As he assembles a more experientially grounded prison image, an inmate also devises a more practical survival strategy. The principal new elements of this strategy include territorial caution, rudimentary impression management skills, selective interaction with other inmates, and a nascent partnership. He also carries over elements of his anticipatory survival strategy, including a continuing resolve to stay out of trouble, a continuing resolve to avoid confrontations with guards and inmates, and a renewed resolve to defend himself in any way possible, if trouble should arise.

Although he becomes better prepared to cope with prison, by virtue of his expanding knowledge and evolving survival strategy, he remains a socially marginal participant of the prison world. He has moved beyond his anticipated practice of complete self-insulation and is now able to interact comfortably with a number of other inmates. In the identity work that he conducts through his intermittent self-dialogue, he stills draws a sharp distinction between himself and the general inmate population, and he continues to feel highly susceptible to the dangers of the prison world. Thus, even several weeks into their sentences, most first-time inmates continue to view the prison world from a more complex version of what is still essentially a preprison orientation—that is, an outsider's view of prison. In the next chapter, we examine how these inmates gradually come to adopt the fundamentally different view of their midcareer prison orientation.

NOTES

1. For a theoretical discussion of impression management, see Goffman, *The Presentation of Self in Everyday Life* (1959). Goffman observes (pp. 3-4) that "regardless of the particular objective which the individual has in mind and of his motive for having this objective, it will be in his interest to control the conduct of others, especially their responsive treatment of him. This control is achieved largely by influencing the definition of the situation which the others come to formulate, and he can influence this definition by expressing himself in such a way as to give them the kind of impression that will lead them to act voluntarily in accordance with his own plan."

2. Similar friendship bonds apparently arise in other total institutions. See Goffman's discussion of "buddy formation" in *Asylums* (1961, pp. 278-279).

3. At the time of our fieldwork, as we noted in Chapter 2, 71 percent of the inmates at Midwestern were white.

4. This is the interpretation held by the new inmates interviewed during the fieldwork; these inmates recognized that there were some exceptions to this generalization. The interpretation is important for this study not as a reflection of objective reality but rather as the accepted guideline for new inmates' behavior.

Chapter V

Prison Orientation: From Violence to Boredom

If we were to draw a sociological sketch of new inmates after two weeks of imprisonment, and then sketch these same inmates three or four months into their sentences, our efforts would yield two remarkably different pictures. After just a few months, these men walk differently, talk differently, and hold different perspectives on the prison, on the outside world, and on themselves. What they believe to be the most important problem presented by their imprisonment has changed and, consequently, the tactics that they employ to respond to their problems have also changed.

This chapter examines how these various changes come about. Part of the answer, as the concept of "prisonization" suggests, is the inmates' extended exposure to "prison culture" and to the regimented schedule of institutional life. But new inmates are influenced by these "universal factors of prisonization" only *after* their emotional response to their imprisonment has changed, as a result of their active efforts to make sense out of the prison world. We begin this chapter, therefore, by extending our analysis of the prior chapter, examining how inmates' prison experiences and survival tactics facilitate the continuous reconstruction of their prison imagery. We then look at the strategic changes they make in response to their reconstructed imagery and reconsider their social marginality during the middle part of their sentences.

REVISING THE PRISON IMAGE THROUGH DIRECT EXPERIENCE

There is no one point at which new prisoners "adjust" to prison life, but the prison environment begins to seem less alien sometime between the first and second months of their sentences. By this time, an inmate will have modified his preprison imagery, incorporating both the official information presented to him through orientation classes and the various forms of prison lore that he has accrued through his own tentative explorations of the prison world. He continues to revise his imagery throughout the early months of his sentence, a process that is facilitated by his experiencing of two early sentence milestones and guided by the still-maturing tactics of his survival strategy.

SENTENCE MILESTONES: CHALLENGES AND OPPORTUNITIES

Every novel prison activity and every venture into unexplored prison territory presents additional survival challenges but also opportunities to learn more about the prison world. Inmates experience two milestone events, cellblock reassignment and a job assignment, about a month into their sentences. Both of these events provide inmates with numerous occasions to exercise their survival tactics and to reduce their uncertainty about the prison world.

Sometime after his first month, a new prisoner will be transferred from the R & O cellblock to another cellblock. At Midwestern prison, unless he is attending a full-time educational or rehabilitation program, this transfer involves a move to "B" hall. The inmate faces the transfer with the same kind of ambivalence with which he confronted his earlier cell reassignment within the R & O unit. The move means that he will again have to adjust to a new and uncertain environment and that he will have closer proximity to the general inmate population which he fears. At the same time, the transfer means that he will be under less intense supervision from prison guards and that he will have a greater range of territory to explore. While he is concerned about the move, therefore, he also welcomes the greater mobility it provides. The cellblock transfer is significant because this to be the "final" cell of his sentence.[1] Thus, an inmate believes that once he has become familiar with the "B" hall environment, he has reached an early sentence milestone.

A second milestone, the inmate's job assignment, also takes place about a month into his sentence. In Chapter 2, we noted the range of jobs that are available through the prison industries and private industries programs, and the maintenance, clerical, and other jobs in which inmates work directly for the institution. A job assignment usually begins with a job classification interview, at which the inmate is asked to describe his job skills, training, and interests. A report from this interview is forwarded to the director of industry personnel, who contacts the inmate for an appointment about a week later. At this appointment, the inmate again reviews his employment background and interests and completes a job application. The personnel director advises him on the jobs currently available; if the inmate decides to interview for one of these positions, he will do so directly at the job site. If he declines to interview for an available position, he is returned to the cellblock and placed on "temporary idle" status, with the option of interviewing for other jobs later. As long as he holds this status, however, he will remain locked in his cell during working hours.

Other inmates secure jobs through alternative recruiting processes, which offer glimpses into both the formal and informal social organization of the prison. Non-industry prison jobs, for example, are posted on cellblock bulletin boards and are usually acquired directly from the prison unit seeking employees. Some of the most desirable industry jobs, on the other hand, are filled through a process that bypasses formal application procedures and makes use of inmate social networks. In these cases, the foreman at a job site may ask his (inmate) workers to seek out new inmates for job vacancies. If a suitable inmate is found, the foreman will ask the personnel director to send that inmate to the job site for his initial job placement. Because they rely on inmate networks, informal recruiting processes also tend to reinforce discriminatory hiring patterns; during the period of our field research, for example, janitorial or foundry positions were likely to be held by African-Americans, while clerical positions were more likely to be held by whites.

A job assignment, like the cellblock reassignment, furnishes an inmate with still more territory to explore as well as interactional possibilities with a larger number of inmates. A prison job, moreover, often allows for these explorations to take place within a more "controlled" situation. An inmate's interactions on the job provide him with further sources of information about prison life, including official procedures, informal guidelines, illicit activities, and "grapevine" gossip.[2] His coworkers usually represent the most heterogeneous group of prisoners he has encountered, including men from various ethnic groups, long-term as well as short-term prisoners, men who have had experience in other institutions, and men who have been sentenced for a variety of offenses. Although the stories he hears from coworkers will be inconsistent and he has learned not to accept most reports at face value, the sheer breadth of the information he receives at his job station nonetheless helps him to "fill in" his imagery of the prison world.

In addition to extending his range of contacts with other inmates, a job assignment serves to integrate a new inmate into the daily tempo of prison life. He is required to report for work at a designated time, take coffee and lunch breaks at specified times, and complete his work at a designated time. Any job, no matter how menial, thus serves to mark the passage of time and to introduce the inmate to the daily work schedule. For most new prisoners, this is preferable to time spent alone in a cell or hanging around the cellblock.

EVOLUTION OF INMATES' SURVIVAL TACTICS

To take advantage of the uncertainty-reducing opportunities offered by a cell reassignment and a job assignment, new inmates must be willing to converse with older, more experienced prisoners. These prisoners have been the very source of their fears, however, so these conversations rarely take place "naturally." Instead, new inmates prepare themselves for these exchanges and initiate them gradually. We described the survival strategy used by new inmates in Chapter 4, noting that each tactic has both a protective and an information-seeking function. Inmates continue to employ "territorial caution" and "selective interaction" in their new cellblocks and on the job. Interactions with other inmates are especially fostered, however, by the newcomer's increasingly sophisticated impression management skills and by his growing reliance on his partnership as the foundation of his day-to-day life in prison.

Impression Management

Even before they arrive at prison, first-time inmates, like most males in our society, already have some "street experience" at masking their fears in uncomfortable situations. Impression management in prison is simply an extension of this experience, nourished by a greatly amplified level of intimidation and, consequently, a perception that the costs of failure are considerably higher. A new inmate's first efforts at impression management, it will be recalled, are both directed at other inmates and modeled after their behavior: he attempts to hide his fear of other prisoners by trying to look and act like them.

Within a few months, most new inmates, especially younger ones, become quite adept at impression management. An inmate's resolve to defend himself gives way to a recognition that the impression of a willingness to fight is often more important than actual fighting ability. Encounters between inmates from the general population come to be viewed as a series of confrontation games, in which inmates are attempting either to intimidate others or to prove that they will not intimidated. These "character contests" (Goffman 1967; Athens 1985) are recognized as games, but they are games that inmates believe they must take seriously. Thus, a 23-year-old inmate describes an exchange that took place in the prison cafeteria:

I did run into a little incident ... I sat down in the Indians' sitting group [in the cafeteria]. I didn't know they had ... places where they sit, and I think this is one thing the guards—you know, it's stupid as hell. It shouldn't have happened. I sit down to eat my meal, and here I've got 20 Indians around me, saying "Whatya trying to do, integrate?" and "You're going to have to move." And I said "In a minute," you know. Finally, after a while, I just got up and moved. But here's all these Indians standing around and here's all these guards up here at the front, just acting like nothing's going on.

To lose at these contests is to be viewed as weak, and the consequences of "weakness" range from being the brunt of a continuous barrage of verbal or practical jokes to being the victim of thefts or assaults. Conversely, to win is to avoid physical confrontations through an image of strength, stoicism, and a willingness to fight. As important as the immediate outcome of any specific contest, however, is the impression an inmate leaves with the wider audience of inmates who witness the encounter (Goffman 1959, p. 16).

Beginning with these interactional "games," impression management comes to be a *taken-for-granted* part of an inmate's day-to-day prison behavior. Inmates come to see these self-presentations not only as situational exigencies but as *general principles* of prison interaction. It becomes apparent to inmates that what is "hidden" is just as important as what is "shown." This idea is described by a 26-year-old inmate we interviewed:

> Kindness is a considerable weakness in here. As far as being friendly to any one person—it's a lot, lot harder to do in here than it is outside. You'll get taken advantage of. You have to work with what you have.... One guy said, just walked up to me and said, "Don't let anyone lead you around. You have to make a stand and be your own man—otherwise you're gonna be led around by the nose." I kinda tried to present that I'm not to be led around by the nose.... I like to watch people. I'll watch people's eyes when they ain't watching me—but I don't look into people's eyes very much.

Such masking is especially important when a new inmate is separated from his partner or other prison acquaintances; as one inmate said, "When I am alone, you will not see a smile on my face. I am the coldest looking dude imaginable." Once this desired image is achieved and routinely presented—through the way an inmate walks and looks, through what he says and does not say, through what he shows and hides—casual but restrained conversations with other inmates become feasible. It is when new inmates master these skills that their cellblock, job stations, and other prison locations become transformed from survival challenges into opportunities for expanding their knowledge of the prison world.

Partnerships

Partnerships, like impression management skills, become a taken-for-granted feature of prison life within a few months of a new inmate's sentence. While an inmate's impression management skills are largely directed at placing as much emotional distance as possible between himself and other inmates, his partnership has precisely the opposite effect: it provides him with a relatively authentic relationship within the prison world.

We described in Chapter 4 how an inmate's early, tentative friendships with one or two other inmates help his initial exploration and interpretation of the prison world. Some inmates continue to interact on this basis, widening their social network over time but explicitly avoiding the term "partner" in order to underscore their temporary participation in the prison world. This is the position taken by a 41-year-old inmate, sent to prison on a probation violation:

> "Associations"—because I don't want anything to do with anybody in this place when I leave here. But, you know, I can't go two years without talking to somebody so long. I visit some people and they visit me. We walk around the yard. I play tennis every day, so there's eight or 10 of us out there. Discuss our problems, you know, every day out there, take out our frustrations on the tennis court.

For most new inmates, however, the mutual dependence fostered by their early explorations strengthens at least one of these associations into an acknowledged partnership. These partnerships are further reinforced by the recognition they receive from other inmates and from guards, often expressed through jokes about the nature of the relationships. Although partnerships rarely involve homosexual behavior, for example, other inmates may refer to an inmate's partner as his "girlfriend," "lady," or "ho." In some cases, familial terms, such as "dad" or "son" are also used to describe a partnership.[3]

The tentative friendships that inmates form early in their sentences may go through a process of trial and error, but most partnerships, once established, tend to remain exclusive. More specifically, it is to an inmate's advantage to develop a small circle of acquaintances in prison but only one principal partner. There are several reasons for this. Although three or more inmates may form a friendship group, these groups tend to generate conflict and evolve into a dominant partnership and one or more secondary relationships. The dyadic structure is also practical, in that prison cells are simply too small to be regularly occupied by larger friendship groups, and larger groups will draw the attention of guards. Finally, within the unpredictable world of the prison, most new inmates find some security in having a single relationship within which they can speak freely, pay less

attention to managed impressions, and, to some extent, "be themselves."
On the other hand, the unpredictability of the prison world renders the
dyad vulnerable. An inmate's partner may be transferred to another
cellblock at any time:

> My main partner moved to a different cell hall two weeks ago. It was kind of a strange
> experience. It helped me realize that we were a lot tighter than I had imagined. We
> had spent almost all our time together, going to meals, watching T.V., playing
> backgammon, walking to work, and then suddenly we hardly ever saw each other.

The loss of a partner, through transfer or release, encourages an inmate
to strengthen his ties with a limited number of other inmates.

Above all else, an inmate's partner is someone with whom he can share
his prison experience. This occurs on a material level, in that partners
routinely share food and other canteen items, giving each other the com-
binations to their cells and granting each other free entry and borrowing
privileges. But it also takes place on an *emotional* level. Thus, partners also
exchange news from home, prison information, advice, personal
thoughts, and emotions. Over time, inmates come to rely on their partners
for many kinds of support. As stated by one inmate:

> My partner will do anything for me excluding homosexual atrocities. If someone is
> giving me shit, my partner is there to back me up, and I'm there when he needs me.

In return, they give license to a partner in ways that are not extended to
other prison acquaintances.

> Sometimes it is almost like he is my mother, warning me to watch out for this guy, quit
> taking chances if you're not getting anything out of it, mainly just nagging me. If any-
> body but my partner was telling me this, I would tell them to get fucked, and mean it.
> But with my partner, I'll probably tell him to lay off, and then think about what he said
> later, and realize that he was saying it for my own good.

Considering that most new inmates did not anticipate any meaningful fel-
lowship in prison, it is noteworthy that many inmates told us that they
believed their partnerships would remain intact after both partners were
released from prison.[4]

As an inmate's partnership bond strengthens, its prominence in his
daily adaptation to the prison increases. Within a few months' time, many
inmates—although they may not be entirely candid with their partners on
all matters—are more likely to confide their thoughts and feelings to their
prison partners than they are to their outside friends. This development is
important in several respects. An inmate's partnership is the single most
significant breach of his preprison imagery regarding other inmates. It
means that he has established an emotional bond within the prison world,

possibly at the expense of his outside ties. It also means that his partnership will continue to play a pivotal role in his ongoing interpretation of the
prison world.

AN EXPANDED UNDERSTANDING OF
THE PRISON

The process of adjusting to prison is primarily one of making greater
sense out of the prison social world—of reducing the uncertainty and
apprehension that dominated the inmate's prior expectations about
prison and his experience during the orientation period. Reducing
uncertainty is a conscious goal of new inmates and it is effected, in
large part, through their active attempts to increase their prison knowledge, especially through exploring unknown territory, developing a
wider circle of prison acquaintances, and seeking additional information about the prison from these people. A change in cellblock and a
job assignment extends an inmate's territorial range and expands his
pool of potential acquaintances. Inmates' maturing survival tactics,
especially impression management and partnerships, guide their explorations of these people and places. The knowledge they acquire
through these efforts reduces their uncertainty by enabling them to
piece together an imprecise but greatly expanded conceptualization of
the prison world.

This knowledge-acquisition process does constitute "prison socialization," but it is by no means a simple matter of learning and then adopting the norms of a monolithic prison culture. An inmate culture does
exist, to be sure, and new inmates must come to terms with it, as a matter of survival. But first-time, short-term inmates, as we have emphasized all along, are never more than marginal members of the prison
social world, and they never become fully socialized into its culture.
Moreover, as Zerubavel (1991, p. 77) has pointed out, socialization
involves learning a culture's "distinctive classificatory schemas" as well
as behavioral norms. It is these "norms of focusing" (Zerubavel 1997, p.
50) more than behavioral proscriptions that new inmates acquire
through their extended interactions with more experienced prisoners.
They learn to *see* the prison world in different and more complex ways
than their preprison imagery allowed. Among the key elements in their
expanded imagery are the prison economic system, the social organization of inmate groups, and a further revision of their imagery of
guards, inmates, and prison violence.

PRISON ECONOMIC SYSTEM

Inmates were given a basic outline of the prison economic system in their orientation classes. As we noted in Chapter 2, all inmates are given the opportunity to work, and most of their wages are deposited into a personal spending account because cash is not allowed in the prison. Anything they buy will be through vouchers that draw upon this account. Food and toiletries can be purchased at a canteen located within the prison. There is also a commissary, where clothing and manufactured goods, such as television sets, may be ordered through catalogs.

An inmate's job helps him to learn more about the prison economy by enabling him to participate in it. Most inmates find that their wages, although low by outside standards, are generally sufficient for their daily needs in prison and may even allow them to save for an occasional luxury item. Inmates with low-paying jobs and those with "expensive" tastes (for example, those who smoke heavily, use drugs, or gamble) may have to supplement their income in one way or another. Through their own needs or their conversations with others, inmates extend their knowledge about how the prison economy works. They learn, for example, that some inmates pursue hobbies or crafts that result in goods for sale or barter. Paintings, jewelry, or leather work are routinely traded for canteen orders, cigarettes, material goods, laundry services, or other handcrafted items. They learn which illegal products (such as drugs and alcohol) are available, and how they may be acquired through bartering or purchased with contraband cash. They come to see gambling as not just a pastime but an integral part of the prison economy; although technically illegal, gambling is so prevalent that most of it takes place entirely in the open. Thus, card games and sports betting pools are almost continuously available on the cellblocks, usually involving cigarettes or other low-stakes wagers.

New inmates' may never comprehend how the prison economy works in its entirety, but their knowledge of it after several months in prison far exceeds what they knew before their arrival or what they were told during orientation classes. They gradually learn to recognize the different realms of economic activity that exist in prison, and some of the more specific distinctions that exist within each realm. For example, even though the general availability of drugs was apparent to them almost from the beginning of their sentences, they only gradually become aware of the gradations in drug traffic that surround them. They learn that some inmates receive small amount of drugs from visitors, for their personal use or for sharing with partners. They eventually hear about inmate-dealers, who will trade limited quantities of drugs for cigarettes, canteen orders, or cash. And they may even hear occasional rumors of larger drug shipments that are smuggled into the prison. Most drug traffic—and most other illegal economic activity—has little direct relevance to the day-to-day lives of new inmates, but their expanding knowledge of these activities nonetheless adds detail to their prison imagery.

SOCIAL ORGANIZATION

New inmates see indications of racial and ethnic stratification from their first days in prison, and they soon learn that most interaction takes place within racial group boundaries. Beginning with this observation, they become able to make increasingly finer distinctions within a few weeks time. From the perspective of white inmates (a majority at Midwestern Prison and in our sample), several generalizations becomes apparent. Whites, despite their numerical majority, are the least cohesive group, with the greatest number of subgroups. The most recognizable of these are the bikers, whose status within the prison social organization is officially sanctioned through a designated "biker day." The prison population also includes members of the Aryan Brotherhood, a group that overlaps with but is by no means identical to the bikers. With these exceptions, however, interaction among most whites occurs in informal, loose-knit groups, based on such factors as age or type of offense. Latinos and Asians remain especially isolated, because they are so few in number and because de facto segregation is enforced by all of the ethnic groups. On the other hand, Native Americans and African Americans play more prominent roles in the prison social structure, but these must be understood in terms of subgroup organization.

As they expand their own social and geographic range within prison, for example, white inmates see young Indians cutting in at the head of lines, physically ejecting other inmates who wander into their territories, and generally doing as they please, with little or no interference from either guards or other inmates. They conclude from this that younger Indians are both powerful, in their control of prison territory, and people who should be avoided, because they are "crazy" and therefore unpredictable. Older Indians, however, are viewed as less problematic. In a similar fashion, African Americans are viewed as two distinct subgroups: a core group of young, streetwise blacks and a smaller group of more conventional, and generally older, black inmates. White inmates see the streetwise group as tight-knit, easily recognizable by their appearance, mannerisms, and dialect, and likely to be involved in drug dealing and other prison hustles, while the remaining blacks are viewed as a less cohesive group and as more approachable.

New inmates recognize that there are exceptions to all of their generalizations, including those pertaining to younger Indians. They learn that intergroup interaction does in fact take place in prison, especially on the job and during some athletic activities. As men who are clearly on the fringes of the prison social organization, however, they are searching for general rules, not exceptions to those rules. Most of their own interaction, consequently, remains within racial boundaries.

As they meet and talk with a greater number of prisoners, new inmates also learn the generally accepted meanings given other aspects of inmate social organization, including the distinction between "long-timers" and "short-timers" and the even finer differentiation between "inmates" and "convicts." They learn, for example, that inmates like themselves (i.e., short-time, and especially first-time, inmates) are thought to be more focused on their outside relationships, more concerned with impressing prison authorities, more cautious about engaging in illegal activities in the prison, and more likely to be victimized. In contrast, long-time prisoners (or "old-timers"), especially those who have served more than one prison sentence, are seen to be less intimidated by the prison, less focused on the outside world, more interested in making their lives in prison as comfortable as possible, and hence more likely to be involved in illegal activities but less likely to place themselves in situations where they might be victimized. They also learn that the majority of prisoners who are considered to be "inmates" can be contrasted with a much smaller group of "convicts," a "vanishing breed" of old-timers who still believe in the ideas of "inmate solidarity" or the "inmate code." Convicts, in turn, are said to be instrumental in such prison activities as betting pools, to insist that all guards and prison staff are the enemy, to believe in the necessity of "dealing straight" with other convicts, and to look down on the majority of inmates as being too concerned with themselves and their presentations to the program review authorities. Although new inmates sometimes find it difficult to discern these various distinctions in specific cases, the general knowledge they acquire about inmate social organization continues to fill in their understanding of the prison social world.

New inmates' conceptions of inmate social organization are unavoidably incomplete, and they recognize that exceptions exist to all of the generalizations or group distinctions they learn. The generalizations are nonetheless important, not only because they add to their knowledge of the prison social world but because they subtly shape their participation in it. As they learn and accept insider distinctions among inmate groups, for example, they gauge the approachability of inmates from other racial or ethnic groups in terms of this classificatory system. They know that inmates with longer sentences are given higher status within the prison social organization, so they are likely to discuss their own sentences in terms of the maximum time they could be incarcerated rather than the actual amount of time they will serve. Perhaps most important, they know that convicts and most long-term inmates believe that prisoners who orient themselves toward the outside world aggravate the circumstances of their imprisonment, so they consciously depreciate the importance of their own outside contacts when talking with these inmates. In this manner, the "focusing norms" that allow new inmates to see the prison from an insider's perspective translate easily into conversational or interactional norms—and these, in turn, represent incipient behavioral norms in the inmates' midcareer accommodations to their imprisonment.

GUARDS AND INMATES

As inmates begin to understand the "bigger picture" of prison economy and social organization, they continue to refine their images of the major participants in their world: prison guards and inmates.

We have already described how inmates develop a more differentiated image of guards; as an inmate's sentence continues, he is able to make even more precise distinctions. Through his expanded social network of inmates, he learns which specific guards will overlook infractions, which follow the rule book to the letter, which are looking for excuses to discipline prisoners, and which behave most consistently. Unlike his other image modifications, however, his elaborated image of guards has little effect on his behavior: most new inmates continue to avoid guards because of the institutionalized animosity that exists between these two groups. Moreover, he fears that even a simple conversation with guards might be interpreted by other inmates as snitching. Whether this fear is realistic or not, new inmates know they cannot afford to be so labeled. Guards do have direct power over prisoners, of course, so most prisoners, especially first-time inmates, do not attempt to antagonize them. Rather, new inmates will speak to guards when they are addressed by them but will rarely initiate conversations.

We have also described, in a general sense, how inmates alter their pre-prison imagery of inmates. When he first entered prison, the new inmate saw himself pitted against a hostile and violent inmate population; he insisted that he was not like other inmates, and he expected to serve his time in virtual isolation from them. He softens this stance during the orientation period, sometimes even during the first few days of his sentence, when he meets one or more other new inmates who have similar backgrounds and a similar apprehension of prison life. During the early weeks of his sentence, these acquaintanceships typically develop into a number of casual friendships and perhaps a partnership. By themselves, these friendships do provide some comfort, although the general inmate population is still defined as an alien group. As his circle of friends widens, however, and his casual interactions with other inmates increase, he begins to accept the *normalcy* of most other inmates. He discovers that the prisoners he meets at work or in the gym are not inherently vicious men, but rather, in many respects, much like himself.

The acceptance of fellow prisoners as normal is not absolute. A new inmate still generally avoids some groups of prisoners—certain ethnic groups, some long-term inmates and inmates convicted of certain offenses. He also avoids some individual prisoners entirely, based on their reputations or on his observations of their behavior. And even among those with whom he does have contact, he may still draw some idiosyncratic distinctions; other prisoners, for example, may appear immature or even childish. Nonetheless, the difference between a belief that most inmates are essentially normal and his initial image of most inmates as violent and abnormal constitutes a remarkable shift in identity boundaries (Zerubavel 1991, p. 14). This change in his imagery leads to a marked reduction in his uncertainty and apprehension and substantially changes his day-to-day behavior in prison.

PRISON VIOLENCE

As new inmates expand their understanding of the prison social world and modulate their imagery of guards and inmates, the intense fear that characterized the beginning of their sentences diminishes. As we described in Chapter 4, however, any complacency they experience is invariably decimated by the recurrence of a rape, murder, or other dramatic event. Incidents that occur within the first month or two of an inmate's sentence shock him back to the tumultuous "reality" of his preprison imagery and interrupt (or even reverse) his progress in reducing his uncertainty and apprehension about prison. In the wake of these early dramatic events, an inmate concludes that he has been operating under a false sense of security, and he approaches his daily activities with renewed vigilance. He enters familiar territory with greater precautions and is more tentative in his casual interactions with other inmates. After a dramatic event, in other words, the prison world suddenly makes less sense to a new inmate than it did before the incident.

The only way that a new inmate can overcome the shock effects of a dramatic event is to make sense of prison violence itself. He is able to do so, to some extent, because his expanding social networks give him access to other inmates' interpretive "explanations" of these incidents. He may hear, for example, that the homicide that occurred the night before was a result of the victim's welshing on a drug deal:

> The murder that occurred while I was here was a stabbing that took place out in the yard. A guy was trying to collect a five-dollar drug debt; the other guy wouldn't pay, so he killed him.

A rape in the next cellblock can be "justified" by the victim's injudicious participation in the prison economic system:

> The guys ask for it. They receive favors from these guys and get into debt. One day, they want the debt repaid. Well, they know you don't have any money, so they say pay up or put out.

* * *

> Look at P.C.U. [Protective Custody Unit]. Why do you think that place is packed? They aren't all pretty boys that can't take care of themselves. But they get into debt, and when collection time comes, the bill collector brings along his companions. The guy either pays up, puts out, or gets raped. Not much of a choice but he deserves what he gets.

Such explanations, taken from conversations recorded in our field research, serve both to insulate an inmate from the emotional shock of a violent incident and to teach him something about life in prison. These lessons are also applied to specific incidents:

> I was in the hall waiting to go to the theater when they dragged him to the hospital, but I didn't know what was going on. After the movie, as soon as I got back to the cell hall, I heard the story. Most inmates felt the guy deserved it. The stabbing was a mat-ter-of-fact thing, no sadness or remorse; he deserved it. It was a lesson to us all. If you rip someone off, this is what happens.

The victim's "crime" may be a debt of only a few dollars or some other seemingly innocuous offense, but the fact that an inmate "hears the story" is profoundly important, for it allows him to classify the incident as an "explained" rather than a random act of violence.[5]

Most of the prison explanations for dramatic events undoubtedly hold some degree of truth, but they have a functional value over and above their validity, in that they reduce a new inmate's apprehension and uncertainty of prison life. If the victim of an incident deserves his fate because he has violated inmate norms, then the incident does not represent something that could happen at any time to any inmate. And if most dramatic events can be explained in this manner, it becomes possible to rationalize that *all* dramatic events have an explanation. Homicides, assaults, and rapes are explained by the victim's behavior—"burning" another prisoner in a drug deal, failing to pay a gambling debt, or snitching. Suicide victims may be prisoners who have been transferred from a state hospital and thus are "special cases," or lifers who have "nothing to live for." For incidents that lack an immediate explanation, a general rationalization will suffice:

You are ready for these things to happen after a while. You expect them, almost as if they are normal occurrences. I guess there is no reason to expect that murders, suicides, or rapes wouldn't happen in here, since they happen on the outside. As long as [they] don't happen to you or your partner, there is little concern after you have been here a while.

Besides emotionally insulating inmates from these incidents, prison rationalizations can also be given as assurances to friends on the outside, who are concerned about prison dangers.

By virtue of the explanations and rationalizations an inmate learns, as well as the simple fact that violent incidents recur with some regularity, dramatic events gradually lose shock value for new inmates during the middle phase of their sentences—as suggested by the following passage from Jones' prison journal:

> Something happened today that does happen from time to time, but I can see that my reaction to the event has changed from when I first entered the prison. I am talking about a piping. Two guys tried to see how hard each other's head was, and both ended up in the hospital. This was the first time I knew both parties. It was the result of an argument over a drug deal. My reaction was one of laughter but I don't know why.... I figure both had it coming because they both are a couple of fools.

Aided by the knowledge he acquires from other prisoners, a new inmate finds that each successive incident has a less intense effect on his image of the prison world and his sense of well-being. Particularly vicious incidents or those involving acquaintances continue to be emotionally difficult, but the inmate finds himself increasingly unaffected by the same kind of incidents that once caused him to fear for his life. Dramatic events, in effect, come to be viewed as a normal component of prison life.

It requires many months and many specific incidents before prison violence loses most of its shock value. And even when this occurs—when incidents no longer result in a sudden increase in the prisoner's uncertainty and apprehension—they still retain *dramatic* value, as this fieldnote excerpt makes clear:

> The reactions to the suicide were that of excitement. It's news, breaks up the monotony. When something of this sort happens, the news spreads fast. People joked about it on the way to breakfast that morning. Others seemed to think the guy was better off dead. No one was upset about it or sad about it.

An explained dramatic event furnishes a colorful topic for conversation, adds fresh material for the prison grapevine, and "breaks up the monotony." Although dramatic events continue to provide some reaffirmation of prison dangers, they simultaneously provide some relief from an increasingly tedious prison routine.

THE PRISON ROUTINE

New inmates' uncertainty about the prison world is also diminished simply by their everyday participation in the prison routine of work, meals, and recreation. This routine, in fact, influences both their prison imagery and their behavior in more far-reaching ways as well. They begin to experience these larger effects, however, only after they have *already* reduced their uncertainty and apprehension about prison life through the information-seeking and image reconstruction activities that we have described.

The standard weekday schedule for an inmate at Midwestern prison is detailed in Table V.1. This schedule essentially outlines inmates' lives for the duration of their sentences. But while the schedule itself remains constant, inmates' *responses* to it shift significantly within a few weeks' time. Their initial reaction, immediately following their cellblock reassignment and job assignment, is to dread all "public" activities—or at least to approach them warily—because they bring them in closer proximity to the general inmate population. As they acquire more information about prison and enlarge their understanding of it, this response soon gives way to another: their daily schedule offers a welcome orderliness, an hour-by-hour predictability, to their days in prison. Within a few weeks, however, inmates begin to see their daily schedule in yet another way: the sameness of each day, combined with their physical isolation from the outside world, comes to be viewed as one of the hardships of their imprisonment.

There is, of course, nothing inherently inhumane about the prison schedule: it is not unlike a weekday schedule for many people on the outside. Rather, the ennui of prison life stems from the lack of even minor variations in these activities and the lack of hope for any meaningful break from this routine in the foreseeable future. An inmate can refuse to go to work on any day, but this means he will remain locked in his cell from 7:00 a.m. to 4:30 p.m. Thus, as the following excerpt illuminates, most inmates submit to this schedule most of the time:

> It is strange how you can get used to a place, even if it's a place you can't stand. When I first got here, I would wake up in the morning, shake the sleep from my head, see the bars, and say "Damn, I'm really in prison." Now, when I wake up, I already am aware that I am here. I just seem to go through the motions everyday. It doesn't take much thought to wake up when the bell rings, go to chow when the bell rings, go to work when the bell rings, and go to your cell when it rings. There really isn't much choice or alternatives; you either do or you don't.

This resigned *acceptance* of a regimented daily schedule as the condition of one's life represents a viewpoint on imprisonment that is fundamentally different from that of inmates' preprison imagery.

Table V.1. Weekday Schedule

6:00 a.m.	Wake-up bell
6:20 a.m.	Cells are unlocked; inmates have until 7:00 to exchange linen and go to breakfast
7:00 a.m.	Inmates return to cells, make beds, clean cells
7:20 a.m.	Bell rings; inmates go to work
7:30 a.m.	Workday begins
9:15 a.m.	Coffee break (15 minutes)
10:50 a.m.	Morning work ends
11:00 a.m.	Lunch begins for workers
11:30 a.m.	Inmates return to cells for count
11:50-12:00	Inmates return to work (nonworkers to lunch)
1:45 p.m.	Coffee break (15 minutes)
3:20 p.m.	Workday ends; inmates return to cells
3:30 p.m.	Count; mail is distributed
4:30 p.m.	Supper; yard and gym open
4:30-10:00	Sports (until 8:30); showers; card playing; television, etc.
8:30 p.m.	Inmates return to cellblock
9:55 p.m.	Warning bell
10:00 p.m.	Count; lockup for evening

The effects of the prison routine, which are well documented in the sociological literature (Cohen and Taylor 1972; Clemmer 1958), are most often attributed to long-term prisoners, who find it increasingly difficult to envision a life outside of prison. These "prisonization" effects are also exhibited by first-time inmates within a few months of their imprisonment. Some of them are visible behavioral manifestations: inmates take on a slower walk—the "jailhouse shuffle"—and their language increasingly includes prison argot and profanity. Underlying these outward changes is a growing lethargy, which is often recognized by the inmates themselves:

> I just realized that I haven't been going outside much anymore. When I first got the privilege of going out, I spent a lot of time in the yard, but for some reason this has changed. I guess when I'm outside, I think more of the things I miss—especially my freedom.

Some inmates attempt to counter their lethargy with intensive participation in athletics, artistic expression, or even religion, but many succumb to it and spend all of their spare time watching television or lying in their cells. Typically, inmates also experience a corresponding emotional apathy about the outside world and their own circumstances. Many inmates stop reading newspapers and curtail their outside contacts, in distinct contrast to their behavior at the beginning of the sentences. These changes are so remarkable that, to a casual observer, first-time, short-term inmates in the middles of their sentences become indistinguishable from long-term inmates and recidivists.

IMPRISONMENT REDEFINED

We outlined the differences between new inmates' preprison imagery and their midcareer prison imagery in Chapter 3. The most profound difference, we noted, is a change from the belief that prison is a violent world to the belief that it is a fundamentally *boring* world. We have now demonstrated more precisely how this change comes about. It happens because the survival tactics they followed at the beginning of their sentences have been successful, both as protective measures and as information-seeking measures. As new inmates make use of these tactics to confront novel prison experiences—most notably, their moves to a different cellblock and their job assignments—they familiarize themselves with various prison locations, expand their circles of prison acquaintances, discuss the information they acquire with their partners and others, and thereby come to see the prison in a different light. They also become accustomed to, and then adversely affected by, the unchanging rhythms of the daily prison schedule. Based on both their active interpretive work and their passive submission to the prison routine, in other words, their conceptualization of the prison world gradually comes to approximate that of more experienced prisoners.

As we will see later in this chapter, their prison orientation also differs from that of long-term inmates in important ways. Nonetheless, within a few months, new inmates have transformed themselves from "outsiders" who possess only a vague but intimidating image of the prison world to prison "insiders" who have a larger, more complex, and more experientially grounded imagery. Most important, they share with more experienced inmates the idea that the essential problem resulting from imprisonment is not surviving its unpredictable violence but rather enduring the boredom that results from its uniformity, its unwavering sameness day after day. As they reassess the problem they face, they also employ insiders' adaptation tactics to address this problem.

AN ENDURANCE STRATEGY

As a new inmate comes to perceive prison as unchanging, colorless, and boring, his survival strategy, though still extant, becomes less salient to his daily activities. Instead, he adopts a more diffuse adaptation strategy, aimed at psychological rather than physical survival. To cope with prison during the middles of their sentences, prisoners actively search for diversions from the prison routine and impose a kind of "thought control" on themselves.

Diversions

There is only a limited number of diversions, legal and illegal, available in prison. Many inmates make use of the prison athletic facilities: the gym, weight room, tennis courts, handball courts, and athletic fields. Athletics provide both physical release from the tedium of the prison day and the opportunity for competition, which offers temporary transcendence of the prison world. Although competition is usually restricted to intramural teams of prisoners, teams from the outside world are sometimes allowed in, and these occasions provide diversion for both participants and spectators. The effects that weight lifting and other athletic diversions have on a prisoner's physique can also contribute to his impression management capabilities.

There are nonathletic diversions as well. Movies and other special events are attended primarily for their diversionary value. Inmates who still prefer solitary activities read or watch television in their cells for hours on end. More sociable inmates play cards frequently, often for extended periods of time. Gambling is a common diversion, in conjunction with these games and in other forms, such as betting pools on sporting events. Some inmates pursue hobbies or programs of study as diversions from the boredom of their daily lives.

"Getting high" is a popular and readily available means of escaping the prison routine, and its prevalence in prison motivates many new inmates to violate their earlier resolves against using drugs. In the words of two inmates, both in their 20s:

> I don't think too many people go in [prison] for a year, without doing [drugs] for a whole year. There's just too much of a mind strain without relaxing your mind. You know, a lot of people can't relax their mind by sitting there and trying to meditate. Just about everybody will get high or do a pill or drink something.

* * *

> Got high for the first time today. It was bound to happen sooner or later. I allowed the old peer pressure to grab ahold of me. The guy who is training me in [on a prison job] and I were on one of our runs and a friend of his turned us on to a doobie. It was nice, got real high, but looking back it wasn't really worth it, and the easiest way not to is is to not buy it. I'm sure after a while the people will quit asking me. Saying no doesn't seem to matter to anyone. They understand you're trying to get through with no hassles. As long as you're cool, and not a snitch, everything is O.K.

Even religious activities, which may contribute to an inmate's adaptation in several respects, can be viewed as a form of diversion from the prison routine. Although not all religious activities are directly sanctioned by prison officials, they are generally within the prisoners' rights and hence constitute "legal" diversions.

Thought Control

Gambling, athletics, and other diversionary activities enable prisoners to avoid thinking about their plight, at least for limited periods of time. Inmates cannot engage in diversionary activities all the time, however, so they regularly find themselves ruminating over the lengths of their sentences, the injustices to which they have been subjected, or their relationships with persons on the outside. They recognize that this kind of thinking, particularly about their lack of influence over events in the outside world, adds to their discomfort in prison. Conversations with more experienced inmates reinforce this idea, as noted in this fieldnote excerpt:

> Speaking of counting, I was talking with [a long-term inmate convicted of murder] and he was telling me that he doesn't usually hang around short-timers because they are so preoccupied with time. He said it took him a long time to get over counting the days, weeks, and months, and that he doesn't really like to be reminded about it.

Such conversations suggest to new inmates that coping with their imprisonment will require them to regulate their own thoughts, about their situation, about the outside world, and about time itself.

Drawing upon the reports of long-term and repeat prisoners, Meisenhelder (1985) has argued that imprisonment affects the experience of human temporality, primarily because it removes the inmate from any meaningful connection with future events that take place outside the institution. Consequently, these inmates focus instead on the past or, especially, on the present. He further argues that there are two essential experiential characteristics of imprisonment. The first, "waiting," is a consciousness of the time that must pass before an inmate will be released, and an associated consciousness that the outside world (including his friends and family) is changing while he remains in prison. The second is a "sense of time as a burden," which must be made to pass. An inmate who tries to maintain connections with the outside world "is forced to live in two equally alien places at once, surely a disorienting and uncomfortable way of existing" (Meisenhelder 1985, p. 45). What (long-term) inmates do instead, Meisenhelder suggests, is to respond to their "temporal encapsulation" with various forms of "creating time" (e.g., creating present-time events such as a rule violation which they can control) or "marking time," for example by noting their progressing skills levels in a sport or hobby.

First-time, short-term inmates differ from long-term inmates precisely because they are never as temporally removed from the outside world. Because of their positions at the periphery of the prison world as well as the differences in their sentences, they do not have the same range of time-creating and time-marking options available to them. By the middle of their sentences, nonetheless, most of these inmates adopt a present-time orientation, rather than one that is focused on their post-prison futures. They do so primarily by attempting to "control" their thoughts about their own predicaments and the outside world. As stated succinctly by one inmate:

> There is no more thinking about time, and nothing to be optimistic about. What I need to do is just get into a groove and hope the time passes.

Apart from diversionary activities, there are no particular "tricks" which inmates use to control their thoughts; they simply, and consciously, block out thoughts that are painful. As we consider in the next section, however, this practice has implications for inmates' outside relationships and for their identity work in prison.

SOCIAL MARGINALITY AT MIDCAREER

After new inmates have been in prison for several months, and have come to view the prison in a manner similar to long-term inmates, their social marginality in both the prison and outside worlds is apparent: they are literally "between worlds." They are now at their most estranged from the outside world, as is evident from the nature of their outside contacts at midcareer and from the periodic identity work that they conduct during the middle of their sentences. Although their position in the prison world is at its least marginal point, most new inmates nonetheless remain at the periphery of this social world. Their continuing "outsider" status—despite their "insider's" pronouncements—can be demonstrated most directly through a closer look at how they conceptualize the prison at midcareer and what they believe to be their principal problem.

Outside Contact

Receiving a letter or visit—or not receiving an expected outside contact—can have an enormous emotional impact on new inmates at the beginning of their sentences. We described this emotional roller coaster, and inmates' growing discomfort with it, in Chapter 4. The nature of visits and other outside contacts tends to change substantially within the first several weeks of the inmate's sentence. Even visits that occur early in this period, although they are greatly appreciated, can lead to mixed emotions. A 42-year-old inmate describes his response to visits in these terms:

> Sitting real close together with a whole bunch of people, it's not really private and it's really—it's fun to see somebody from the outside, no question about it and—but it's also very emotional, and you find that the emotional part hangs with you when they leave and you leave and go back to your cell, and it was hard.

Subsequent visits, for a variety of reasons, can become more difficult. The inmate is still apprehensive and uncertain about prison, but he wants to protect his visitors from his personal fears; consequently, he begins to use his impression management skills with visitors as well as with other inmates. As simply stated by a 26-year-old inmate we interviewed:

> I've come to the realization that the truth is too unbelievable. Sometimes it makes you sound crazy. Sometimes I'd lie.

A 23-year-old inmate described how controlling information to outsiders also takes place in letters written by inmates:

> When you're writing to your grandma and your parents, it's a strain. It's more of a mind strain when you're in prison, because you have to keep everybody in a way happy; that they are thinking that you are doing O.K.; that there is no reason to whine about it because you're here and there is nothing they can do about it. So you have to write them and let them know that you are doing O.K. and you feel O.K., even if you don't. Especially to your grandma, somebody who's 80 years old. Just to sort of relax their minds, you know, to make them feel good even if you feel rotten and you're depressed and everything else. You still have to let them know you're O.K.

By restricting information about their lives, inmates thus contribute to their own alienation from their former social worlds.

Outsiders similarly become cautious about relating too much information about the outside world, to avoid accentuating the inmate's isolation from his family and friends. In this interview excerpt, a 26-year-old inmate describes how news of an important family event was almost withheld from him:

> They tell me about my sister's wedding, but I found out later that they didn't plan on telling me, because they knew I'd get bummed out. Yeah, they control that and there's stuff they talk about that they know I can handle.

In part through this reciprocal control of information, it becomes increasingly apparent that the inmate is living in a separate world and that the longer he *is* in that world, the less the inmate and the outsider have in common.

As they reach the middle of their sentences, inmates come to accept the typical insider's present-time orientation, and they engage in the practice of "thought control" to avoid thinking about their loss of control over future events in the outside world. This change in their prison orientation, combined with the changing nature of their outside contacts, leads inmates to minimize the importance of these contacts, to themselves as well as in their conversations with others. An inmate's inability to influence outside events—or even to predict when he will receive a letter or visit—adds to the uncertainty of his life in general. Depreciating the importance of outside contacts makes this uncertainty more bearable and insulates him from two of his most specific fears. First, he has been concerned from the beginning that his visits and letters would decrease over time. Based on what he has learned from long-term inmates, this concern appears to be realistic. Second, he knows that there is always a possibility that a visit or letter could bring bad news. It is not unusual for an inmate to break off an intimate relationship to avoid worrying about that relationship every day; this thinking is illustrated in the following statement by a 37-year-old inmate:

> I think it would be almost impossible to carry on a relationship, a real close relationship, being here for two years or a year and a half. It's literally impossible. I think that the best thing to do is to just forget about it, and if the relationship can be picked up again once you get out, that's fine. And if it can't, you have to accept that.

Although a few short-term inmates manage to maintain daily contact with the outside world, a far greater number of them—borrowing from the adaptation strategies of long-term inmates—begin to tell themselves and others that they would almost prefer no outside contacts to uncertain contacts.

Like a number of reactions to their imprisonment throughout their sentences, their midcareer thoughts about outside contacts are actually ambivalent. They may declare that they would be better off without these contacts, but most would be disappointed if their contacts actually ceased. Their declaration can instead be viewed as an expression of fear about losing touch with family and friends, and an available protective rationalization if these contacts do decrease significantly. By asserting their emotional distance from the outside world, however, inmates reduce the value of letters and visits for reaffirming their outside ties, further exacerbating their marginality. In the middle of their sentences, inmates now see the outside world as having the kind of illusory quality that they had once assigned to the prison world.

Identity Work

A new inmate's separation from the outside world is also underscored by his limited identity work at midcareer. Through his self-dialogue, a convicted felon begins to differentiate himself from other inmates even before his arrival at prison, and he continues this differentiation process through the beginning of his sentence. For a number of reasons, his self-dialogue all but disappears after a few months, and when he does engage in self-reflection, his analysis is likely to cast doubts on how different he is from other prisoners.

Inmates engage in self-dialogues less frequently and less intensely because they no longer need or want the same level of introspection. The interpretive function of their self-dialogues is less vital, both because they believe that they now understand the prison world and because any new information they confront can be interpreted in conjunction with their partners or others, rather than through isolated self-reflection. As they have modified their images of other inmates through their experiences, they feel less compelled to differentiate themselves from others. Finally, their acceptance of a present-time rather than a future-time orientation and their practice of "thought control" encourage them to suppress self-reflection when it does arise.

Despite all of this, inmates do engage in identity work at midcareer, even if they reflect upon it less often. Most significantly, their taken-for-granted use of impression management itself constitutes a form of identity work. A new inmate sees his impression management as a means of hiding his "true" identity from others, as well as the temporary adoption of a more suitable identity for the prison world (an identity preservation strategy we analyze in a later chapter). Most new inmates are fully conscious of their impression management efforts, recognizing both the artificiality of the prison identity and the costs of assuming it. As one inmate stated, "For once, I would just like to be myself. It sucks the way we have to go around here like bad asses." The initial cost of adopting a prison identity is the inmate's inability to "be himself." This is particularly frustrating because the inmate knows that *other* inmates are engaging in exactly the same forms of impression management, as suggested in this excerpt from our fieldnotes:

> It's funny, but it seems like everyone in here is acting. Wouldn't it be nice if they all decided just to cut it out. It would be such a mellow place.

Inmates thus recognize that interactions with other inmates constitute, in Goffman's terms (1959, p. 10), a necessary "working consensus" of the definition of the situation.

As the assumed prison identity becomes second nature, an inmate may also reflect on the possibility of a much greater cost of his role pretense: an inability to revive his suspended identity at the conclusion of his sentence. Sometimes this takes the form of a concern that the inmate is losing his sense of self, an interpretation that is evident in this inmate's statement:

> I had a visit from _____ today, and like all visits I told how this wasn't all that bad a place to be, that it won't be that hard to do my 10 months. But no matter how many times I tell myself or others that, I don't think I really believe it. As I sit here in my cell, I wonder how in the hell I am going to make it. It seems such a waste. It is almost as if I can feel myself deteriorating, little by little, week by week.

Other inmates are concerned that they are becoming "hardened" in prison, including this 25-year-old inmate convicted of burglary:

> That's what I worry about a lot. Because I just didn't want to change.... I'm still fighting it, 'cause from what I understood before, I wasn't that bad—I wasn't even violent. But I have people say stuff to me now, before I used to say "O.K., O.K."—but now it seems like I got to eye them back, you know.

Within a matter of months, then, a new inmate's feelings of uncertainty have shifted from a concern for his physical well-being to a concern for his identity. As stated by one inmate: "I wonder if I will be the same person when I leave that I was when I arrived here." Reflections of this kind, whether they occur in conversations with friends or during periods of solitude, constitute a crucial change in the inmate's view of the prison world, and of himself.

THE PARADOX OF ROUTINE
AND UNCERTAINTY

Our analysis in this chapter has shown how new inmates, after several months in prison, come to focus more on the invariability of the prison routine than on unpredictable violence, and how they come to see their primary problem as one of endurance rather than survival. In these respects, they do share the prison perspective of long-term inmates. Their midcareer prison orientation, however, has been rather thinly superimposed over the preprison orientation with which they began their sentences. These inmates do look at the prison world differently at midcareer, but they have by no means reached the point where they view prison as an entirely *predictable* world. Fending off boredom may be the immediate challenge of their day-to-day lives, but survival remains their underlying concern. Dramatic events may lose most of their shock value but they nonetheless serve as reminders that anything may happen in prison. It is this juxtaposition of a totally monotonous daily routine within a milieu that is still fundamentally uncertain and unpredictable that delineates new inmates' cognitive and emotional responses to prison at the middle of their careers.

Inmates often speak of a kind of psychological tension that emanates from prison life, because of its monotony and because it affords inmates virtually no control over even the most minute details of their environment.[6] Below, we cite several examples from our fieldnotes to illustrate what inmates mean by this tension. By the middle of their sentences, inmates report that day-to-day prison life no longer terrorizes them but it nonetheless "gets on their nerves."

> I can honestly say that I am sick of this place and the people that are in it. It is really difficult to see the same people day after day with no variety whatsoever. You have heard every story a number of times and there is nothing else to talk about. Plus, there are a bunch of people who you just can't tolerate. Either they stink from not showering, or they have terrible manners, or maybe they just have big mouths. Even with your partners, sometimes they have annoying little quirks that just get to you at times.

How much tension they experience as a result of their confinement varies tremendously, however, from day to day. Although it may always be present in some degree, it is sometimes imperceptible and sometimes overwhelming:

> The noise in this place is getting to me today for some reason. I am not able to shut it out. When I try to read, it breaks through my concentration. When I try to watch T.V., it drowns out the sound. Then there are the people continuously walking past the cell. There is one fool who just walks up and down the tier; I'm so sick of seeing him. Of course, then there are the assholes who can't speak in a normal tone. They have to scream when the guy he is talking to is sitting right next to him. This is so upsetting to me that I could scream. It is driving me crazy and I don't know what to do about it. I really feel helpless because I know there isn't anything I can do.

When it reaches this level of intensity, the stress experienced by inmates renews their preprison fear of "going crazy." A number of inmates talked about the need to break through this psychological tension in some way, but most claimed they had found no effective means of doing so:

> There isn't really any way to relieve the tension while you're in here. You can try to work it off physically, but usually it ends up in mind games. It is like a cancer, eating away at you.

What inmates do, in response to this tension, is to engage in the same diversionary activities they use to escape the prison routine. The limitation of this tactic is that the prison routine is so overpowering that it soon encompasses even these diversionary activities, and inmates find themselves shooting baskets, playing cards, or using drugs with the same people, at the same time, day after day.

New inmates view the psychological tension of imprisonment, to the point of "going crazy," as a personal problem that results from an unvarying prison routine. But they also acknowledge that *other* prisoners experience these phenomena as well, which has the paradoxical effect of reemphasizing the unpredictability, and therefore the danger, of prison life. If all inmates are subject to this kind of tension, at varying levels of intensity, then routine interactions with others—interactions essentially similar to those that take place every day—can suddenly erupt into flared tempers or impulsive behaviors. An extended passage from our interviews, rich in both descriptive and interpretive detail, illustrates this possibility:

> I was out at the tennis court earlier.... Two Indians got along one end of the tennis court and they were throwing the football back and forth, totally out of place—just, you know, the whole yard out there to throw the football on and here these guys don't have much room from the baseline to the fence. The end of the court is for horseshoes, basketball, and the football is forever coming out on the court. Somebody's going to get hurt. Well, finally it bounced off of there and I hollered at them. I says, "Get that football out of here," you know, I just let them know right there and then to get that damn football out of there.... I just told them to get that football out of there before somebody gets hurt. He thought I meant me challenging him, me hurting him. I didn't, you know, [I meant] some of the tennis players getting hurt, throwing that thing around. He right away challenges me. He says "Yeah, it might be you." Well, I could see where he was coming from right then and there. I wasn't afraid of the guy, let it go at that. I figured—he stood down there for a couple of minutes, he went and told his buddy what I said. Well, I happened to have played tennis with the guy he was playing catch with, so I wasn't really too concerned about it.... It was that kind of bullshit. It had gotten very, very tense. I could feel myself just very, very upset. There's no reason for that kind of bullshit. It's nothing major, but it could have been. Here you got a group—not a group but two Indians and they're going to think that the white is coming down on them and God only knows what's going to happen. Maybe one is in for life and he's looking for a little excitement. Who knows?

In this instance, a near-altercation is attributed both to the specific situation and to underlying intergroup frictions. Under slightly different circumstances, this exchange might well have escalated to a prison "dramatic event."

In the following interview excerpt, another inmate describes an incident that progressed somewhat further toward violence.

> I had one experience about two weeks ago. An old man here who spent three and a half years here threw me up against the wall with a jack—had a jack in his hand, bigger than that. I had flashbacks. Well, you made it 19 months.... I suppose this is the end of the line and basically that's what it was all about. I figured that he put me here

to kill me, that there was no other reason, and I figured that this old fool was going to do it. Luckily, they stopped him. He wasn't mad at me either—he was maybe mad at his wife or something else. They're crazy and they put normal people in here and we're the targets.

In this incident, irrationality is attributed to a specific individual (or a specific type of individual—"they're crazy") rather than the immediate situation, but both situational factors ("he was maybe mad at his wife or something else") and the man's longer-term imprisonment are also cited in the interpretation. New inmates also refer to a "craziness" that occurs on a collective basis:

Some real craziness around here today. Somebody threw a couple of homemade smoke bombs at the sergeants' desk today. It hit one of the guards and he was taken to the hospital. That is one of the weird things that happens around here from time to time. It is really a ridiculous act. Nothing will be accomplished by it and something can be lost. Who knows how the guards will react to this?

New inmates recognize that other inmates face the same hardships of imprisonment, or greater ones, and they know that others' day-to-day responses to these hardships remain unpredictable, despite the fundamental sameness of every day in prison.

The paradox of an unchanging daily routine within an environment that remains fundamentally unpredictable symbolizes new inmates' existential reality during the middle of their sentences. Like more experienced prison insiders, they believe that their principal problem is enduring the boredom that results from an invariant prison routine. Immediately beneath this problem, however, is the belief that on any given day they might still walk into a violent confrontation with other inmates. In this sense, new inmates remain marginal in the prison world even when they have constructed an insider's orientation to this world.

SUMMARY AND DISCUSSION

Within a few months' time, new inmates progress from an *outsider's orientation* toward the prison, characterized by a violent prison image, a belief that their fundamental problem is one of survival, and a strategy designed to ensure their survival, to what is essentially an *insider's orientation*, through which inmates look at the prison in terms of its invariable, repressive routine; believe that their most significant problem is endurance of the boredom that results from this regimentation; and employ an adaptation strategy designed primary to combat their boredom. Their principal adaptive tactics by midcareer consist of a search for legal or illegal diversions and a self-imposed "thought control," to restrain their ruminations about their lives in prison and about the outside world.

Despite the similarity between their prison orientations and those of longer-term inmates or recidivists, first-time, short-term inmates remain marginal members of both the outside and the prison social worlds. Their connection to the outside world grows more tenuous through a reciprocal control of information, in which both inmates and their family and friends become increasingly reticent to share the details of their lives with one another. Moreover, the identity work that they conduct at midcareer, through taken-for-granted impression management and intermittent self-reflection, also raises doubts about their ability to return to their former lives. Although their immediate focus—like that of long-term inmates—is on the boredom of prison, they remain concerned about survival and are highly conscious of the incongruity between their unchanging daily routine and the essential unpredictability of the prison world. In Chapter 6, we examine what happens to these inmates' experiential orientations as their return to the outside world becomes imminent.

NOTES

1. In fact, there are a number of reasons why an inmate could be transferred to still another cell, on a temporary basis or for the duration of his sentence. An inmate might request a transfer, or he might be reassigned to another cell for administrative purposes. If he is victimized or threatened by other inmates, he could be placed in a protective custody cell. He also might be placed in a segregation cell for disciplinary reasons. Toward the end of his sentence, he might apply for a transfer to the Minimum Security Unit, a procedure we discuss further in Chapter 6.

2. Clemmer (1958) notes that the idea of the prison grapevine is often exaggerated into a mysterious and highly effective mode of communication but that it is actually a marginally effective word-of-mouth information exchange. We are using the term in the latter sense; a job assignment offers a new inmate greater and more direct access to word-of-mouth prison information.

3. We found no evidence to suggest that the presence of surrogate family relationships among inmates, such as those documented in women's prisons by Giallombardo (1966). Rather, we found that inmates use familial terms in the same way that they use sexual terms: as a form of humor that also serves to reinforce the partnership bond.

4. This expectation tends to fade later in the inmate's sentence. In the middle of their sentences, however, many inmates see their partnerships as their only genuine friendships. The belief that a partnership will extend beyond the prison world further authenticates this relationship.

5. Hearing and telling stories of this kind also constitute the structure of a larger moral framework within the prison. Wieder (1988) has suggested that although inmates and former inmates talk about the convict code as something that is real, the actual basis for its existence is its use in after-the-fact explanations and justifications of behavior. In this sense, inmates'

use of the convict code may be parallel to the way delinquents make use of the legal code to neutralize the moral implications of their behavior (Sykes and Matza 1957).

6. Parisi (1982, pp. 10-16) argues that pressures on inmates result in a combination of institutional deprivations, management concerns, sentencing and parole policies, post-release concerns, and both inmate and staff coping styles.

Chapter VI

Postprison Orientation: Looking Out

In the last two chapters, we documented the journey which a new, short-term inmate takes *into* the social world of a maximum security prison. We now turn to his journey out of this world. The inmate begins his sentence with a "preprison orientation" that he formulated prior to his arrival at the institution. He refines this outsider's orientation through his early experiences in prison, concretizing his prison imagery and elaborating his survival strategy to include a number of tactics that serve both to protect him and to allow him to acquire additional information about the prison world. Over several months' time, he acquires sufficient experience and knowledge to expand his understanding of the prison world and to revise his prison imagery (from a violent world to a routine one), his definition of the problem of imprisonment (from survival to endurance), and his adaptive tactics (continuing to rely on impression management and his partnership but adding diversionary activities and the practice of "thought control"). This insider's "prison orientation" does not negate his earlier concerns entirely but it does change the way he looks at his imprisonment on a day-to-day basis.

By definition, a short-term inmate's days in prison are highly limited—at least from the perspective of other prisoners. This fact, along with the equally important attribute that this is his *first* prison sentence, accounts for the inmate's inability to achieve more than a marginal status in the prison world. As we have seen, by the middle of his sentence, a new inmate also has become marginalized in the outside world. At the conclusion of his prison career, he faces the daunting challenge of coming to grips with the *contrast* between his insider's and outsider's orientations.

At Midwestern prison the "contrastive work" that an inmate performs at the end of his sentence is facilitated by a Minimum Security Unit, which we will examine next. This transitional unit, which is located on the prison grounds but outside the prison wall, enables an inmate to "look back" at the maximum security prison and his own experiences there. At the same time, any inmate in the final months of his sentence (whether in the Minimum Security Unit or not) must begin to "look ahead" to his future outside of prison. It is through these contrasts—between maximum and minimum security, between the prison and outside worlds, between an insider's "present-time" focus and an outside future—that the inmate's orientation changes once again. This is not an easy transition and, like the inmate's earlier shift from his preprison orientation to his prison orientation, it is one that takes place gradually, partly through his own efforts (especially his contrastive work) and partly as a result of what happens to him during the course of his sentence.

This chapter examines the emergence of the inmate's "postprison orientation," a process that includes two distinct but overlapping cognitive elements, in which he comes to accept that his sentence is in fact ending and begins to anticipate his return to the outside world. As the inmate shifts to a postprison orientation, he begins to focus on the uncertainty of his future and the specific problem of reintegrating himself into the outside world. As he does this, he alters his imagery of the prison world and his adaptive tactics once again, begins to reassemble a conceptualization of the outside world, perhaps makes some generalized plans for what he will do once he is released from prison, and engages in the most difficult and troubling identity work of his prison career.

THE MINIMUM SECURITY UNIT

The minimum security unit (MSU) at Midwestern is intended to help prisoners prepare for their transition to the outside world. Not all prisoners participate in this unit, although most first-time, short-term inmates elect to participate (and are eligible to do so because they have been convicted of relatively less serious offenses). Inmates must apply for a transfer to MSU, and their acceptance depends both on the crime for which they were sentenced and an evaluation of the prisoner's potential for success at MSU. To apply, a prisoner asks his caseworker to set up an interview with the prison classification committee. If the classification committee approves, he is then interviewed by a committee of MSU staff members; if this committee accepts him, the transfer must still be approved by the Associate Warden of Operations and the Warden. Acceptance of a prisoner's application and the timing of his transfer also depend on the available space at MSU.[1]

New inmates have known about MSU at least since their orientation classes at the beginnings of their sentences. At that time, when all of their energies are focused on daily survival, they give little attention to the possibility of an eventual transfer to an end-of-sentence program located somewhere outside the prison wall. As they progress through their sentences and move from a preprison orientation to a prison orientation, MSU is one of a multitude of prison topics that they hear about in their conversations with other prisoners—and, like any other topic, the "inside" version differs considerably from the official version. The prison grapevine regularly conveys news of what is going on at "the farm." (The unit was formerly operated as a prison farm and is still referred to by that name by both inmates and staff.) Inmates hear stories from prisoners who have been at minimum security but have been transferred back, voluntarily or otherwise, to maximum security:

> Today, a guy who returned from the farm was trying to tell me how crazy I was to want to go to the farm. He said that he would rather do his time in here than have to kiss ass for a half-freedom.

They hear, for example, that life in minimum security is even more boring than life in the secure institution, that the house rules at minimum security are petty and degrading, and that it is better to serve your time in maximum security than to live under the pretense of greater freedom in the Minimum Security Unit. Like all other prison information, these stories are not accepted unequivocally, but they nonetheless color the inmate's image of the Minimum Security Unit. Yet, despite such stories, the idea of a facility without bars and a program that offers not only greater visiting privileges but even home visits has obvious appeal to someone who is only months away from completing his sentence.

An inmate's application for minimum security illustrates both his acceptance of an insider's prison orientation and the conditional nature of the acceptance. The very act of applying for a transfer expresses his desire for the greater privileges afforded by minimum security, as well as his dawning recognition that his sentence is coming to a conclusion. But although the Minimum Security Unit may symbolize his hope for the future, his use of thought control makes him reluctant to place too much emotional stock on this symbolism. In conversations with others, he will instead refer to MSU as simply a "change in surroundings," which may have some value in breaking the monotony of the prison routine.

This lack of enthusiasm may be explained in part by the vagaries of the application process itself. No inmate knows for certain if or when his transfer will be approved. Suppressing enthusiasm about a possible transfer is thus similar to suppressing excitement about an expected visit, in that it serves to reduce disappointment if expectations are not met. A transfer, like visits, is beyond the direct control of the inmate himself.

Focusing too heavily on the possibility of a transfer can lead to disappointment, as reflected in this journal passage:

> I really feel that I have been aced out. Mike went to the farm today. I am happy for him, but feel I have been screwed. Mike got here about a month after I did and he has already gotten out there. I haven't even got an interview yet. I guess it really makes a difference who you get for a caseworker. It is bad enough that we have to try to motivate ourselves in this pit, but it is outrageous that we have to also be responsible for motivating the staff. I am getting very tired of saying good-bye and good luck to people. This is one of the toughest things to handle around here, to see people leave while you have to stay here.

Even when a transfer is approved, the inmate's optimism remains guarded. The prison world is unpredictable, and the inmate know that prison authorities may revoke or postpone their decision at any point.

If an inmate does express enthusiasm about his transfer, to his partner or other prison acquaintances, he is likely to receive reactions that reflect the caution and controlled emotion of the prison orientation they share:

> When I found out, I had to tell everyone. I received mixed emotions from them. Some were happy for me while others would say that a lot can happen between now and then and that I am not out there yet.

These responses reinforce the inmate's own caution about his transfer:

> My excitement about going out there has gradually been reduced. When I found out I was accepted, I was very happy, but I feel a number of people have spoiled that for me. They bring up all sorts of negative things about the place—half-freedom, kissing ass, etc.

Within the parameters of his prison orientation, in other words, the inmate labors, with partial success, to attribute only minimal significance to his application for minimum security.

INMATES' AND VISITORS' INITIAL
REACTIONS TO MINIMUM SECURITY

Just as he carried his preprison orientation into the prison at the beginning of his sentence, an inmate brings along much of his prison orientation to minimum security. In doing so, many inmates provoke a discordance between how they and their visitors view the minimum security unit. That is, both visitors and inmates engage in "contrastive work" in the final months of an inmate's sentences, but visitors do so at a faster pace and from a different angle of vision.

For visitors, the prison experience has consisted of regular or intermittent trips to the prison, passing through a metal detector, incidental observations of the visiting room and the perimeter of the prison facility, and supervised conversations with an inmate. Their knowledge of the prison social world rests entirely on the limited information given to them by the inmate. They receive much of this information, moreover, during their earliest visits, at which the inmate typically describes the general features of the prison world but "spares" visitors from knowing about his deepest fears about prison life. Later visits became less informative, as we discussed in Chapter 5, because of the inmate's suppressed emotion about visiting and his use of impression management tactics during visits. As visits become awkward and sometimes even strained, outsiders typically attribute an inmate's recalcitrance to the conditions of his confinement. This "explanation," however, is no longer available following an inmate's transfer.

At MSU, visitors can park directly outside the residential building and enter it (after a preliminary clearance) with only a signature at the front desk. Once inside, a visitor sees a physical and social environment that is remarkably distinct from the maximum security prison. The residential building itself is located outside the prison wall, and its rear windows provide a view of the maximum security complex. The view from the front windows, in contrast, includes an athletic playing field and the rolling hills of a golf course. There are no bars on the windows and no gates at the door, and although there are territorial restrictions on the inmate's movement, he is free to leave or enter the residence as often as he pleases after work and before dark. (In fact, because most residents work in the prison industries program which is located in a warehouse several hundred feet from the residence, they are *required* to go outside every day, when they walk to and from work.) Immediately inside the front door is a commons area, with tables and banks of telephones; to the right of this is a residents' lounge and the canteen. To the left are offices, a kitchen, and an informal cafeteria with outside windows and hanging plants. A stairway leads from the commons area to the sleeping rooms upstairs and the activities rooms downstairs. Residents can be seen watching television in the lounge, shopping at the canteen, reading newspapers, or using the telephones, in an atmosphere that seems casual and relaxed. The visits themselves take place in the lounge or cafeteria rather than in a separate visiting room.

Visits at MSU are thus entirely unlike those at maximum security, where outsiders felt constrained by the metal detectors and other security procedures. Compared to the imposing environment and regimentation of the maximum security prison, the casual atmosphere at MSU seems almost idyllic. Many visitors, in fact, find this contrast to be so great that they experience an immediate sense of relief when they first walk into the minimum security residence—and it comes as a surprise to them that the inmate they are visiting does not appear to share this relief.[2] Similarly, visitors see the transfer itself as a significant sentence milestone and are often taken aback by the inmate's cynical approach to it. For these reasons, it is common for an inmate's visitors to become concerned about how the inmate has "changed" as a result of his prison experience and how these changes will affect him in the future.

Inmates' reactions to minimum security are based on an alternative perspective. The social world of the maximum security prison has been their primary world for a period of many months. During this time, they have progressed from a preprison orientation, including a survival strategy designed to meet their fears of physical or sexual violence, to a prison orientation, with an adaptation strategy directed toward enduring a prison existence which is monotonous but still fundamentally unpredictable. It is from this latter vantage point that even short-term inmates view their transfer to minimum security.

Most components of inmates' midcareer adaptation strategies remain intact during the transfer. The emotional caution that they cultivated about the possibility of transfer is extended to the transfer itself, as suggested by this inmate:

> I came out here with some reservations and had some negative expectations that had been instilled by some inmates I had talked to on the inside. For one thing, I hate programs, the idea of earning privileges and moving through steps or phases. I also hate the idea that they have this thing that they can hold over you. "If you mess up, then we can send you back in...." Actually, to play down the transfer, I didn't really expect a whole lot from this place. The main thing I wanted was the visiting privileges that they have here, and for the most part, that is the only real advantage of this place.

New arrivals typically offer disparaging remarks about the MSU residents they see meticulously grooming themselves in anticipation of a "special duty" (a pass for an accompanied trip to the local community for shopping or dinner) or a home visit—especially after they discover that they will not be allowed similar privileges for some time.[3] It is precisely these kinds of remarks that lead visitors to become concerned about the effects of imprisonment.

Adaptation tactics that govern inmates' interactions with others are also brought along to minimum security. Their practice of avoiding interaction with prison staff, which inmates have followed since their arrival at the institution, is easily maintained. Impression management skills, which have become both more sophisticated and taken for granted, continue to guide their early interactions with other residents and visitors. In fact, the only significant element of the inmates' adaptation strategies that is not carried directly to minimum security is the reliance on partnerships, because partners are rarely transferred simultaneously. These adaptation tactics are not superficial customs; they were consciously formulated by inmates in response to their interpretive understanding of prison life. An inmate will continue to rely on them until his understanding changes or the tactics no longer prove useful.

Following their transfers, inmates' daily lives do change in significant ways and their prison orientation does gradually give way to a new, "postprison" orientation. We examine these changes in subsequent sections of this chapter. But there are a number of features of daily life in minimum security—some new and some familiar—for which the inmates' prison orientation remains well-suited. For example, a new hardship they confront in minimum security (though they may have been warned of it while still in maximum security) is the "half-freedom" of an open prison setting. A casual social atmosphere does not negate the hard fact that they are still in prison. If they should leave the minimum security grounds, if they should be involved in disciplinary infractions, or if the staff should consider them to be inappropriate residents for any reason, they can be immediately returned to maximum security, without anything like a due process hearing. They will eventually be given a taste of the outside world through "special duty" passes or home visits, but these provide only brief respite from their imprisonment. Their (insiders') response to these highly conditional "freedoms" is to devalue them and to emphasize instead the difficulty they present to inmates, as suggested in this fieldnote excerpt:

> ____ mentioned how he wouldn't want to be at MSU for very long. He agrees with many of us on that point. We really wonder how some of the guys are able to do a lot of time out here. Doing time anywhere is a drag, but doing it out here can at times be extremely difficult to do. You're just too damn close to the streets.

In much the same way that they learned to devalue outside contacts when they were in maximum security, inmates downplay the importance of these minimum security privileges in order to stabilize their emotional response to their continuing imprisonment.

There are other "new hardships" in minimum security. Inmates find that the lower security and less institutional living arrangements at MSU are accompanied by greater visibility of their actions. For example, the personal privacy they gain by having doors on bathroom stalls is countered by the reduced privacy of dormitory-style sleeping facilities, in which the residential floor is divided into sleeping cubicles by partitions that do not extend to the ceiling, and a new arrival must share his sleeping quarters with a roommate. Their freedom of movement inside and outside the residential building is countered by the small size of the MSU, which means that their actual range of movement is less than it was in maximum security. Within this restricted territory, the staff are in a better position to observe and respond to acts that would have been overlooked in maximum security, including profanity, verbal aggression, minor challenges to authority, gambling, or drug use. Residents' lack of anonymity means that they are subject to frequent informal head counts as well as the formal counts of the routine prison day. Finally, residents are also faced with a much more detailed set of regulations, many of which seem petty, irrelevant, or demeaning. They resent the requirement (for most residents) of having to attend chemical dependency classes. They see the "step program," through which they must earn program privileges, as superficial and childish. They view rules regarding domestic chores or general deportment as absurd:

> I received my first incident report today. The reason—failure to dust the desk of the unoccupied part of my cubicle. Shame on me, 50 lashes with a wet noodle.

Residents have to attend to these policies, because a sufficient number of infractions of even the most trivial rules can result in a return to maximum security. When viewed from the perspective of an insider's prison orientation, however, it is difficult to take these rules seriously.

In response to these new hardships, residents initially rely on adaptation tactics formulated in maximum security, including presentation of a prison identity created through impression management and a self-imposed thought control which minimizes emotional reactions and discourages both thoughts and emotions about the outside world. Through their maximum security experience, in other words, inmates have learned to place considerable distance between themselves and their immediate circumstances. With this refined detachment, inmates now view minimum security with a sense of unreality, much as they viewed the maximum security prison when they first arrived.

Besides the new hardships, residents find that some of the older ones continue to exist as well. Foremost among these is a fundamental lack of control over their own lives and daily activities. On matters large and small, they remain at the mercy of prison staff, as illustrated by the following incidents:

> I ordered Christmas cards from the canteen and they arrived today. The assholes sent me two cards for my wife, two for your first Christmas, 11 for my sweetheart, four for my kids, and five all-purpose cards.

* * *

> What a day: I sent in a voucher for $12 and Inmate Accounts sends it back saying I have no money. Hell, two weeks ago they said I had $28. They never have their shit together, but that's O.K., it's only the inmate who suffers.

Incidents of this kind reinforce the continuing validity of inmates' prison orientation.

Another familiar hardship is the boredom of a fixed daily routine. Although MSU does offer a number of new activities, there are actually fewer sanctioned diversions available. Thus, in exchange for such new activities as photography classes or participation in a Jaycees organization, residents find that they no longer have access to a theater or a gym and that they have fewer opportunities for exercise. After the novelty of the new sensory stimuli has worn off, therefore, residents typically assert that their daily routine is just as boring as it was in maximum security, as suggested in this journal entry:

> It was kind of a bummer day in general. Not that anything bad happened to me, it is more about what is not happening. After sitting around most of the day playing solitaire and listening to the radio, I just had this feeling of total uselessness. And of course, I just heard from Karen, who just got a job, and Luke is also getting some job offers. That is where I should be at now. It seems like such a waste, just sitting around doing nothing but getting fat. It seems that my knowledge could be put to better use. For me, this doing nothing is the severest of punishments that the state has to offer me.

To deal with the familiar concern of boredom, the familiar tactic of diversionary activities, including involvement in illegal activities, is used. Participating in these activities becomes logistically more difficult in minimum security, but the diversions themselves are still available. In maximum security, for example, inmates could consume drugs in any number of locations, including their own cells. In minimum security, drug use is likely to be confined to specific areas, such as the adjoining golf course or work stations, or transformed into a planned group activity, requiring the selection of a suitable time and place and the designation of a "lookout."

Within the contrastive framework held by visitors, activities such as drug use often seem to be a senseless risk of new-found freedoms. Within the prison orientation that inmates carry over from maximum security, such activities are viewed as a reasonable response to the relentless monotony that still dominates their daily lives. Minimum security residents also share a rationalization for their illegal activities, learned in maximum security from returning inmates: they have only a few months left to serve and they have already established their ability to survive maximum security, so a temporary return to the secure prison is not really much of a sanction. This rationalization not only enables residents to participate in illegal activities but also allows them the option of rejecting the "pettiness" of minimum security at any time, and diminishes the amount of control that prison officials have over them.

Differences in visitors' and inmates' initial reactions to the minimum security unit thus highlight the strength and residual effects of inmates' prison orientation, as well as raising questions about the personal effects of imprisonment. Immediately following the transfer, visitors grant enormous significance to the contrast between maximum and minimum security, and they are concerned that inmates do not seem to share their views. But in spite of their emotional reticence and apparent cynicism, inmates do engage in their own contrastive work, which they initiate even before their transfers take place.

RECASTING THE PRISON IMAGE

An inmate's midcareer prison orientation, as we have seen, is a present-time orientation. He believes that thinking about the outside world, and especially about his future on the outside, will make his time in prison more difficult. He has never been able to eliminate such thoughts entirely, of course, but he attempts to suppress them when they occur. As an inmate approaches the final months of his sentence, his thought control becomes less effective. While he is still in the maximum security prison, he begins to reflect on his prison experience and to speculate about life on the outside. He does not give free rein to this thinking, to be sure, but he cannot avoid becoming more future-time conscious as he begins to acknowledge to himself that his sentence is coming to an end. A transfer to the Minimum Security Unit, with its noninstitutional open campus and informal social atmosphere, greatly facilitates this self-acknowledgement.

THE "LOOK BACK" FROM MINIMUM SECURITY

Recently transferred inmates, as we have described, carry their prison orientation with them to minimum security, and they initially address both familiar and new prison hardships with the adaptation tactics that were refined in maximum security. Despite the residual influence of their prison orientation, however, the minimum security program clearly, if gradually, alters their perceptions and behavior. MSU creates opportunities for the inmate to look back at maximum security both literally, in that it is located outside the prison wall, and figuratively, in that it removes an inmate from the social milieu of maximum security. These effects begin with the transfer itself. No amount of thought control or suppressed emotion can completely obscure the significance of packing up all one's belongings in preparation for departure from the prison complex that has served as the absolute boundaries of one's world for many months. Walking through the front gate, out the front door of the prison, and past the wall—regardless of the seeming "unreality" of the situation and the inmate's long experience with avoiding thoughts of the outside world—is recognized as a significant event, even if the inmate refuses to examine its larger implications in any detail. This is, after all, the first time that inmates have had an unobstructed view of the scenery beyond the wall.

> We were taken to the farm in a station wagon. It was really strange walking out the front door. Since I had come here at night, I really didn't see much of what the prison looked like from the outside. The place looked much as I expected.... It was real nice to see some trees. They were real pretty, all different colors.

The trip to minimum security is brief; the unit is located directly adjacent to the maximum security wall, a few blocks from the maximum security entrance. In spite of the inmate's reluctance to admit too much enthusiasm about the transfer to himself or others, he is not blind to the symbolic value of this journey.

Inside the minimum security residence, a transferring inmate cannot help but note the obvious dissimilarities in environment:

> One thing that you notice right away is the noise factor; it is very quiet around here. Another difference that you notice is the almost total absence of uniforms, either on the inmates or on the guards. Actually, there are no guards here, they are considered staff.

Other contrasts are equally apparent. The same features that leave such an impression on visitors—the lack of bars or security checkpoints, the large windows with the golf course view, the comfortable furniture, green house plants, and so on—catch the inmate's attention as well. He may not express or feel the same delight at these differences that visitors do (an emotional reserve that often causes consternation to his visitors), but he includes them in his own contrastive work.

Some contrasts, although noticed immediately, nonetheless require additional time to filter through the inmates' prison orientation before they are fully appreciated. Transferring inmates, for example, typically see a number of familiar faces, some of them personal acquaintances, from their time in maximum security. For reasons that are not always immediately understood, these other inmates now seem changed. In part, this is simply because they are now dressed in civilian clothes rather than prison uniforms and they are being viewed in a new environmental context. But they also appear to *act* differently with one another (and toward the transferring inmate), in a way that is both more casual and more reserved. This was described by a newly transferred inmate whom we interviewed:

The crowd out here seem to mind their own business. I've only been here a couple of days, but there doesn't seem to be a lot of games and stuff going on. Most of the guys want to stay here and they know what they have to do to stay here and they don't want to go back inside and they don't take any chances.

In the weeks following his transfer, the inmate comes to understand that daily life in minimum security, for himself and his fellow residents, *is* distinctly different than it was in maximum security.

Numerous other differences, large and small, reinforce this contrast. The simple fact that he can now make canteen purchases with cash rather than an account slip signifies that he is moving experientially away from the prison world and toward the outside world. Newspapers are plentiful in the unit, and residents pay greater attention to outside events than they did in maximum security. And outsiders themselves are everywhere: from their first day at MSU, residents are given greatly increased opportunities for outside contact, including more liberal telephone privileges, unlimited visiting hours, and an unlimited number of visitors.

Perhaps most important, new residents gradually discover that they no longer experience the ongoing tension, resulting from the juxtaposition of routine and uncertainty, that was at the heart of their prison orientation—even though many aspects of their daily lives remain unchanged. After the novelty of the MSU environment wears off, for example, they again experience boredom, resulting from a relatively fixed daily schedule and fewer sanctioned diversions. Their lack of control over their own lives also ensures some continuing uncertainty. What is no longer present, however, is their basal uncertainty about prison violence. The newly transferred resident comes to accept that other residents pose virtually no danger, because any act of aggression will result in a return to maximum security. The resulting reduction in daily tension, perhaps more than any other factor, convinces the inmate that he is no longer imprisoned in quite the same way.

DISSIPATION OF ADAPTATION STRATEGY

As transferred inmates come to look at maximum security as an experience in their *pasts*, they change both their behavior and their prison imagery. An important component of their shift to a "postprison orientation" is their disuse of many of the adaptive tactics they developed in maximum security. This is by no means an immediate cessation. Inmates, as we have seen, carry their prison orientation with them to minimum security, and it is their insiders' response to the nonprison-like MSU environment that often causes concern for their visitors. In fact, some of their insiders' tactics continue to be relevant throughout their sentences, particularly their use of legal and illegal diversionary activities to alleviate boredom. But the strategic changes they do make are important ones, because they constitute a transformation in how inmates experience their imprisonment.

The reliance that an inmate places on his partnership—a central tactic in most inmates' midcareer strategies—is the first casualty of this transition. An inmate is separated from his partner by virtue of his transfer. That is, his partner either is still in maximum security or was transferred to minimum security earlier, and has therefore been undergoing his own change in experiential orientation. More to the point, the less threatening environment of minimum security, and the greater contact with the outside world it affords, means that an inmate will be functionally less dependent on his partner. If an inmate's partner has already been transferred to MSU, the partners usually remain friendly but the relationship is likely to become less intense.

The Minimum Security Unit's nonthreatening environment also affects an inmate's relationships with other prisoners because it removes the situational necessity of his maximum security presentation of self. An inmate's impression management skills were developed and refined to mask his fear and vulnerability. His original concern was with avoiding confrontation and covering weakness, through the self-control of simple behaviors such as eye contact. Over time, he learned to project an image of stoicism, toughness, and independence, through manipulation of body language, physique, speech patterns, and language—presentations that became taken for granted in prison interactions and regularly incorporated into his visits with outsiders as well. After a brief time in minimum security, the inmate comes to accept that presentations of this kind are no longer required. There is no real threat from other prisoners; there are no dangerous territories within the unit, and consequently, there is no longer an underlying fear to the resident's daily life. Interactions with other residents gradually become less patterned and more casual. Inmates' maximum security presentations of self are not easily shrugged off, of course, and we will return to the question of their identity work later in the chapter. The fact that they no longer *automatically* assume maximum security postures in their interactions with others is, nonetheless, a crucial development for inmates' postprison orientation.

The most significant change that an inmate makes, in terms of his movement toward a postprison orientation, is that he progressively relinquishes his use of thought control. Although this process actually begins in maximum security, it greatly accelerates following his transfer. To a large extent, this change in cognitive practice is the *point* of the Minimum Security Unit, in that the noninstitutional environment and greater visiting privileges make it difficult for a resident *not* to think about his time in prison and his impending return to the outside world. (From an insider's prison perspective, this is also the burden of "half-freedom" imposed by minimum security. In the words of an inmate we quoted earlier, "You're just too damn close to the streets.") In the final months of his sentence, therefore, an inmate finds himself regularly returning to the kind of self-dialogue that characterized the beginning of his prison career. The cognitive work that he conducts through this dialogue includes a revision of his prison imagery, the reconstruction of an outside image, and more intensive identity work.

CONSTRUCTING A CONCLUDING IMAGE

Each new inmate begins his sentence with a vague picture of a violent prison world, based largely on outsiders' meanings of imprisonment. The inmates retain the basic contours of this imagery during the early weeks of their imprisonment, using their early experiences in prison to fill in details. As they acquire information through their increasing participation in the prison world, this preprison imagery gives way to an insiders' view of prison as an unchanging, boring world. Their midcareer imagery, once established, remains stable for most of their sentences. In their final months or (especially) weeks, however, they transform their prison imagery again, in a manner that is really quite remarkable. Although their concluding image contains few new dimensions, it is nonetheless distinctly dissimilar from the images of their preprison and prison orientations. It is, rather, a synthesis of these earlier images.

As inmates reflect back on their imprisonment, they retain several features of their midcareer imagery. The most notable is the idea that the prison world was—and is—inherently boring. Despite the new experiences afforded by MSU, they see their transfer as only a temporary interruption of prison boredom. Even outside furloughs eventually come to be viewed as nothing more than periodic interruptions of the minimum security routine. They continue to view prison as an uncertain world as well; even more than at midcareer, this uncertainty is seen primarily in the lack of control they have over their lives rather than with respect to violence. For this and other reasons, most MSU residents also continue to view their own sentences as a personal injustice (an understanding developed during their prison orientation) rather than as a personal misfortune (a perception of the preprison orientation). The belief that their imprisonment is arbitrary and unjust may even be intensified at minimum security, as inmates become perplexed and angered by the early release of repeat or long-term offenders because of prison overcrowding.

It is not particularly surprising that inmates would hold onto much of their insiders' prison imagery after their transfer. What is more noteworthy is that they begin to incorporate elements of their *preprison* imagery back into their concluding imagery. Thus, as inmates look *back* at the maximum security prison, this institution again comes to be viewed as a spatially separate world that is quite distant from the residents' current lives in minimum security. In contrast to the beginning of their sentences, residents now know what life is like within the prison walls, but even with this knowledge, prison again starts to appear as an alien and somewhat illusory world. As they look *forward* to their lives after prison, residents also return to their preprison understanding of their sentences as time that has been taken away from them—as a disruption of the normal flow-of-time that exists in the real world. Their insiders' approach to temporality, which we described in Chapter 5, becomes irrelevant.

Similarly, as residents are separated from their partners and other prison associates and begin to think about reestablishing ties with relatives and friends on the outside, they return to their preprison view of their sentences as a disruption of their prior networks of social relationships. The most striking reversion in a resident's imagery is in his conceptualization of other inmates, particularly those in maximum security. After gradually breaking through his preprison stereotypes, learning to distinguish among several different kinds of inmates, and conceding that most men in prison are "normal," he returns to more categorical thinking in his postprison imagery. He does not reaccept the violent stereotypes of his preprison image entirely, but he again believes that he has little in common with maximum security inmates. This disidentification, as we discuss shortly, is crucial to his postprison identity work.

Residents themselves become aware of their interpretive revisions on those occasions when maximum security somehow reasserts itself into their consciousness. This journal excerpt describes one such occasion:

> We played the inside team in broomball today. It was quite an experience going back inside. I must say it is a lot different hearing the door slam behind you when you know you will be going right back out. Of course, things haven't changed much. The same people walking the halls, same guards, and the same guys in the gym. Of course, there are new faces interspersed, but I do believe that I could come back a year from now and things would be much the same. We had to be searched going in, the first time for a long time. It is so degrading.... Talk about invading your "space."

These kinds of reflections—on the unchanging "sameness" of the prison world itself but also on the resident's changed reactions to both the noise of a slamming cell door and the strip search—point out the social and emotional distance that the resident has already traveled from maximum security.

Reports of prison incidents provide similar occasions for cognitive reflection and underscore residents' marginality in both the prison and the outside worlds. If an incident itself is "newsworthy," residents will be able to contrast official and unofficial versions of what happened. Many MSU residents (unlike most maximum security prisoners) regularly read newspapers and watch television news programs, and understandably take a particular interest in stories about the prison. Because of their continuing ties to the prison grapevine, residents can contrast the "real" story of an incident with the newspaper or television report. They may know, for example, that a reported suicide was really a homicide, or they may have heard a very specific motive for what is reported as an unexplained homicide. This insider's knowledge marks both their separation from the outside world and their residual affiliation with the prison world. On the other hand, dramatic events have now lost all of their shock value, denoting the distance that residents have come from their maximum security concerns. Compare this flippant description of prison violence with how inmates described such incidents earlier in their sentences:

> When things start to get a little dull on the inside, something always seems to happen to brighten things up. Someone nicked himself shaving and then stumbled off the 4th tier in B Hall. In other words, he was stabbed and pushed off. There wasn't much of a reaction to this out here, except for some joking. When it comes to the dangers of the prison, the prison itself seems very remote to the residents out here. I guess that it is a place that most of them would like to forget.

Dramatic events in maximum security come to seem far removed from residents' daily concerns—in exactly the way that newspaper reports of a prison incident have little significance to the daily lives of most outsiders.

A first-time, short-term inmate's concluding imagery does not travel "full circle" back to his preprison imagery, but it does complete a surprising portion of this journey. He began his sentence with a simple, abstract image, grounded largely in an outsider's stereotypes about a violent prison world. Through his information-seeking tactics and prison experiences, his prison imagery became more concrete and more complex. Although he certainly has not lost the insight of his prison knowledge and experience, minimum security offers him the opportunity to look back on maximum security with some physical and social distance. This simultaneous decreasing participation in the prison world and increasing participation in the outside world, and the contrastive work this change inspires, provide the bases for his concluding imagery. Thus, to say that the concluding image is a synthesis of the anticipatory and midcareer images is simply to recognize that it is a synthesis of outside and inside meanings. An inmate cannot return completely to the public stereotype with which he entered prison, because he has become a part of the prison world and he knows the stereotype to be inaccurate. Nonetheless, as his orientation returns to the outside, his concluding image becomes clouded once again by an outsider's stereotype of prison.

RECONSTRUCTING AN OUTSIDE IMAGE

Inmates' preparations for their future on the outside, like their reflections on their prison experience, begin while they are still in maximum security. Throughout their sentences, inmates periodically fantasize about what they will do when they get out of prison. Toward the ends of their sentences, they begin to speculate more frequently about life on the outside and to discuss their outside plans with others. Their insiders' adaptation strategy inhibits them from pursuing this line of thought too deeply while they remain in maximum security, but their transfer to minimum security promotes it, in the manner we have described.

Meisenhelder (1985, p. 53) has argued that "the most significant aspect of the lived temporality of prison is its lack of a future." This assertion is undoubtedly true for long-term inmates, and we have found it to be surprisingly valid for short-term inmates as well, for much of their sentences. The most important temporal characteristic of a short-term inmate, however, is that he has never been separated from the outside world—in one direction or the other—for more than a year. At the end of his sentence, especially after his transfer to minimum security, he gradually but inevitably abandons his practice of thought control (as well as other maximum security tactics) and, thus, opens himself not only to reflections about his prison past but also to projections about his outside future.

In order to plan for his future, even a short-term inmate has to reconstruct an image of the outside world. His outside imagery is much less developed than his prison imagery, but there are nonetheless parallels to his cognitive processes at the beginning of his sentence: he again finds himself about to become involved in a different social world, and he anticipates this involvement with some fear and a great deal of uncertainty. It is on the basis of his imagery, moreover, that he again begins to formulate a strategy for adaptation to the outside world. There are, of course, some obvious differences between the beginning and end of an inmate's prison career. Prior to his arrival at prison, he had no direct knowledge of the prison world, so his earliest imagery was constructed from incomplete and often distorted information received from others and from fictional or journalistic presentations. At the end of his sentence, he is faced with the task of *reconstructing* an image of a world in which he has already participated. He clearly has an advantage here, but he must nonetheless confront the question of how much the outside world, particularly his intimate social world of family and friends, has changed in his absence. His analysis of this question affects (and is affected by) his interactions with outsiders during visits at MSU and, eventually, by his own visits to the outside world.

CHANGING NATURE OF VISITS

The minimum security program—regardless of the complaints that an inmate may have about it—does foster an inmate's reconceptualization of the outside world. Residents not only think about the outside world more but become more directly engaged in it, before actually reentering it, through increasingly "natural" conversations with others. As residents let go of their patterned use of impression management, they begin to converse more freely with visitors about a greater variety of topics:

> I am finding myself becoming more interested and aware of what is going on on the outside. This is kind of a switch from when I was in the prison. I feel a need for more contact with family and friends, and also a desire to make new friends. For one thing, there are basically the same people [here] that were in the prison (and I can't say that I was all that fond of very many people in there). Also, most of the guys that are here maintain close contacts with family and friends and don't seem to really need anything from the other residents.

These conversations, in turn, encourage a resident to look forward to his first outside leave:

> Well, I think I am starting to soften up a little bit. I believe the identity I picked up in the prison is starting to leave me now that I have left the world of the joint. I find myself becoming more and more involved with the happenings of the outside world. I am even getting anxious to go out and see the sights, just to get away from this place.

Residents with families have time to get reacquainted with them, because of the unlimited visiting hours at MSU. There is even a separate house on the prison grounds, in which a married inmate can spend a weekend with his wife, before he becomes eligible for a home visit.

Although the changing nature of visits is an important preparation for an inmate's return to the outside, it is not without some cost. As suggested in this journal excerpt, the more that an inmate lets the outside world into his daily thoughts, the greater the burden he feels about his continuing lack of control over outside events:

> There are times that I really feel very helpless. When I hear from a friend and hear that there are problems, I do so much want to help. But there isn't anything I can do while I am out here. Sure, I can listen to them on the phone, but you can't help unless you are there. One thing that I had always prided myself about was that I was always there, or would be there, when a friend needed me. I am not there now. I know that

my friends do understand, but I must wonder if they wonder if I will always be absent when I am needed.

Despite the emotional difficulty entailed, however, it is precisely through such reflections—about the inmate himself, his friends and family, and his relationship to them—that a resident begins to reconstruct an understanding of his outside social world and to reengage himself in it.

PRELIMINARY VENTURES OUTSIDE

The inmate's first direct participation in the outside world is likely to be a "special duty" into the local community, provided that he can arrange for a staff member or volunteer who has completed the institution's "escort training" to accompany him for this activity. Special duty passes are typically granted for such activities as attending church services or going shopping.

On the day of his first special duty, or perhaps even the evening before, the inmate finds himself agitated about what will happen. He wonders whether others will know that he is from the prison, and about his ability to talk with outsiders. Like the MSU residents he once laughed at, he takes great pains to present himself "properly," making sure that he is well-groomed and "dressed up" (at least by wearing something other than a prison uniform or jeans). The few hours that he spends on the outside offer familiar but almost-forgotten sensory experiences:

> I went on my first special duty today. We went to a bookstore and then to the mall.... It was strange being out in public. Walking down the main street was nice, doing a little window shopping.

A special duty pass thus gives the inmate just a taste of what it is like not to be in prison. For this reason, some residents find their first outing to be somewhat anticlimactic because of the inflated, though ill-defined, expectations they had allowed to develop. Nonetheless, most prisoners view this introductory outside visit as a positive experience.

Following their first and subsequent special duty outings, most residents have little difficulty returning to the daily schedule of the minimum security unit. The effects of the special duty are short-lived, but inmates value them because they offer temporary relief both from the daily prison routine and from the inmates' intensifying self-dialogues.

An inmate's first three-day furlough is quite another matter, because it promises his first involvement with his own social world of family and friends. He anticipates this furlough in much the same way that he did his first special duty, except that his excitement starts to build several days before the event itself. His preparation for the furlough is also similar, in terms of his desire to present a nonprison image to the outside world. The accompanying self-dialogue, however, is understandably more intense, centering on the inmate's fears that he will be returning to a world in which he no longer belongs. Conversely, friends or relatives, not knowing how the inmate has changed or what he expects, also approach the initial furlough cautiously:

> I have no idea of what I want to do. I hate to plan anything. I guess I would just like to let things happen. But they really want to make this special for me. And it's kind of odd, they are kind of handling this with kid gloves. I guess I will just have to wait and see what happens.

During their initial furloughs, inmates are often invited to parties or gatherings at which they are called upon to relate their prison experiences to others. There are rules prohibiting alcohol or drug use on home visits, but inmates who are so inclined seem to have little difficulty indulging in these pleasures. Although violation of these rules can result in a return to maximum security, their defensive rationalization—that they have only a limited time left on their sentences and that they have proven that they can survive in maximum security—renders this threat relatively ineffective.

An initial furlough often provides an inmate with a reading of his outside relationships. Most inmates fear that changes will have occurred in these relationships but nonetheless cling to the hope that their lives on the outside will be essentially the same, or better, than they were before prison. This hope, of course, is easily translated into expectations that can be shattered during a home visit. What actually happens on the furlough depends on many factors, including the inmate's expectations, the expectations that friends and family have of the inmate, and any changes in their relationships that have taken place during the inmate's imprisonment.

However enjoyable a first home visit is, inmates are fully cognizant that they have to return to prison, in most cases for several months. When an inmate does return—usually at the last possible minute—he is likely to remain awake for several hours, reliving the events of his furlough and thinking about his return to freedom. Just as he did prior to his imprisonment, he thus finds himself engaged in an extended self-dialogue, through which he imaginatively constructs an imagery of a world he is about to enter.

REINTEGRATION PLANNING

In the days immediately following their first home visits, some inmates continue to experience euphoria over their first real outside contacts while others become mildly depressed by the reality of being back in prison:

> Talk about a long day. I realized today just how hard it is to come back to this place. I sure am glad I don't have much time left because after the furlough I really don't know how long I could deal with this place. One thing that does help is that I know I will be going on furlough again in a couple of weeks. I guess that does give me something to look forward to.

In either case, inmates begin to think more about what their lives will be like after prison. Some of their thoughts are devoted to practical matters, including residential and occupational plans. This is not the first time that short-term inmates have thought about their occupational plans, of course, but it is the first time since their arrival at prison that occupational planning has been a necessity. In maximum security, their reveries about their future tended toward generalized possibilities, often grandiose and impractical. As their return to the free world becomes imminent, however, their plans tend to becomes more specific and more realistic.[4] Many minimum security residents, following their first home visits, begin to read the employment want ads in newspapers, call on acquaintances about job leads, and initiate mail or telephone contacts with employers. They also typically resolve to devote part of future home visits to looking for jobs.

Beyond their immediate needs for a job and a place to stay, inmates are also concerned with other dimensions of their lives on the outside. Although a few inmates may decide to move away and "start over" and some may be released to a halfway house as a condition of their supervised release, most expect to return to their preprison communities of residence and networks of family and friends. They understand, however, that reintegrating themselves into these communities will take some work. In maximum security, most inmates placed considerable emotional distance between themselves and at least some of their outside relationships; as a consequence, these relationships have diminished in intensity as well as frequency of contact. In some instances, inmates even terminated personal relationships, to avoid having to maintain them at a distance from prison. Now inmates must decide which of these relationships should be reestablished, determine whether they can be reestablished, and consider how to go about reestablishing them. An initial home furlough forces an inmate to confront these questions, and impending furloughs represent circumstances in which they must be addressed.

It is when inmates begin working on the practical details and relation-ships of their outside futures that they fully appreciate the discomfort of "half-freedom." Although they presumably have a far easier end-of-sen-tence transition than long-term inmates, even short-term inmates some-times regret giving up the present-time orientation of maximum security prison life. Occasionally an MSU resident will ask to be transferred back to maximum security, in order to postpone the difficult process of reestab-lishing an outside future. Similarly, MSU residents (and others) often attribute this motive to inmates who are involuntarily transferred back, because of serious rule infractions or an "escape" (i.e., walking away from the facility, or not returning from a furlough). For the majority of resi-dents who continue to struggle with the existential problems of anticipat-ing their return to the free world, it becomes increasingly difficult to avoid thinking about the outside. As a consequence, the remaining weeks or months of their sentences seem particularly arduous, consisting of a daily routine that is still viewed as boring but is punctuated by periodic home visits and frequent ruminations about the future.

Subsequent furloughs tend to be less frenetic than the first. They still typ-ically include parties or other social events, but these become less awkward as inmates begin to feel more at ease in their interactions with friends and family. Inmates have less trouble separating themselves from the prison world, and it becomes even more difficult for them to return to the prison. Inmates come to believe that they are no longer part of the prison world, and they view the remaining time on their sentences as simply a final ordeal that must be overcome. On home visits and at MSU, they continue to plan for their futures but, to a large extent, the final weeks of their sen-tences are spent simply marking time until their release. Throughout this final period of "waiting," however, inmates continue to engage in self-dia-logues about the outside world, about their relationships, and about how they have been affected by their imprisonment.

IDENTITY WORK: THE STRUGGLE TO REVIVE PREPRISON IDENTITIES

Short-term inmates engage in identity work, in one form or another, throughout their entire prison careers. In each of their experiential orien-tations to prison, their identity work is intricately related to their concep-tions of the prison world. In their preprison orientation, they initiate a self-dialogue well before the beginning of their sentences, in which their fear of being changed in prison is intertwined with their analyses of the bio-graphical events leading to their imprisonment, their concerns about fam-ily and friends, their efforts to construct an image of the prison world, and their concerns for survival within that world. They therefore enter the prison with a belief that they have nothing in common with other inmates and a resolve to insulate themselves from others. They regularly return to this self-dialogue during their first weeks in prison, as their primary means of making sense out of the prison world and differentiating themselves from other inmates. In so doing, they gradually fashion a survival strategy, including a reliance on impression management tactics, that allows them to maintain a good measure of insulation from other prisoners.

In their midcareer prison orientation, inmates' identity work takes place largely through impression management, which comes to be taken for granted as a basis for interaction with others. They no longer view most inmates as being very different from themselves and they actively suppress introspective analyses; they do, however, experience occasional doubts about whether they are, in fact, changing as a result of their imprisonment.

In the postprison orientation, these doubts come to the forefront of their renewed self-dialogues, as inmates strive to ascertain how their time in prison will affect their participation in the outside world. As in their earlier orientations, their identity concerns at the ends of their sentences are intermingled with other cognitive issues, particularly the revision of their prison imagery.

We have already noted two constituent elements in an inmate's identity work in minimum security. The first is the dissipation of his maximum security adaptation tactics, particularly his declining use of impression management in his interactions with others. The second is a return to categorical, stereotypic thinking about maximum security inmates and the concomitant process of differentiating himself from them. Both of these changes are part of the inmate's postprison contrastive work, through which he compares the perspectives of the outside and inside worlds. These contrasts generate a host of specific questions. If he no longer needs to present himself as he did in maximum security, how should be act toward others? That is, once he lets go of his "prison mask," what lies behind it? How much of the inmate's "old self" remains? How is he different from other prisoners? How has he changed in prison? How will others react to these changes? He addresses these and other questions both introspectively, through his renewed self-dialogue, and interpersonally, through his prison visits and outside furloughs.

As an inmate's orientation shifts gradually from the prison world back to the outside world, his identity work can be seen in his changing view of special duty passes and furloughs. Where he once laughed at other residents dressing up or getting excited about a trip to town or a weekend home, he now eagerly looks forward to his own participation in these activities. His anticipation, however, also prompts the kind of self-assessment that characterized the beginning of his prison career. Some of his concerns are similar, particularly those about the effects of his sentence on family and friends, and how his prison experience may change his relations with others. Although he hopes that his family and friends will welcome him back as if nothing has happened, he fears that this may be impossible. He realizes that he will have to make some important personal decisions—including where to live and what kind of job to look for—very soon. These thoughts, as described in the following journal passage, can be intimidating:

> I'm in kind of a strange mood tonight. I think I'm just a little scared. I've been thinking about my future on the outside and I guess I have some doubts about my ability to make something of my future. I really wonder what impact this prison stay will have. I really don't worry too much about the prison stigma—only when applying for jobs and maybe with certain women. The really big fear is that I have been very lazy and lackadaisical. Everything has been planned out for me and all my needs have been provided for the past year. How will I handle being responsible for myself?

Home visits themselves also promote self-reflection, as recounted here:

> I've been thinking a lot about seeing [an ex-inmate] at that pizza place [during a first furlough]. I know that I didn't want to go up to him because I thought it might be uncomfortable. We all want to put this prison experience out of our minds as much as possible, and who needs any reminders? I wonder if this means my self-esteem has lowered a few notches. I don't really suppose that I should feel uncomfortable running into former fellow inmates. There is no reason we couldn't exchange formalities, and there is no reason to mention our prison experiences. This is one area that I am going to have to work on. That is, to remind myself that I am not inferior, that I am as good as others regardless of my prison experience.

These kinds of fears, about what will happen when he returns to the outside world, constitute the predominant emotional response of the inmate's postprison orientation.

An inmate's self-dialogue intensifies as his release date approaches and it comes to be dominated, above all else, by the question of how he has changed as a result of his imprisonment. He feels that he is essentially the same person he was when he entered prison, but he also knows that he has had to alter both his behavior and his thoughts to adapt to prison life. In this interview excerpt, a 37-year-old inmate reflects on his time in prison:

> I saw changes in myself because I couldn't constantly be giving people what they wanted all the time. I couldn't just constantly give them cigarettes and stuff. I just decided to become a little bit colder. And more selfish ... the people on the outside have made it extremely difficult for me to spend my time here.

What he doesn't know for certain is how permanent these changes are, whether he can ever really be the same as he was before prison, and how others will react to him.

Like the self-dialogue at the beginning of his prison career, an inmate's thoughts and analyses do not take place in an organized, logical fashion; they take place, as suggested by this excerpt, during intermittent periods of reflection:

> While sitting at work this morning pondering my usual, boring daily routine, I wondered what my day would be like once I gained my freedom. We all have some expectations of what our new lives ... will hold for us. These expectations are laced with many hopes and also some fears. What will it be like not to be constantly surrounded by 75 other males, to not have the bell ring at 6:15 every morning, to not have to shower, shave, shit and piss with others...?

> I think there is some danger in the idea that we all expect so much from our new lives. In looking back, my life wasn't filled with total joy and excitement. Yet, we seem to think that that is what awaits us once we obtain our freedom. I am afraid that many of us may be in for quite a letdown; we have set our expectations much too high. Hell, anything will be better than what we have now, but anything will wear off quickly. It won't take much to put a real damper on things, such as failure to get a job, failure to find that woman or women you have dreamed about during incarceration, among other things. All in all, it will be an interesting experience, one which I am looking forward to.

Some thoughts, especially fears about changes in relationships, are suppressed. Others recur regularly. What is significant is that the inmate is beginning to direct his thoughts again toward the outside world, and his place in it.

SUMMARY AND DISCUSSION

First-time inmates enter prison as outsiders. Drawing upon "public knowledge" about prisons, they construct a vague image of the prison world and a crude plan for surviving it. Over a period of several months, building from their own experiences and the knowledge they acquire from others, they transform this *preprison orientation* into an insider's *prison orientation*, with a very different understanding of what prison is all about, and different tactics for dealing with the problems presented by their imprisonment. In the final months of their sentences, as they engage in the contrastive work of looking back at their prison experience and forward to their outside future, they devise still another orientation to their imprisonment. Their *postprison orientation*, which is facilitated by a transfer to the Minimum Security Unit, includes (among other things) a decreasing use of their insiders' adaptation tactics and a revision of their prison imagery.

Although inmates now have a much fuller, insider's understanding of prison than they did at the beginning of their sentences, their postprison imagery nonetheless encompasses a number of features from their pre-prison imagery, including the categorical belief that they have little in common with most maximum security inmates. Thus, at the conclusion of their prison careers, inmates again incorporate an outsider's view of the prison into their own orientations. Although inmates' preprison, prison, and postprison orientations are quite dissimilar from one another, each is affected by the inmates' social marginality, in both the prison and outside worlds. We take a closer look at the relationship between their marginality and their adaptation to prison in Chapter 7.

The postprison orientation is a look forward as well as backward, and it includes an inmate's efforts to reconstruct a picture of his outside world and at least some preliminary planning for his reintegration into it. It is this look into their futures—after an extended period of intentionally suppressing such thoughts—that provides the emotional tone of the postprison orientation: an increasing apprehension about returning to the outside. At the center of this apprehension is his postprison identity work, which focuses on a consideration of how he has changed as a result of his time in prison. The stakes of this identity work are enormous, in that it will define how prison will continue to affect the inmate's life after their release. We return to questions of identity in Chapter 8.

Inmates' concerns about their identities and outside relationships do not, of course, negate their raw excitement about getting out of prison. As their release dates approach, inmates continue to think about the outside world, go on weekend furloughs, and engage in self-dialogues. Many of the inmates we studied were transferred to a prerelease program, with job-seeking and other reintegration classes, and even more liberal furlough policies, for the final three weeks of their sentences.[5] Whether or not inmates go to this program, their final days in prison are dominated by the emotional anticipation of their freedom. We thus close this chapter with the final two entries from Jones' prison journal:

> I can do this standing on my head. It is amazing. I have been waiting so long for this day to come around. I didn't do anything at all today but sit around and watch T.V. A fitting way to end my prison experience. I have really been watching the clock. Just ten more hours to go.

* * *

> I just crossed off the last day on my prison calendar. I just want to scream, I'm so damn happy. I had really hoped that I would be more settled on the outside—with a job, that is. But at the present time, I really don't care. At least I have a place to live; I know that I am going to make it. I have no real plans for today, except that I would like to party with my friends.... Well, 15 minutes to go.

NOTES

1. Our fieldwork and interviews included discussions with prisoners who had transferred to MSU, prisoners who would complete their sentences in maximum security, and prisoners who were not yet eligible to apply for transfer to MSU. Our description of the prison career focuses on those who have transferred. One reason for this focus is that Jones transferred to MSU, providing us with the opportunity to extend our fieldwork into the minimum security unit. A second reason is that first-time, short-term prisoners, because they have been convicted of relatively less serious offenses, are typically eligible for MSU.

2. The differences between visits at MSU and visits at the prison are actually greater than many visitors realize. For visits at MSU, the inmate, after being called by staff, walks unescorted from his job station to the visiting site. Unlike maximum security, he is not required to have a pass and he is not subjected to a strip search either before or after the visit. Many visitors, however, were unaware that these maximum security procedures ever took place.

3. Assuming adequate progress through the steps of the MSU program, a newly transferred inmate can expect to receive special duty privileges in about a month, and his first furlough in three to four months.

4. These same changes have been noted among longer-term prisoners. Irwin (1970, pp. 104-105) discusses how prisoners' plans become more conventional just before their release from prison.

5. Inmates who are completing their sentences in maximum security may also be transferred to this facility for the final weeks of their sentences.

Chapter VII

Adapting to the Prison Experience

In his discussion of the practicality and goal directedness of everyday life, Schutz (1962) argues that people experience situations in practical terms, as a project they are working on in that world. So it is for new inmates in a maximum security prison. Inmates' experiential orientations, which we presented in the preceding chapters, consist of their subjective understanding of the prison world, the practical problems they feel compelled to resolve as a result of this understanding, and their strategies for resolving these problems. Our analysis makes it evident that "doing time" is not simply a matter of being in prison. It is, rather, a creative process through which inmates must invent or learn a repertoire of adaptation tactics that address the varying problems they confront during particular phases of their prison careers. Throughout this analysis, we also have emphasized how each of the inmates' prison orientations was shaped by their *social marginality* in both the prison and outside worlds. In this chapter, we examine inmates' adaptation strategies more fully, demonstrating how inmates make use of their social marginality, and the sociological ambivalence that results from it, to forge highly delimited adaptations to the prison culture.

MARGINALITY, EXPERIENTIAL ORIENTATION, AND PRISON ADAPTATIONS

Inmates' subjective understandings of the prison world are important because they provide a basis for action (Blumer 1969). Figure VII.1 summarizes how inmates' adaptation strategies emanate from their changing understandings of the prison world. For example, in response to the violence of their initial outsider's imagery, their earliest survival tactics are protective and defensive in nature. As cultural outsiders, however, new inmates also recognize their need for more information about the prison

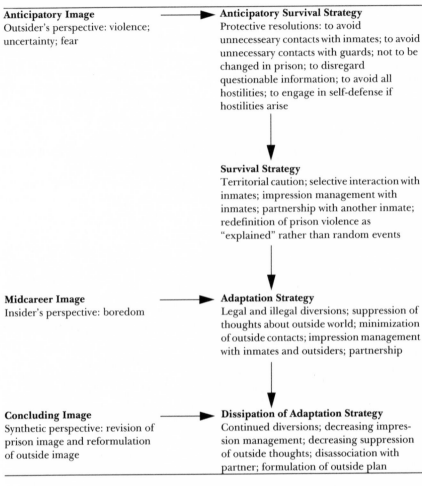

| Anticipatory Image | → | Anticipatory Survival Strategy |

Anticipatory Image
Outsider's perspective: violence; uncertainty; fear

Anticipatory Survival Strategy
Protective resolutions: to avoid unnecesseary contacts with inmates; to avoid unnecessary contacts with guards; not to be changed in prison; to disregard questionable information; to avoid all hostilities; to engage in self-defense if hostilities arise

Survival Strategy
Territorial caution; selective interaction with inmates; impression management with inmates; partnership with another inmate; redefinition of prison violence as "explained" rather than random events

Midcareer Image
Insider's perspective: boredom

Adaptation Strategy
Legal and illegal diversions; suppression of thoughts about outside world; minimization of outside contacts; impression management with inmates and outsiders; partnership

Concluding Image
Synthetic perspective: revision of prison image and reformulation of outside image

Dissipation of Adaptation Strategy
Continued diversions; decreasing impression management; decreasing suppression of outside thoughts; disassociation with partner; formulation of outside plan

Figure VII.1. Prison Images and Strategies

world, and virtually all of their early survival tactics serve as information-seeking as well as protective measures. Thus, territorial caution, impression management, and the new inmate's partnerships guide their ventures into the cafeteria, the yard, the gym, and other unexplored areas of the prison. Selective interaction with other inmates, impression management and their partnerships help them to confront such prison experiences as cell transfers, legal and illegal recreational activities, and participation in the prison economy. The barrage of often-conflicting information they receive through these tactics is the raw material out of which they continuously revise their prison images.[1] Although they continue to view prison with essentially an outsider's perspective, their survival tactics allow them gradually to acquire an insider's knowledge of the prison and to modify their adaptation tactics accordingly.

A common form of prison adaptation is the creation of a survival "niche" (Seymour 1977) that allows inmates some measure of activity, privacy, safety, emotional feedback, structure, and freedom within the larger, hostile environment of the maximum security prison (Johnson 1987; Toch 1977). Because of their inexperience, new inmates are particularly ill-equipped to find such niches (Johnson 1987, p. 114) and new short-term inmates are further handicapped by their continuing marginality in the prison world, which restricts their ability to exert personal control (Goodstein et al. 1984) and inhibits their acceptance by other inmates. But short-term inmates, in contrast to those facing years of imprisonment, need only to develop a *transient* niche in prison. The problems they face are similar—understanding the prison status hierarchy and recognizing their place in it, learning whom to trust and whom to avoid, determining how to evade trouble in a trouble-filled environment—but their solutions do not need to be as enduring. The inmates in our study are able to achieve such transient "accommodation without assimilation" (Gibson 1988) within a few months time. To a casual observer, moreover, they soon became indistinguishable from long-term inmates, relying on such adaptive tactics as legal and illegal diversions and conscious efforts to control their thoughts about the outside world. Their relative integration into the prison world is short-lived, however, and their marginality within this world again becomes evident as they prepare for departure from prison. Like more experienced inmates, their preparatory concerns include both practical problems, such as finding a job and a place to live, and existential concerns, about how the outside world has changed and how the inmates themselves have changed during their time in prison (see Irwin 1970). Faced with these problems, it becomes increasingly apparent to inmates that most (though not all) of the adaptation tactics associated with their prison orientation are inadequate for dealing with the outside world.

Based on this general pattern, it is tempting to infer that inmates' adaptations change simply because their reference group changes. This is essentially the explanation suggested by Wheeler's (1961) finding of a curvilinear relationship between institutional career phase and conformity to staff expectations. By this logic, inmates come to abandon the beliefs, values, and norms of the outside world as they acquire more information about, and eventually achieve membership in, the prison world. In similar fashion, they abandon the beliefs, values, and norms of the prison world when they are about to regain membership in the outside world. Our analysis has challenged this explanation in a general way by using a close-up focus on inmates' continuous and active work to *interpret* prison life. The idea that inmates simply alternate between conventional and prison reference groups becomes even more unsatisfactory when we introduce into our analysis the *ambivalence* that inmates experience throughout their entire prison careers.

AMBIVALENCE AND PRISON STRATEGIES

In its most general sense, ambivalence refers to the experience of being pulled in psychologically different directions; because inmates *share* this experience, it becomes sociologically as well as psychologically significant. The ambivalence of new inmates flows directly from their transitional status between the outside and prison social worlds: it is an ambivalence grounded in the marginality of "people who have lived in two or more societies and so have become oriented to differing sets of cultural values ... [or] of people who accept certain values held by groups of which they are not members" (Merton and Barber 1976, pp. 11-12). Although inmates' ambivalence affects their prison imagery and strategies in various ways, its principal effect is to limit behavioral changes by inhibiting new inmates from becoming fully assimilated into prison culture.

Feelings of ambivalence characterize the thoughts, emotions, and sometimes actions of new inmates, throughout their entire prison careers. Their adaptations to prison express both the outsider's perspective they prefer and the insider's perspective they provisionally accept. Because their strategies are guided by their imagery, their outsider's perspective is most apparent in their behavior at the beginning of their sentences, while their insider's perspective is most apparent during the middle of their sentences. Their behavior during the final months of their sentences is a mixture of nonprison forms of interaction and prison adaptive tactics, because their concluding imagery is a synthesis of outsider's and insider's perspectives. Yet, a closer inspection of inmates' evolving strategies reveals that the simultaneous influence of the outside and inside worlds is not restricted to the end of their sentences. At every stage of their prison careers, their actions are influenced by the underlying ambivalence that results from their marginal position in both the outside and prison social worlds. Table VII.1 presents the various manifestations of this ambivalence that occur throughout the prison career.

PREPRISON ORIENTATION

New inmates' ambivalence begins before they arrive at prison. Like most outsiders, they view prison as a world quite different from their own and

Table VII.1. Experiences of Ambivalence During Prison Career

	Career Experiences	Reported Ambivalence
Preprison	• Conviction and sentencing • Detention in county jail • Transportation to prison	• Desire to postpone sentence versus desire to proceed with sentence
Early months of sentence	• Holding cell • In-processing • First night in cell • Orientation classes (first week) • Initial correspondence and visits with outsiders	• Desire to insulate self versus desire for sociability • Desire to proceed with new experiences versus relief at security of close supervision during first weeks of sentence
	• Transfer to another cell • Assignment to caseworker • First contacts with general inmate population • Job or program assignment • Cellblock transfer	• Desire for greater mobility • within prison versus fear of greater
Middle of sentence	• Work/program participation • Legal and illegal diversions • Correspondence and visits with outsiders	• Desire for greater freedom versus willingness to complete sentence in maximum security
Conclusion of sentence	• Application for transfer to minimum security • Transfer to minimum security • Outside passes • Home furloughs • Transfer to reentry program • Release from prison	• Desire to greater freedom versus willingness to complete sentence in maximum security • Desire to put prison in past and return to free world versus desire to avoid existential concerns about return to free world

have difficulty picturing themselves within that world. In the final days of their freedom, they are faced with conflicting desires: they want desperately to avoid their sentences—to escape or be forgotten about—but they also want their sentences to proceed, because they know this is inevitable. They retain an outsider's perspective but they know that they are no longer full members of the outside world.

Their ambivalent feelings continue throughout their sentences, although the form and emphasis of their ambivalence changes as they progress through their prison careers. But even in their earliest days in prison, the dominant form of their ambivalence emerges: their desire to insulate themselves from the surrounding prison world is countered by their desire for human sociability (see Glaser 1969, pp. 18-21). Throughout their careers, but especially during the first halves of their sentences, both sides of this fundamental conflict between an outsider's detachment and an insider's participation in the prison world influences their behavior. Of importance here is that inmates begin to *act*, cautiously, on their desire for contact with others, even at the very beginnings of their sentences. Their initial contacts with others are quite limited and do not appreciably alter their images or strategies, but these contacts do indicate that their isolation does not need to be as extreme as they had anticipated. A 23-year-old inmate, convicted of narcotics sales, describes his earliest encounter with another inmate:

> There was one guy that they brought in with me, and we sort of talked off and on. He was sort of scared too, and it was his first time too. He was talking to a guard; I over-heard him talking to a guard. I heard him say that he was just basically scared as hell. The guard was trying to calm him down. We were all together in a group; we eat at the same table and everything, and I got talking to him. So I had somebody to talk to.

During their first week in prison, in which they are housed together with other incoming inmates but segregated from the general inmate population, they are able to express their desire for contact with others through limited interaction with both guards and inmates. They learn that not all guards fit their initial stereotypes, and many new inmates encounter one or more fellow inmates with backgrounds similar to their own. They are still intimidated by the prison, particularly by those aspects of prison life that they have not yet experienced, but they begin to reduce their isolation and expand their knowledge of the prison world.

The first week thus enables new inmates, through passive observations and direct interaction, to modify (but not radically transform) both their images and their strategies. Their segregation during this week also leads to yet another variant of their ambivalence: they are relieved at the protection of close supervision but they know that they cannot avoid facing the general inmate population indefinitely, so they are anxious to move on to the next phase of their sentences. Similar feelings of ambivalence resurface with each new experience. When they learn that they will be transferred to a different cell, and later to another cellblock entirely, they look forward to the greater mobility these moves offer but they fear the increased inmate contact the moves will necessitate:

> After only two days, they moved me [to another cell].... With this move came more freedom.... I could go out in the yard and to the dining hall for meals. I was a little apprehensive about getting out. I had made friends with one guy, so we went into the yard together. We were out for about an hour when we were approached by a black dude. He wanted to get us high. I'm sure that's not all he wanted.... It helps to find a friend or two; you feel safer in a crowd.

Their fear mirrors the violence of their prison imagery, while their desire to proceed reflects their acceptance that they are now prison inmates.

The evolution of the inmate's prison perspective continues, and accelerates, through the early months of his sentences. The survival strategy he formulates during these months, like his anticipatory survival strategies, are based on his images of prison. But, increasingly, this strategy leads to the modification of his images. This happens because his strategy continues to be influenced by the same motivational factors: his concern for safety but also his recognition that his prison imagery is incomplete, and his ambivalence, especially his desire to proceed with the new and inevitable prison experience. The same tactics that give him new information also reflect the opposing directions of his ambivalence. The inmate's practice of territorial caution and his rudimentary impression management skills express his apprehension over contact with other prisoners and his desire for self-insulation, but these tactics also allow him to initiate or accept limited interaction with others. His selective interaction with other inmates and his partnership with one other inmate directly expresses the new inmate's desire for sociability while providing him with a means of maintaining social and emotional distance from the majority of the inmate population.

PRISON ORIENTATION

As an inmate shifts from an outsider's preprison orientation to an insider's prison orientation, the focus of his behavioral strategies changes as well. The inmate's midcareer adaptation strategies, like his earlier survival strategies, are based on his prison imagery and his ambivalence. His adaptation strategies differ from his survival strategies because his image changes and because the form and emphasis of his ambivalence changes. His survival strategy was intended to insulate him from the violence of his anticipatory images, but also to allow him to confront new prison experiences and to provide him with new information about the prison world. By midcareer, his imagery is dominated by the theme of boredom rather than violence, and he no longer sees a need for more information.

But boredom is only one of the problems associated with "doing time" at midcareer: the inmate's relationship with the outside world presents him with other difficulties:

> I don't know, but I may be losing touch with the outside. I am feeling real strange during visits, very uncomfortable. I just can't seem to be myself.... My mind really seems to be glued to the inside of these walls. I can't even really comprehend the outside. I haven't even been here three months, and I feel like I'm starting to lose it. Maybe I'm just paranoid. But during these visits, I really feel like I'm acting. I'm groping for the right words, always trying to keep the conversation going. Maybe I'm just trying to present a picture that will relieve the minds of my visitors, I just don't know.

Within a few months, a new inmate comes to share the long-term inmates' belief that preoccupation with the outside world can make his sentence more difficult, resulting in yet another manifestation of his ambivalence: his desire to maintain his involvement in the outside world is countered by a temptation to discontinue all outside contacts so that he can do his own time without the infringement of a world to which he no longer actively belongs. A 26-year-old inmate, convicted of the possession and sale of marijuana, told us:

> When they [the inmate's visitors] left, I felt depressed.... It's a high when they come and you get depressed when they leave. I was wondering if that's good. Maybe I should just forget that there is an outside world—at times I thought that. Maybe as a survival mechanism, to forget that there are good people in the world.

Although most short-term inmates do not discontinue their outside relationships (with the exception of some intimate relationships, as we noted in Chapter 5), the mere contemplation of this act speaks to their shifting prison orientation.

In a matter of months, then, inmates' perspectives undergo a substantial transformation: they are now viewing the outside world from the perspective of the prison world, rather than the reverse, and their adaptation strategies, accordingly, are designed to help them cope with their insider's problems of "doing time" rather than their outsider's fears. Their viewpoints are only an *approximation* of an insider's perspective, however, and their insider's tactics are equivocal, because they never achieve more than a marginal status within the prison world. During the middles of their sentences, they may be tempted to sever all outside contacts to make their time pass more easily but, for the most part, they do not actually follow through on this temptation. And although the relationships they establish in prison, especially their partnerships, might seem more important than their outside relationships, they know that they would not have freely chosen to associate with most of these people on the outside, and they know that they will not continue most of these relationships once they were released from prison. In this respect, the prison relationships of the men we studied are more cautious than those typically formed by long-term inmates (Johnson 1987, pp. 62-63; Cordilia 1983, pp. 13-29); they acknowledge that they do not fully belong to the prison world in the same sense that long-term or multiple-term inmates do, and they recognize that these other inmates do not fully accept them as members of their world. First-time, short-term inmates, in other words, never completely relinquish their outsider's perspective, even in the middle stage of their prison careers when they are most alienated from the outside world.

POSTPRISON ORIENTATION

The inmate's continuing ambivalence is a motivating factor in his decision to apply for a transfer to the Minimum Security Unit in the concluding months of his sentence. His behavior, once again, embodies both directions of his ambivalence: his outsider's perspective is apparent in the application itself, which indicates a desire for the greater privileges and outside contacts available in minimum security, while his insider's perspective is reflected in his emotional caution about his chances that the transfer will be approved.

> As much as I try to, it is very difficult to keep [minimum security] off my mind. I figure that if I don't think about it, it won't be as agonizing waiting for it to happen. It would be much easier if they would give a date to go, but they won't.

If his application are approved, the inmate's ambivalence also influences his response to the transfer itself:

> I am looking at this transfer a little bit differently from my coming to prison and my transfer to "B" Hall. I don't want to expect too much from [minimum security] because then I won't be disappointed. Also, there is one big difference; if I don't like it out there, I can always come back here.

The inmate is aware that his transfer marks the final phase of his prison sentence and a first step toward rejoining the outside world, but he is equally cognizant that he will still be in prison for some time and that he can be returned to maximum security at the whim of prison officials. Consequently, he is reluctant to admit, to himself or others, that his transfer holds great symbolic importance. He arms himself with an insider's rationalization: if he doesn't like minimum security, he can always come back. And if he should be sent back involuntarily, he is now confident of his ability to survive the remainder of his sentence in maximum security.

Once an inmate is transferred to minimum security, he experiences yet another manifestation of his ambivalence, similar to that reported by long-term inmates after they have been placed in halfway houses (Cordilia 1983, pp. 99-100): he wants to put his prison experience behind him and prepare for his return to the free world, but he also wants to avoid the existential concerns raised by this preparation and to complete his sentence by "doing his own time," just as he did when he was in maximum security. This dilemma is described in a journal excerpt:

> Doing time is not as easy as it may sound; actually, it is a rather complicated business. For one thing, you must try to keep yourself busy even though there is very little for you to do.... You would like to plan for the future, but it seems so far away that it

doesn't really seem like it is worth thinking about. Also, thinking about the future tends to make the time drag. You also don't want to think about the past, because eventually you get around to the dumb mistake that got you in here. So, I guess it must be best to think about the present but that is so boring ... that it can lead to depression. You don't want to think too much about the outside because it makes you realize all that you are missing, which can be somewhat depressing. But then, you don't really want to just think about the prison, because there isn't anything more depressing at all.

In the final months and weeks of his sentence, the inmate vacillates between directly confronting questions about his future and avoiding these questions through continuing tactics of thought control and diversionary activities.

Each of the manifestations of ambivalence itemized in Table VII.1 reflects the marginality of the inmates, because each involves a conflict between an outsider's and an insider's point of view. At various stages in their careers, inmates might place more emphasis on one or the other viewpoint but they never fully resolve their feelings of ambivalence. During the middle of their sentences, for example, they might believe that thoughts about the outside world make serving their sentences more difficult (an insider's belief) and they might consciously suppress these thoughts (an insider's tactic) but they do not generally terminate outside contacts, and they would be severely disappointed if their visitors or letters ceased to arrive. Thus, even when inmates place the greatest emphasis on an insider's viewpoint, their perspective (that is, the interdependent relationship between their images and their strategies) expresses their marginality. Similarly, when they place the most emphasis on an outsider's viewpoint, at the beginnings and ends of their sentences, a closer inspection of their perspective again reveals their marginality. Our analysis thus suggests that inmates' changing imagery and strategies do not represent a total conversion to an insider's point of view and a subsequent reversion to a more conventional point of view, as suggested in Wheeler's (1961) cyclical model of prison socialization. Rather, the inmates we studied experienced a subtler transformation in which their movement toward either an insider's or an outsider's perspective was circumscribed by their ambivalence.

DISCUSSION

When new inmates first arrive at prison, they see their central problem as one of surviving the violence and uncertainty of the prison world. As this outsider's preprison orientation gives way to an insider's prison orientation, their adaptation strategy becomes more focused on the problem of enduring the boredom of an unchanging prison routine. At the conclusions of their sentences, this adaptation strategy itself begins to break down, as inmates begin to anticipate their reintegration into the outside world. We have now added to this general model of prison adaptation by showing how an ongoing ambivalence, resulting from inmates' social marginality, limits the kinds of adaptations that inmates make throughout their sentences.

Although using ambivalence as a basis for sociological explanation can be problematic (see Schmid and Jones 1993; Room 1976), the very pervasiveness of ambivalence in social life suggests that its interactional significance must be addressed. The ambivalence experienced by the inmates we studied is derived from a very specific set of circumstances: involuntary but relatively brief confinement in a total institution that is both entirely unknown and absolutely feared. Similar, if less extreme, feelings of ambivalence can emerge whenever human beings become fully immersed in highly demanding but time-limited social worlds or social situations, a point of comparison we will return to in Chapter 9. The issue of primary interest here, for prisoners or others, is how sociological ambivalence affects human action. In our analysis, inmates' feelings of ambivalence serve sometimes to motivate action (for example, to break through their initial isolation or later to apply for transfer to minimum security) and sometimes to inhibit action (not to break off ties to the outside world during the middle of their sentences, despite a temptation to do so). At some career points, the inmates' ambivalence offers them no real choice in behavior (after orientation, inmates are transferred to another cellblock regardless of how they feel about it), while at other points they do face choices (decisions about continuing outside contacts). The principal effect of their ambivalence, however, is to circumscribe their behavior, keeping it somewhere between the more extreme perspectives of the prison outsider and the long-term inmate.

The traditional model of prison socialization suggests that inmates enter prison with conventional values, become socialized to the values of an inmate culture, and then subsequently become resocialized to the values of the outside world. Our research suggests an alternative model of the prison experiences of new inmates, in which inmates continuously and actively interpret the prison world in their efforts to address the problems of imprisonment. Throughout this interpretive process, moreover, their social marginality continuously shapes both their subjective understanding of the prison world and their adaptations to it. Specifically, we argue that the ambivalence that results from these inmates' transitional status limits the behavioral adaptations they make in prison and inhibits their assimilation into prison culture. But this ambivalence has a larger effect as well: in Chapter 8, we consider how inmates' sociological ambivalence also affects their identities.

NOTE

1. In keeping with their marginal position in the prison world, their interpretation of this information is partly individual and partly interactive. When they are alone in their cells, they analyze conflicting information through intermittent self-dialogues that begin before their arrival at prison. Their partnerships provide them with an interactive means of interpreting information. Goffman (1961, p. 286) has observed that "where persons are deprived of knowledge of what is likely to happen to them, and where they are uninformed about how to 'make out' in a situation where making out may mean psychological survival, information itself becomes a crucial good ... it is understandable, then, that buddies in all total institutions give mutual aid by 'wising' each other up." Although new prison inmates find information to be cheap—that is to say, plentiful but conflicting—their partnerships serve a similar "wising" function by allowing them to sort through and interpret this information. Whether alone or with their partners, inmates' refusal to accept fully any single piece of information is the guiding principle of their efforts to understand the prison world.

Chapter VIII

Inmates' Identity Work

Throughout their prison careers, inmates experience prison by actively working to address the problems they encounter. The specific problems that they focus on change with their experiential orientations, beginning with their need to survive a violent and uncertain prison world and evolving into their efforts to endure a boring, never-changing prison routine and, then, their subsequent anticipation of reintegration into the outside world. Their interpretive work, as we demonstrated in Chapter 7, is shaped and limited by their ongoing marginality between the prison and outside worlds and the various manifestations of sociological ambivalence that result from this marginality. At the same time that inmates are struggling to adapt to their changing conceptions of the prison, they are also grappling with questions of who they are, in relation to both the prison and outside worlds. Following Schutz's (1962) argument that a person's sense of self while working toward a goal is experienced as his total self, inmates' adaptive work and identity work can be seen as different components of a single interpretive process. In this chapter, we consider inmates' identity work directly, and demonstrate that the ambivalence that inmates experience throughout their prison careers affects their identity work in the same manner that it affects their adaptation strategies.

A prison sentence necessarily constitutes a "massive assault" on the identity of those imprisoned (Berger 1963, pp. 100-101). This assault is especially severe on new inmates, and we might therefore expect radical identity changes to ensue from their imprisonment. New inmates are generally aware that their identities are being challenged, however, and this awareness affords them some measure of protection against radical identity change. Inmates' identities do change in prison, but this change is as much a product of their own identity work as it is a passive result of their imprisonment. Inmates' identity work, like their adaptive work in general, is a highly conscious endeavor. To be sure, the degree to which inmates are conscious of their own identities varies with phase of the prison career, and from inmate to inmate. During each of the experiential orientations we have described, however, inmates clearly seek to respond to the effects of imprisonment on their identities.

PREPRISON IDENTITY

Our data suggest that first-time inmates have little in common before their arrival at prison, except their conventionality. Although convicted of felonies, most do not possess "criminal" identities (see Irwin 1970, pp. 29-34). Their preprison orientations include only a vague, incomplete image of what prison is like, but this image nonetheless stands in contrast to how they view their own social worlds. The prison image of their preprison orientation is dominated by the theme of violence: they see prison inmates as violent, hostile, alien human beings, with whom they have nothing in common. They have several specific fears about what will happen to them in prison, including fears of assault, rape, and death. They are also concerned about their identities, fearing that—if they survive prison at all—they are in danger of changing in prison, either through the intentional efforts of treatment programs or through the unavoidable hardening effects of the prison environment. Acting on this imagery (Blumer 1969)—or, more precisely, on the inconsonance of their self-images with this prison image—they develop an anticipatory survival strategy (presented in Chapters 4 and 7) that consists primarily of protective resolutions: a resolve to avoid all hostilities; a resolve to avoid all nonessential contacts with inmates and guards; a resolve to defend themselves in any way possible; and a resolve not to change, or be changed, in prison.

An inmate's image and strategy are formulated through a running self-dialogue, a heightened state of reflexive awareness (Lewis 1979) through which he ruminates about his past behavior and motives and imaginatively projects himself into the prison world. This self-dialogue begins shortly after his arrest, continues intermittently during his trial or court hearings, and becomes especially intense at the time of his transfer to prison:

> My first night in the joint was spent mainly on kicking myself in the butt for putting myself in the joint. It was a very emotional evening. I thought a lot about all my friends and family, the good-byes, the things we did the last couple of months, how good they had been to me, sticking by me. I also thought about my fears: Am I going to go crazy? Will I end up fighting for my life? How am I going to survive in here for a year? Will I change? Will things be the same when I get out?

His self-dialogue at this time is also typically the most extensive self-assessment he has ever conducted; thus, at the same time that he is resolving not to change, he is also initiating the kind of introspective analysis that is essential to any identity transformation process.

SELF-INSULATION

The inmate's self-dialogue continues during the initial weeks and months of his sentence, and it remains a solitary activity, each inmate struggling to come to grips with the inconsonance of his established (preprison) identity and his present predicament. Despite the differences in their preprison identities, however, inmates now share a common situation that affects their identities. With few exceptions, their self-dialogues involve feelings of vulnerability, discontinuity, and differentiation from other inmates, emotions that reflect both the degradations and deprivations of institutional life (see Goffman 1961; Sykes 1958; Garfinkel 1956) and their continuing outsiders' perspective on the prison world. These feelings are obviously the result of everything that has happened to inmates, but they are something else as well: they are the conditions in which every new inmate finds himself. They might even be called the common attributes of inmates' selves-in-prison, for the irrelevance of their preprison identities within the prison world reduces their self-definitions, temporarily, to the level of pure emotion.[1] These feelings, and a consequent emphasis on the "physical self" (Zurcher 1977, p. 176), also constitute the essential motivation for inmates' self-insulation strategies.

An inmate cannot remain wholly insulated within the prison world, for a number of reasons. He simply spends too much of his time in the presence of others to avoid all interaction with them. He also recognizes that his prison image is based on incomplete and inadequate information, and that he needs to interact with others in order to acquire first-hand information about prison life. As we discussed in Chapter 7, moreover, his behavior in prison is guided not only by his prison image but also by a fundamental ambivalence he feels about his situation, resulting from his marginality between the prison and outside social worlds. His ambivalence has several manifestations throughout his prison career, but the most important is his conflicting desires for self-insulation and for human communication.

MANAGING A DUALISTIC SELF

An inmate is able to express both directions of his ambivalence (and to address his need for more information about the prison) by drawing a distinction between his "true" identity (i.e., his outside, preprison identity)

148 / *Doing Time*

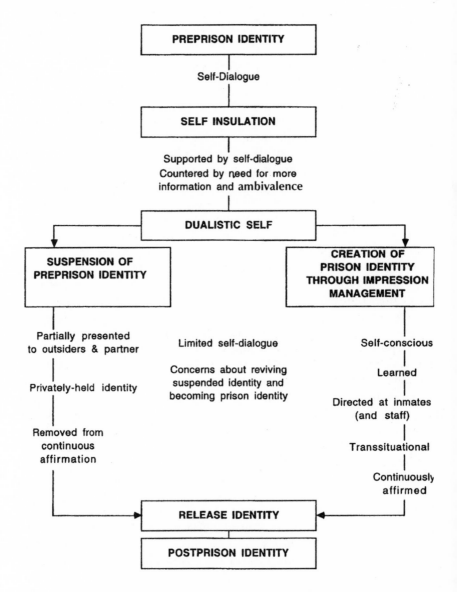

Figure VIII.1. Suspended Identity Dialectic

and a "false" identity that he creates for the prison world. For most of a
new inmate's sentence, his preprison identity remains a "subjective" or
"personal" identity while his prison identity serves as his "objective" or
"social" basis for interaction in prison (see Weigert 1986; Goffman 1963).

This bifurcation of his self (Figure VIII.1) is not a conscious decision made at a single point in time, but it does represent two conscious and interdependent identity-preservation tactics, formulated through self-dialogue and refined through tentative interaction with others.

First, after coming to believe that he cannot not "be himself" in prison because he would be too vulnerable, he decides to "suspend" his preprison identity for the duration of his sentence. He retains his resolve not to let prison change him, protecting himself by choosing not to reveal himself (his "true" self) to others. Expressions of a suspension of identity emerged repeatedly and consistently in both the fieldwork and interview phases of our research. As simply stated by one inmate: "I didn't want nobody to know too much about me. That was part of the act." The inmate's decision to suspend his preprison identity emanates directly from his feelings of vulnerability, discontinuity, and differentiation from other inmates. These emotions foster something like a "proto-sociological attitude" (Weigert 1986, p. 173; Zurcher 1977), in which new inmates find it necessary to step outside their taken-for-granted preprison identities. Rather than viewing these identities and the everyday life experience in which they are grounded as social constructions, however, inmates see the *prison* world as an artificial construction and judge their "naturally occurring" preprison identities to be out of place within this construction. By attempting to suspend his preprison identity for the time that he spends in prison, an inmate believes that he will again "be his old self" after his release.

While he is in confinement, an inmate's decision to suspend his identity leaves him with little or no basis for interaction. His second identity tactic, then, is the creation of an identity that allows him to interact, however cautiously, with others. This tactic consists of his increasingly sophisticated impression management skills, which are initially designed simply to hide his vulnerability but which gradually evolve into an alternative identity felt to be more suitable to the prison world. The character of the presented identity is remarkably similar from inmate to inmate. As described to us by one inmate:

> Most people out here learn to be tough, whether they can back it up or not. If you don't learn to be tough, you will definitely pay for it. This toughness can be demonstrated through a mean look, tough language, or an extremely big build.... One important thing is never to let your guard down.

An inmate's prison identity, as an inauthentic presentation of self, is not in itself a form of identity transformation but is rather a form of identity construction. His prison identity is simply who he pretends to be while he is in prison. It is a false identity created for survival in an artificial world. But this identity nonetheless emerges in the same manner as any other identity: it is learned from others and it has to be presented to, negotiated with, and validated by others. A new inmate arrives at prison with a general image of what prisoners are like, and he begins to flesh out this image from the day of his arrival, warily observing others just as they are observing him. Through watching others, through eavesdropping, through cautious conversation and selective interaction, a new inmate refines his understanding of what maximum security prisoners look like, how they talk, how they move, how they act. Despite his belief that he is different from these other prisoners, he knows that he cannot appear to be too different from them, if he is to hide his vulnerability. His initial image of other prisoners, his early observations, and his concern over how he appears to others thus provide a foundation for the identity he gradually creates through impression management.

Impression management skills, of course, are not exclusive to the prison world; a new inmate, like anyone else, has had experience in presenting a "front" to others, and he draws upon his experience in the creation of his prison identity. He has undoubtedly even had experience in projecting the very attributes—strength, stoicism, aplomb—required by his prison identity (see Majors and Billson 1992). As we described in Chapter 5, however, impression management in prison differs in the totality with which it governs interactions, in the singular audience to whom it is addressed, and in the inmate's belief that the costs of failure are higher. For these reasons, the entire impression management process becomes a more highly conscious endeavor. When presenting himself before others, a new inmate pays close attention to such minute details of his front as eye contact, posture, and manner of walking:

> The way you look seems to be very important. The feeling is you shouldn't smile, that a frown is much more appropriate. The eyes are very important. You should never look away; it is considered a sign of weakness. Either stare straight ahead, look around, or look the person dead in the eyes. The way you walk is important. You shouldn't walk too fast; they might think you were scared and in a hurry to get away.

To create an appropriate embodiment (Weigert 1986; Stone 1962) of their prison identities, some new inmates devote long hours to weightlifting or other body-building exercises, and virtually all of them relinquish their civilian clothes—which might have expressed their preprison identities—in favor of the standard-issue clothing that most inmates wear. Whenever a new inmate is open to the view of other inmates, in fact, he is likely to relinquish most overt symbols of his individuality in favor of a standard issue "prison inmate" appearance.

By acting self-consciously, of course, a new inmate runs the risk of exposing the fact that he *is* acting. But he sees no alternative to playing his part better; he cannot "not act" because that, too, would expose the vulnerability of his "true" identity. He thus sees every new prison experience, every new territory that he is allowed to explore, as a test of his impression management skills. Every nonconfrontive encounter with another inmate symbolizes his success at these skills, but it is also a social validation of his prison identity. Eventually, he comes to see that many, perhaps most, inmates are engaging in the same kind of inauthentic presentations of self (see Glaser and Strauss 1964). Their identities are as "false" as his, and their validations of his identity may be equally false. But he realizes that he is powerless to change this state of affairs and that he has to continue to present his prison identity for as long as he remains in prison.

A new inmate enters prison as an outsider, and it is from an outsider's perspective that he initially creates his prison identity. In contrast to his suspended preprison identity, his prison identity is a *shared* identity, because it is modeled on his observations of other inmates. Like those of more experienced prisoners, his prison identity is tied directly to the social role of "prison inmate" (see Scheff 1970; Solomon 1970). Because he is an outsider, however, his prison identity is also severely limited by his narrow understanding of that role. It is based on an outsider's stereotype of who a maximum security inmate is and what he acts like. It is, nonetheless, a *structural* identity (Weigert 1986), created to address his outsider's institutional problems of social isolation and inadequate information about the prison world.

By the middle of a new inmate's sentence, his preprison orientation has evolved into a prison orientation that is essentially an insider's perspective on prison life. His prison image has evolved to the point where it is dominated by the theme of boredom rather than violence. (The possibility of violence is still acknowledged and feared, but those violent incidents that do occur have been redefined as consequences of prison norm violations rather than random predatory acts.) His survival strategy, although still extant, has been supplemented by such general adaptation tactics as legal and illegal diversionary activities and conscious efforts to suppress his thoughts about the outside world (see Chapters 5 and 7). His impression management tactics have become second nature rather than self-conscious, as he routinely interacts with others in terms of his prison identity.

An inmate's suspension of his preprison identity, of course, is never absolute, and the separation between his suspended identity and his prison identity is never complete. He continues to interact with his visitors at least partially in terms of his preprison identity, and he is likely to have acquired at least one inmate "partner" with whom he interacts in terms of his preprison as well as his prison identity. During times of introspection, however—which take place less frequently but do not disappear—he generally continues to think of himself as being the same person he was before he came to prison. But it is also during these periods of self-dialogue that he begins to have doubts about his ability to revive his suspended identity. We cite two examples:

> I saw the movie *The Deer Hunter* today. One part got me thinking, it was when the guy came back from ... from Vietnam. His friends had planned a homecoming party but when the cab pulled up to his house, he told him to drive on and he spent the night in a motel. I guess he wasn't all that proud of what he had been doing, so didn't really feel he deserved a party. He also wasn't really the same person that had left two years earlier. I wondered if I will have a similar reaction. I'm sure there will be party for me when I get out but I have mixed emotions about it, if it does happen. I can't say that I'm all that proud of going to prison (although I might be fairly proud of surviving the experience). I also probably won't be the same person that entered this institution. I know it will be really strange, just like it is during some of the visits.

* * *

> I realized that strength is going to be an important factor whether I'm going to turn into a cold person or whether I'm going to keep my humanitarian point of view. I knew it is going to be an internal war. It's going to take a lot of energy to do that.... I just keep telling myself that you gotta do it and sometimes you get to the point where you don't care anymore. You just kinda lose it and you get so full of hate, so full of frustration, it gets wound up in your head a lot.

At this point, both the inmate's suspended preprison identity and his created prison identity are part of his "performance consciousness" (Schechner 1985), although they are not given equal value. His preprison identity is grounded primarily in the memory of his biography (Weigert 1986) rather than in self-performance. His concern, during the middle of his sentence, is that he had become so accustomed to dealing with others in terms of his prison identity—that he has been presenting and receiving affirmation of this identity for so long—that it is becoming his "true" identity.[2]

An inmate's fear that he is becoming the character he has been presenting is not unfounded. All of his interactions within the prison world indicate the strong likelihood of a "role-person merger" (Turner 1978). An inmate views his presentation of his prison identity as a necessary expression of his inmate status. Unlike situational identities presented through impression management in the outside world, performance of the inmate role is transsituational and continuous. For a new inmate, prison consists almost exclusively of front regions, in which he must remain in character. As long as he is in the maximum security institution, he remains in at least partial view of the audience for which his prison identity is intended: other prison inmates.[3] Moreover, because the stakes of his performance are so high, there is little room for self-mockery or other forms of role distance (Ungar 1984; Coser 1966) from his prison identity, and there is little possibility that an inmate's performance will be "punctured" (Adler and Adler 1989) by his partner or other prison acquaintances. And, because his presentation of his prison identity is continuous, he also receives continuous affirmation of this identity from others—affirmation that becomes more significant in light of the fact that he also remains removed from day-to-day reaffirmation of his pre-prison identity by his associates in the outside world. The inauthenticity of the process is beside the point: Stone's (1962, p. 93) observation that "one's identity is established when others *place* him as a social object by assigning him the same words of identity that he appropriates for himself or *announces*" remains sound even when both the announcements and the placements are recognized as false.

Standing against these various forms of support for an inmate's prison identity are the inmate's resolve not to be changed in prison, the fact that his sentence is relatively brief (though many new inmates lose sight of this brevity during the middle of their sentences), and the limited reaffirmation of his preprison identity that he receives from outsiders and from his partner. These are not insubstantial resources, but nor are they sufficient to guarantee an inmate's future ability to discard his prison identity and revive the one he has suspended.

IDENTITY WORK

When an inmate's concerns about his identity first emerge, there is little that he can do about them. He recognizes that he has no choice but to present his prison identity so, following the insider's perspective he has now adopted, he consciously attempts to suppress his concerns. Eventually, however, he begins to reassess his capacity to revive his suspended identity; his identity concerns, and his belief that he has to deal with them, become particularly acute if he is transferred to the Minimum Security Unit of the prison for the final months of his sentence. As he moves toward a postprison orientation at the conclusion of his sentence, an inmate shifts back toward an outsider's perspective on the prison world; this shift involves the dissipation of his maximum security adaptation strategy, further revision of his prison image, reconstruction of an image of the outside world, and the initial development of an outside plan. It also includes a fundamental form of "biographical work" (Gubrium et al. 1994), in which the inmate endeavors to reconcile his suspended identity and his prison identity.[4]

An inmate engages in biographical work primarily through his self-dialogue, which becomes what amounts to a dialectic between his suspended identity and his prison identity. Through his self-dialogue, he tries to confront the extent to which these two identities really are different. He does

this in part by trying again to differentiate himself from maximum
security inmates:

> There seems to be a concern with the inmates here to be able to distinguish ... them-
> selves from the other inmates. That is—they feel they are above the others....
> Although they may associate with each other, it still seems important to degrade the
> majority here.

But he recognizes that he *has* changed in prison, and that these changes
run deeper than the mask he had been presenting to others. He has not
returned to his "old self" simply because his impression management
skills are used less frequently in minimum security.

The larger question faced by an inmate, then, is: how permanent are
these changes? This is not a question that he can fully answer while he is
still in prison. As the following interview excerpt suggests, however,
inmates themselves often understand that the answer depends on others'
interpretations:

> I know I've changed a little bit. I just want to realize how the people I know are going
> to see it, because they [will] be able to see it more than I can see it.... Sometimes I just
> want to go somewhere and hide.

Part of his self-dialogue, accordingly, concerns the question of how his
friends and family see him and whether they believe that he has changed.
In similar fashion, he speculates about how much the outside world—
especially his own network of outside relationships—has changed in his
absence. (It is his life, not those of his family and friends, that has been suspended during his prison sentence; he knows that changes have occurred
in the outside world, and he suspects that some of these changes may have
been withheld from him, intentionally or otherwise.) He has questions, if
not serious doubts, about his ability to "make it" on the outside, especially
in his relationships with others; he knows, in any case, that he cannot simply return to the outside world as if nothing has happened. Above all, he
repeatedly confronts the question of who he is and who he will be in the
outside world.

An inmate's struggle with these questions, like his self-dialogue during
his preprison orientation, is primarily a solitary activity. The identity
that he claims at the time of his release, in contrast to his prison identity, cannot be learned from other inmates. Also, like his earlier periods
of self-dialogue, the questions he considers at the conclusion of his sentence are not approached in a rational, systematic manner. The process
is more one of rumination—of pondering one question until another
replaces it, and then contemplating the new question until it is replaced

by still another, or suppressed from his thoughts. There is, then, no final resolution to any of the inmate's identity questions. Each inmate confronts these questions in his own way, and each arrives at his own understanding of who he is, based on this unfinished, unresolved self-dialogue. In every case, however, an inmate's identity at the time of his release is a synthesis of his suspended preprison identity and his prison identity—just as the prison image of his postprison orientation is a synthesis of the images he formulated during his preprison and prison experiential orientations.

POSTPRISON IDENTITY

An inmate begins constructing his postprison identity while he is still in prison. Because each inmate's identity is the outcome of his own identity dialectic, we cannot provide a profile of the "typical" release identity. But our data do allow us to specify some of the conditions that affect his identity at the time of his release and afterwards. Reaffirmations of his preprison identity by outsiders—visits and furloughs during which others interact with him as if he has not changed—provide powerful support for his efforts to revive his suspended identity. These efforts are also promoted by an inmate's recollection of his preprison identity (i.e., his attempts, through self-dialogue, to assess who he was before he came to prison), by his desire to abandon his prison identity, and by his general shift back toward an outsider's perspective. But there are also several factors that favor his prison identity, including his continued use of diversionary activities; his continued periodic efforts to suppress thoughts about the outside world; his continued ability to use prison impression management skills; and his continuing sense of injustice about the treatment he has received. Strained or cautious interactions with outsiders, or unfulfilled furlough expectations, can also inhibit the revival of his preprison identity. And he faces direct, experiential evidence that he has changed: for example, when a minimum security resident recognizes that he is now completely unaffected by reports of violent incidents in maximum security, he acknowledges that he is no longer the same person that he was when he entered prison. Turner (1978, p. 1) has suggested three criteria for role-person merger: "failure of role compartmentalization, resistance to abandoning a role in the face of advantageous alternative roles, and the acquisition of role-appropriate attitudes;" at the time of their release from prison, the inmates we studied had already accrued some experience with each of these criteria.

Just as we cannot define a typical release identity, we cannot predict these inmates' future, postprison identities, not only because we have restricted our analysis to their prison experiences but also because each inmate's future identity is inherently unpredictable. What effect an ex-inmate's prison experience has on his identity depends on how he, in interaction with others, defines this experience. Some of the men we studied will be returned to prison in the future; others will not. But all will have been changed by their prison experiences. They entered the prison world fearing for their lives; they depart with the knowledge that they have survived. On the one hand, these men are undoubtedly stronger persons by virtue of this accomplishment. On the other hand, the same tactics that enabled them to survive the prison world can be called upon, appropriately or not, in difficult situations in the outside world. To the extent that these men draw upon their prison survival tactics to cope with the hardships of the outside world—to the extent that their prison behavior becomes a meaningful part of their "role repertoire" (Turner 1978) in their everyday lives—their prison identities will have become inseparable from their "true" identities.

DISCUSSION

As identity preservation tactics, an inmate's suspension of his preprison identity and development of a false prison identity are not, and cannot be, entirely successful. At the conclusion of his sentence, no inmate can ever fully revive his suspended identity; he cannot remain the same person he was before he came to prison. But his tactics do not fail entirely either. An inmate's resolve not to change, his decision to suspend his preprison identity, his belief that he will be able to revive this identity, and his subsequent struggle to revive this identity undoubtedly minimize the identity change that would otherwise have taken place. As we discuss further in Chapter 9, inmates' identity work in prison suggests an identity transformation process that differs from both the gradual, sequential model of identity transformation that characterizes most adult identity changes and from models of radical identity transformation.

NOTES

1. This is a matter of some theoretical interest. Proponents of existential sociology (see Douglas and Johnson 1977) view feelings as the very foundation of social action, social structures, and the self. From this theoretical framework, a new inmate would be viewed as someone who has been stripped to that core of primal feelings that constitutes his existential self; the symbolic constructions of his former world, including his cognitive definition of himself (learned from the definitions that others hold of him) are exposed as artificial, leaving the individual at least partially free to choose for himself what he wants to be and how he wants to present himself to others. Whether or not we view the feelings of vulnerability, discontinu-

ity, and differentiation as the core of an inmate's self, or even as attributes of his self, we must note that the inmate does not reject his earlier self-image (or other symbolic constructions) as artificial. He continues to hold on to his preprison identity as his "true" self and he continues to view the outside world as the "real" world. It is the prison world that is viewed as artificial. His definitions of the outside world and the prison world do change with his experiential orientations, but he never fully rejects his outsider's perspective.

2. Recall Clemmer's (1958, p. 299) definition of "prisonization" as the "taking on in greater or less degree of the folkways, mores, customs, and general culture of the penitentiary." As the term is generally used, it refers to a gradual socialization process that takes place over many months or even years of inmates' sentences. Yet, new inmates begin to "take on" these things almost immediately, as part of the impression that they are attempting to present to other inmates. Thus, we would argue instead that prisonization (meaning assimilation to the prison world) begins to occur for these inmates when their prison identities become second nature—when their expressions of prison norms and customs are no longer based on self-conscious acting. A new inmate's identity concerns, during the middle of his sentence, is essentially a recognition of this assimilation. For other examples of problems associated with double identity, see Warren and Ponse (1977) and Lemert (1967); Adler and Adler (1989) describe self-diminishment problems, as well as self-aggrandizement effects, that accompany even highly valued identity constructions.

3. This finding stands in contrast to other works on total institutions, which suggest that inmates direct their impression management tactics toward the staff (see, e.g., Goffman 1961, p. 318; Heffernan 1972). New inmates certainly interact with guards and other staff in terms of their prison identities, but these personnel are neither the primary source of their fear nor the primary objects of their impression management. Interactions with staff are limited by a concern with how other inmates will define such interactions; in this sense, presentation of a new inmate's prison identity to staff can be viewed as part of the impression he is creating for other inmates.

4. A methodological issue in this regard is how the research interviews contribute to an inmate's balancing of inside and outside identities. Gubrium and colleagues (1994) note that social science interviewing itself can be a form of biographical work and that an interviewer can often present a particular biographical model through his or her choice of questions and use of follow-up prompts. Because our interview questions were derived directly from our fieldwork discoveries, we are fully confident that the distinction between inmates' suspended preprison identities and their shared prison identities accurately represents their interpretive framework. It is, of course, possible that the interview process further reinforced this distinction for the inmates in our interview sample.

Chapter IX

Prospects and Promise

In the preceding chapters, we examined how new inmates experience the social world of a men's maximum security prison as they progress from a preprison to a prison and then a postprison orientation. Our purpose in this final chapter is not to summarize our findings but rather to look back on them and comment on their relevance for three bodies of knowledge: the social science literature on prisons, correctional policy and programs, and social psychology.

THE PRISON LITERATURE

In his review of the current state of prison research, J. Thomas (1999, p. 14) observes that most studies can be characterized as "policy-driven," "theory-driven," or "ideology-driven." He argues that all of these traditions, while contributing to social science knowledge about prison life, nonetheless "begin from a set of premises that are shared and serve to format a core set of assumptions and expectations about prisons whose meanings do not originate in prisons or with prisoners." He adds that recent research has placed less emphasis on the prison culture and on the interactional processes through which prison life is created. Our study stands in contrast to these trends. It originated from a very specific and personal set of circumstances, which we discuss further in the appendix. It was guided neither by policy nor by ideological concerns, and its theoretical framework developed gradually, as our research progressed. Most important, it is grounded in the meanings and experiences of inmates themselves. As such, it is a study of the interactional processes and, ultimately, the culture of prison life, as that culture is experienced by new inmates.

What can the experiences of this category of inmates tell us about the prison world? These inmates are obviously not in the best position to map the contours of the inmate social structure as a whole, or to provide insight into local prison culture traditions. Research on these matters would more appropriately begin with the perspectives of inmates who participate more fully in the prison world, including long-term inmates and those who have served prior sentences in the same or other institutions, and in both men's and women's prisons. But first-time inmates, and particularly those with relatively brief sentences, are ideally situated to tell us about the experience of imprisonment itself. These inmates enter prison with intensified versions of the same prison imagery that most of us hold, and they find themselves in the position of attempting to retain their outside cultural moorings while also having to learn and survive in the very different cultural framework of the prison. In this sense, they view and experience prison life through the "fresh eyes" of cultural sojourners.

INMATE SOCIAL STRUCTURE, PRISON CULTURE, AND SOCIALIZATION

The prison research tradition that our study is most closely associated with is the body of work that examines the inmate social structure, its associated culture, and patterns of inmate adaptation to the prison world. The idea that inmates form their own social structure, with social arrangements not fundamentally different from those of the outside world, essentially emanates from Donald Clemmer's (1958) work in the 1940s and 1950s. Clemmer argued that men who are sent to prison experience a socialization process through which their established values, beliefs, and attitudes are stripped away and replaced by the cultural values of the prison, a process he referred to as the "prisonization ordeal." In other words, as inmates come to adopt behavior patterns that are consistent with the prison culture values of manipulation and deceit, they also become increasingly further removed from conventional behavioral patterns. Within this conceptualization, Clemmer hypothesized that the longer a man was incarcerated, the more prisonized he would become and, therefore, the more difficult it would be to alter his behavior in a socially acceptable direction.

Much of the ensuing research on inmate socialization was designed to examine how the amount of time served is associated with the adoption of prison culture. Stanton Wheeler's (1961) work has been particularly influential because it suggested that the relationship between these two variables is not a simple linear one. Wheeler developed an index of prisonization based on the extent to which inmates expressed opposition or low conformity to staff norms. He presented a sample of inmates with a series of hypothetical conflict situations, in which to do one thing would be to conform to staff expectations and to do otherwise would be to act in opposition to staff expectations; respondents were asked to choose from four alternative response categories, which represented degrees of approval or disapproval of the behavior depicted. Wheeler's data generally confirmed Clemmer's observations that the longer inmates are exposed to inmate culture (i.e., the more time they have served), the more prisonized they become. His data also supported another of Clemmer's hypotheses, that inmates who become more involved in the informal organization of the prison become more prisonized than inmates who remain socially isolated in the prison world.

But Wheeler discovered something more important as well. He found that prisonization was related not only to the length of time inmates had served but also to the length of time they had left to serve. He divided the inmate population into three phases of their institutional careers: (1) inmates who have served less than six months of their sentences (early phase); (2) inmates who have less than six months remaining to serve (late phase); and (3) inmates who have served more than six months and have more than six months left to serve (middle phase). This procedure allowed him to examine any changes in prisonization that may occur as inmates are preparing for their return to the outside world. His data indicated that, for many inmates, there is a curvilinear relationship between institutional career phase and conformity to staff expectations, with the greatest amount of conformity appearing in the early and late phases of the institutional career. Wheeler found that this U-shaped pattern, which he interpreted to mean that inmates first take on and then shed the prison culture, characterized the careers of both first-timers and recidivists.

Garabedian's (1963) research provided further empirical support for this U-shaped "adaptive response" to prison, and he extended this line of inquiry further by examining how prison socialization patterns varied with prisoner roles within the inmate social system. He looked at five specific roles: the "square John," who has had little systematic participation in criminality and primarily holds conventional values; the "right guy," who has an extensive criminal history and is most in tune with inmate culture; the "outlaw," who is self-oriented and rejects both staff and inmate norms; the "politician," who is likely to have committed sophisticated crimes based on deceit and manipulation; and the "ding," a residual category. Using methods similar to Wheeler's, Garabedian found that both square Johns and right guys exhibited the U-shaped adaptive pattern, while outlaws exhibited a linear prisonization pattern, in which their conformity to staff expectations decreased steadily throughout their prison careers. The other groups displayed alternative patterns: politicians generally conformed to staff expectations throughout their prison careers, while dings' conformity to staff expectations increased steadily throughout time in prison.

As Wheeler, Garabedian, and others (see Akers et al. 1977; C.W. Thomas 1977; Tittle and Tittle 1964) sought to test and interpret Clemmer's hypotheses on prisonization, a more complex conceptualization of inmate socialization emerged, in which inmate social structures were viewed as collective responses to the prison environment; patterns of adaptation to prison culture were demonstrated to vary with inmate roles in the social structure; and inmate roles were understood to be shaped, at least in part, by values, beliefs, and behaviors brought into the institution by incarcerated offenders. These understandings later congealed into two theoretical models of inmate adaptation.

THE DEPRIVATION AND IMPORTATION MODELS

The deprivation model is most closely associated with the work of Gresham Sykes (1958) and Sheldon Messinger (Sykes and Messinger 1960), who argue that the inmate social structure is a functional response to the inherent deprivations of imprisonment: the loss of liberty, goods, services, heterosexual contact, autonomy, and security. Although inmates react to these deprivations individually, Sykes and Messinger observe that they also do so collectively, through the cultural theme of inmate solidarity and the normative prescriptions of the inmate code. The various social roles that constitute the inmate social system are essentially a system of classifying how individual inmates respond to prison deprivations, including the extent to which they conform to or violate the inmate code. Thus, the "right guy" is an individual who epitomizes the inmate code, while the "rat" or "squealer" is someone who violates the norm of loyalty to one's fellow inmates. Other role designations are applied to those who threaten or exploit inmates through violence ("tough" and "gorilla") or commerce ("merchant" and "peddler"), those who engage in homosexual behavior ("wolf," "punk," "fag"), those who continuously defy authorities ("ball-buster"), and so on. A considerable number of empirical studies have been devoted to testing the deprivation model, including investigations on the sexual and drug habits of prisoners (Akers et al. 1974), informal systems of contraband distribution (Williams and Fish 1974; Kalinich 1986), and inmate adjustments to prison deprivations (Tittle 1969; C.W. Thomas 1977). In general, this body of research supports the usefulness of the deprivation-functional model for explaining how inmate social systems develop and the purposes they serve in the prison environment.

Other prison researchers have contended that the deprivation model gives insufficient consideration to what inmates bring to the prison environment. This "importation response" emphasizes how the experiences and values of prisoners prior to their incarcerations affect their adaptations in prison and, ultimately, inmate social structure and culture. In an early statement of this model, Irwin and Cressey (1962) identify three ideal-type subcultures within the inmate social structure: the thief, convict, and legitimate subcultures. Members of the thief subculture identify with a larger criminal subculture that extends well beyond the boundaries of the prison world. These men value (at least in principle) the ideas that criminals should not cooperate with police or prison authorities and that they should be reliable and "solid" in the eyes of other inmates. Their interests lie in resolving group conflicts and promoting behavioral norms that contribute to making life easier for themselves while serving time. In contrast, members of the convict culture are oriented primarily to the prison itself and seek to acquire status within reference groups inside the prison. Members of this subculture are men who have spent extensive time behind bars, including time at juvenile institutions. Their values, which are "imported" from the "hard-core" lower class, result in a utilitarian and manipulative approach toward the prison world, for the purpose of personal advantage and influence. According to Irwin and Cressey, the remaining inmates, who make up a large percentage of the prison population, reject the values of both the thief and convict subcultures, isolate themselves from members of these subcultures, generally follow prison rules, and seek to do their time with as little trouble as possible; these are the men classified as members of the "legitimate subculture." Building on this conceptualization, a number of researchers have documented how external values and experiences contribute to prison adaptation patterns (Jacobs 1977; Wellford 1967; C.C. Thomas 1975; C.C. Thomas and Foster 1973; Schwartz 1971), leading Hawkins (1976) to conclude that the available empirical evidence favored the importation over the deprivation model.

Although both models have empirical support and it has become conventional for researchers to cite and give credence to both models (see Parisi 1982), there is also increasing dissatisfaction with the "deprivation versus importation" terms of the debate. J. Thomas (1999) observes that this conceptual framework has essentially limited efforts to develop a broader understanding of prison culture and notes that a great deal of recent research has shifted its focus from prison culture to matters of prison power, administrative organization or specific prison problems. There is also evidence that inmate social structures are themselves changing in ways that render earlier empirical descriptions within either the deprivation or the importation model less relevant. Irwin (1980), for example, has observed that prisons are no longer comprised of the three dominant subcultures that he and Cressey had identified. Rather, as a generalized extension of the importation model, inmate social systems are increasingly constituted by specific groups or gangs of prisoners, each with its own identity and purpose (see, e.g., Davidson 1974).

Experiential Orientations

Our research on inmates' experiential orientations does not speak directly to the deprivation versus importation debate but it is informed by, and contributes to, the same research tradition. Like all of the studies we have cited, our project examines inmate adaptations to the conditions and deprivations of prison life. Lending broad support to the importation model, our analysis documents the importance of what inmates bring with them to the prison—in the case of the inmates we studied, an outsider's stereotypic imagery of prison life and a tentative plan of action grounded in this imagery. More generally, the men we studied could be classified as members of what Irwin and Cressey called the "conventional" or "legitimate" subculture in prison, although their inexperience would relegate them to the margins of even this segment of the prison world. In contrast to the usual importation model analysis of how outside norms or values are translated into prison adaptations, however, our study examines how new inmates, as outsiders, define the problems of imprisonment and how they then act on these definitions. As we have seen, the inmates in our study initially did these things on an individual basis, because of their limited prison knowledge and experience. Even as their sentences progressed, however, and they did learn about prison culture and participate in collective responses to their imprisonment, their marginal position in the prison and outside worlds continued to shape their adaptations.

Our study adds two sociological themes to the research on prison culture and inmate adaptations. The first is that inmates' changing orientations to prison life are better characterized as active efforts to interpret the prison rather than as the passive response to prison culture suggested by Clemmer's concept of prisonization and subsequent research on prison socialization. The second is that inmate orientations, at least for new inmates, reflect the interplay and continuous influence of both the outside world and the prison world throughout their sentences. This simultaneous influence is inadequately recognized not only by the "prisonization pattern" of a linear, progressive socialization into prison culture but also by the U-shaped "adaptive pattern" (through which prisoners are seen to be prisonized and then deprisonized) suggested by Wheeler's and Garabedian's research. It is also insufficiently addressed by the "deprivation versus importation" framework for examining prison culture.

Both of these themes are conspicuous in the prison experiences of new inmates during their preprison orientations, during which they attempt to envision and prepare for prison life, and again in their postprison orientations, during which they engage in contrastive work about the prison and outside worlds and attempt to assess the impact that their prison experience will have on their future lives. There is, to be sure, a period in the middle of their sentences when their response to the prison routine suggests a more passive form of prison adaptation such as that represented by the term "prisonization." As we indicated in Chapter 5, however, this takes place only after inmates have already altered their emotional response to the prison as a result of their interpretive work; in addition, as we discussed in Chapter 7, it is countered by their ambivalent but continuing identification with the outside world.

Our analysis in Chapter 6, which demonstrates that these prisonization effects dissipate at the end of inmates' sentences, lends general empirical support to Wheeler's (1961) finding of a curvilinear relationship between institutional career phase and an outside world orientation (represented in his study as conformity to staff expectations). Our interpretation of this pattern, however, is different. To explain these results, Wheeler and subsequent researchers have suggested that inmates enter prison with conventional values but then are subjected to socialization processes that transmit the rules and values of an inmate code; this socialization, in turn, shapes inmate responses to the deprivations of incarceration. At the end of their terms, inmates then relearn or reaccept the values of conventional society. At the risk of oversimplifying, this explanation implies that over the course of their incarceration, inmates learn, then unlearn, how to live as prisoners. Our investigation, which focuses on inmates' experiential realities and their orientations to the practical problems of everyday prison life, suggests an alternative way of understanding the changes in inmates' outlooks and behavior. Rather than attributing inmates' behavior to rules and values in some deterministic sense, our findings indicate that inmates are more actively engaged in social life and social action as interpretive processes. Thus, their evolving experiential realities and the changing problems and concerns of everyday prison life provide the basis for inmates' changing adaptations to the different phases of the prison experience. The cyclical pattern of socialization, therefore, entails something more than a passive alternation between conventional and criminal values: it involves inmates' continuous and active work to interpret the prison world within which they act and interact. As indicated by our analyses in Chapters 7 and 8, moreover, their interpretive work, including both their adaptation strategies and their identities, is shaped by the simultaneous influence of the outside and prison worlds at every stage of their prison careers.

As inmate social structures and prison cultures continue to change, inmate adaptation patterns will change as well, and the "deprivation versus importation" analysis will be increasingly less productive as a conceptual framework. Our analysis of how new inmates experience prison represents an empirical step toward expanding this framework by focusing more directly on the interactional basis through which inmates respond to (and ultimately construct) prison life.

CORRECTIONAL POLICY AND PROGRAMS

Deriving policy or programming implications from any single study is always a precarious undertaking. At the same time, the increasing reliance on imprisonment as a crime control strategy in the United States and elsewhere and the growing consensus that this strategy is a costly social failure means that applicable social science research must be examined carefully for its correctional implications. In this section, we briefly examine the social policy of imprisonment and then consider the relevance of our study for this policy as well as for correctional programming within prisons.

Imprisonment as Social Policy

The United States is incarcerating prisoners at an unprecedented rate, more than tripling its prison population since 1980 despite the fact that crime rates during this period have remained level or declined (Dyer 1999). Imprisonment is now clearly established as the sentence of choice for a wide variety of offenders: in 1990, 71 percent of all felons convicted in state and federal courts were sentenced to incarceration (Langan et al. 1994). Both new court commitments and the number of offenders who are returned to prison because they have violated the conditions of their release have increased dramatically. For example, the percentage of prison admissions represented by "returnees" rose from 17 percent in 1980 to 30 percent in 1990 and accounted for more than a third of the growth in prison admissions (Gillard and Beck 1994). Although rates vary significantly from state to state, the overall rate of adult incarceration in the United States is now in excess of 519 per 100,000 residents (Mauer 1994), and is likely to increase further (DiIulio 1991; Cullen et al. 1996).

Rising incarceration rates are fueled by stricter sentencing policies (Forer 1994; Gordon 1994; Skolnick 1994) but do not have a direct relationship to rates of serious crime (Blumstein 1995; Zimring and Hawkins 1991). Among the most frequently cited explanations for the burgeoning prison population is the sentencing reform movement of the 1970s. In this movement, indeterminant sentencing policies came under attack from both conservatives and liberals, and determinant sentencing came to be viewed as more impartial and as a greater deterrent to crime. Although determinant sentencing plans varied from state to state, they were generally characterized by a fixed period of incarceration for specific offenses, from which there could be little or no deviation, and the elimination or substantial reduction of parole discretion. As a result of these changes, many offenders who previously might have been placed on probation or sentenced to community-based programs were now being sent to prison instead. In many determinant sentencing jurisdictions, the average sentence length also increased. In addition, the abolition of parole in many states had the unintended consequence of also eliminating an institutional release mechanism to relieve prison overcrowding (see Goodstein and Hepburn 1985; Forer 1994).

Changes in sentencing policies for drug offenders, as part of the "war on drugs," have also had an enormous impact on incarceration rates (Currie 1993; Gordon 1994; Irwin and Austin 1997). Zimring and Hawkins (1995) have determined that two categories of offenders—recidivist property offenders and drug users who have been convicted of drug or property offenses—account for the majority of all prison sentences in the United States. They note that, unlike other offense categories, the number of people arrested and convicted of drug offenses varies dramatically over time, as policies change. Thus, not only has the number of drug arrests increased steadily in recent years, but the proportion of prisoners who are incarcerated for drug crimes has increased more rapidly since the mid-1980s than ever before in United States history (Zimring and Hawkins 1995, p. 162).

As the prison population continues to grow, overcrowding has come to be viewed as a "modern correctional nightmare" (Durham 1994, p. 31), with 39 percent of states reporting in 1990 that they were operating at or beyond 100 percent of their highest capacities, and several states reporting overcrowding levels at more than 150 percent of their capacities (Durham 1994, p. 37; see also Camp and Camp 1994). In response to these pressures, state governments and the federal government have responded by building new prisons at a rate of approximately 50 new facilities each year (Cullen et al. 1996, p. 32) and by making use of private correctional facilities to house inmates (Christie 1993; Welch 1990). As correctional budgets are being strained by these trends, the economic and social costs of these facilities are coming under increasing scrutiny. Mauer (1994, p. 6) estimates that $26.8 billion was spent on prison costs in the early 1990s. Gottfredson (1995) reports that the California corrections budget increased by 25 percent from 1990 to 1994, while that state's education budget declined by 25 percent. Zimbardo (1994, p. 7) has calculated that, including interest paid for a construction bond debt, it costs $333 million to build one new prison in California. He illustrates the social cost of this construction by noting that it is equal to 8,833 new teachers who could have been hired in the state's educational system, or 89,660 children who could have been supported to enroll in Head Start programs.

Beyond the financial expense of building new prisons or otherwise expanding prison capacity are the personal and social costs of imprisonment itself, which are undoubtedly exacerbated by the impact of over-crowding (Paulus 1988). As Richards and Jones (1997) point out, imprisonment carries both direct and indirect consequences for inmates. While they are incarcerated, inmates lose nearly everything that is dear to them in the outside world, including the intimacy of family and friends (see Holt and Miller 1972; Parker and Lanier 1997), and they are con-fined in institutional environments that are often characterized by vio-lence (Silberman 1995; Fleisher 1989; Flanagan 1983; Sawyer et al. 1977) and sexual victimization (Jones and Schmid 1989; Nacci and Kane 1983; Lockwood 1980). Indirect consequences include the numerous docu-mented "effects of incarceration," some of which may not be experienced until inmates are released from prison. Among these collateral conse-quences are the physical and psychological effects of imprisonment, including institutional dependency (Wormith 1984; Goodstein and Wright 1989; Walker 1983; Zamble and Porporino 1988); extended diffi-culties in relationships with family (Cobean and Power 1978; Homer 1979; Schafer 1978; Burstein 1977; Conrad 1981; Holt and Miller 1972); various disabilities, disqualifications, and legal restrictions (Allen and Simonson 1995; Burton et al. 1987); inadequate financial resources at the time of release (Lenihan 1974); and postprison unemployment (English and Mande 1991; Dickey 1989; Grogger 1989; Smith 1984; Dale 1976; Tropin 1977; Pownell 1969).

Drawing upon these and other analyses, criminologists and other social scientists have declared the prison system to be a failed policy of crime control (Dyer 1999; Rieman 1998; Irwin and Austin 1997; Allen 1981; Bottoms and Preston 1980; Foucault 1977). Increasingly, correctional practitioners are also coming to this position. As Garland (1990, pp. 4-7) has observed, prison systems throughout the western world have experi-enced a "crisis of self-definition" over the past decades, as they have aban-doned the goal and even the language of rehabilitation, and failed to establish a satisfactory new rationale for penal sanctions. The underlying issue of this crisis, Garland asserts, is not whether the prison system can be reformed but the larger question of whether crime and deviant behavior can be effectively addressed through a technical institutional solution. The very existence of prisons, he notes, inhibits us from thinking about other possible solutions to these problems. As we argued in Chapter 1, the idea that prisons are places to which we send criminals is a fundamental part of our shared cultural awareness of our own society, and the violent images we have of prisons are lodged in this awareness.

In his call for a revitalized sociology of punishment, Garland (1990) argues that we need to understand that prisons are shaped by a variety of social forces and exist for a variety of purposes, of which crime control is only one. Prisons are, above all else, "a way of punishing people—of subjecting them to hard treatment, inflicting pain, doing them harm—which is largely compatible with modern sensibilities and conventional restraints upon open, physical violence" (Garland 1990, p. 289). What is needed, he maintains, are detailed analyses of punishment as a social institution, a view that is shared by J. Thomas (1999, p. 16), in his call for research on how the prison culture itself operates as a punitive mechanism. It is in this regard, we believe that our study contributes to discourse on the larger issues of imprisonment as social policy. Although Midwestern prison has a reputation as a progressive correctional facility which offers an array of programming options and employment opportunities, inmates who are sentenced there, like prisoners elsewhere, experience their imprisonment as punishment. Our delineation of their experience serves as a phenomenological counterpoint to a correctional ideology that has led to the imprisonment of almost two million people in the United States.

As the inmates we studied progressed from their preprison through their prison and postprison orientations, some of their evolving understandings and adaptations may well embody the intended punishing or correcting effects of incarceration. Others clearly do not. The men in our study, for example, entered prison viewing their sentences as personal misfortunes but nonetheless accepting responsibility for their offenses. After witnessing numerous sentencing, administrative, and release inequities, most of these men came to view their sentences in terms of personal injustice rather than simple misfortune, an assessment that stands in direct opposition not only to the fading objective of correctional rehabilitation but to the moral foundation of an impartial punishment objective as well.

Prison Programs

Even as we question the wisdom of imprisonment as a crime control strategy, search for a new correctional philosophy, and entertain noncorrectional social responses to the problems of crime, it is clear that we will continue to rely on imprisonment as our most severe legal penalty, short of capital punishment, for sanctioning criminal offenders. In this context, it is incumbent upon us to ensure that imprisonment is a *humane* form of punishment, which facilitates rather than obstructs the eventual social reintegration of inmates. Our research holds programmatic implications for this goal in two respects. Because of its experiential focus, our investigation shows how the punishment of prison is received and interpreted by its recipients, rather than how it is intended by those who prescribe and implement it. Additionally, because new inmates themselves desire to retain their conventional preprison identities and to minimize the influence of imprisonment on their lives, our research points to specific issues that should be addressed by prison reintegration programs and provides temporal clues about when intervention regarding these issues can be most effectively provided.

Although the experiences of the inmates we studied do not represent those of all prisoners, there are several reasons why their experiences should nonetheless be examined carefully for correctional implications. First, as we have noted, their outsider status at the beginning of their sentences offers an exceptional vantage point for viewing prison life and for understanding the phenomenological impact of imprisonment. Second, the category of inmates we studied—first-time prisoners serving relatively brief sentences—warrants particular attention from correctional practitioners, precisely because of their outsider status. Compared with other inmates, these men generally have stronger ties to the outside world and fewer ties to prison or criminal subcultures and, consequently, have the greatest potential for successful reintegration. Finally, it is likely that key elements of the prison experience are fundamentally similar for new inmates and recidivists. If, as Irwin and Austin (1997, p. 143) assert, most prison inmates aspire to modest and conventional lifestyles, then the correctional implications of our work may apply to other categories of inmates as well.

The first program that inmates typically encounter is an orientation program designed to introduce them to the prison world gradually and to monitor their reactions to it. Ideally, these programs not only help the prison staff to manage the inmate population, but also help inmates prepare for the experiences ahead of them. Johnson (1987) has argued that prison officials have a responsibility to help inmates cope with the psychological hardships of imprisonment by promoting mature and conventional ways of adapting to prison life. Such "mature coping," he argues, requires inmates to recognize the common adjustment problems that all prisoners face, to understand that they must not resort to violence or deception as coping mechanisms, and to learn that caring for both self and others is important to successful adjustment to prison life. Toch (1982, pp. 26-27) has proposed that orientation programs should promote "constructive anxiety" by presenting inmates with information about the problems they are likely to face in prison and the resources available to them, and then encouraging inmates to work out their own plans to meet these challenges.

Ethnographic research on prison life, inclusing our study, is a useful referent for orientation programming because it presents understandings of the prison world that are derived from inmates' meanings and experiences. Our research, for example, provides a detailed examination of new inmates' own views of the problems they face and their initial plans for facing them as they begin their sentences. That these views are based on violent prison images that they have constructed from widely available cultural resources rather than on the actual conditions of the prison they are entering does not diminish their influence on inmates' behavior. The immediate implication of our analysis of inmates' preprison orientation is simply this: prison cannot be a humane form of punishment if it is an act of terror. The prison imagery that new inmates bring with them is often so violent and emotionally consuming as to overpower the more temperate depiction of prison life presented through orientation classes. (Indeed, one of the principal challenges facing new inmates is their need to sort out the conflicting information they receive from various sources, including the orientation program.) New inmates' violent prison imagery and the survival and identity preservation problems that emanate from it must be dealt with directly by orientation programs before longer-term guidelines for coping with prison life can be effectively conveyed.

A second implication of our research for orientation programming stems from our delineation of the survival tactics that new inmates use to address the practical problems of imprisonment, and our analysis of how both their understanding of these problems and their survival tactics evolve over time. As we have observed, the inmates whom we studied entered prison with conventional identities and, for the most part, they relied on conventional tactics to confront their problems. The tactics they employed in the early part of their sentences—territorial caution, selective interaction, impression management, and partnerships—operated both to protect them and to provide them with new information about the prison world. Each of these tactics is also a form of "mature coping."

The survival tactics we described could easily be incorporated into orientation programs that seek to advise inmates on the resources available to them to meet prison challenges. For example, an inmate we quoted in Chapter 4 described a potentially violent confrontation in the cafeteria and suggested that prison guards could have prevented the incident by informing new inmates that specific seating areas were controlled by particular inmate groups. He was right. Although prison officials might choose not to sanction territorial claims by providing precise details, both the fact that territorial claims are made and the tactic of territorial caution are topics that should be included in orientation classes. More generally, orientation programs should be designed in ways that give greater attention to the availability and use of space, including the value of areas that can be used as "critical space" (McCorkel 1998) for inmates' coping strategies and identity work.

In their presentation of coping resources to inmates, orientation programs should also emphasize the interactional contexts that exist in prison. While simple "how to" instructions might be of limited value, recognition of successful practices that inmates actually use, including selective interaction and impression management would be useful orientation information, especially if presented by prison inmates. In a similar fashion, our analysis of prison partnerships can be viewed as an ethnographic delineation of a particularly successful coping tactic. Partnerships, which represent one variation of a prison niche (Seymour 1977; Toch 1982), are the most prominent and continuous adaptation tactic used by the inmates we studied. Partnerships are routinely acknowledged by both staff and inmates at Midwestern, and are even incorporated into unofficial orientation advice. The value of carefully selected associations with other inmates should be presented through the official orientation program as well, as a problem-solving resource and as an example of a mature coping tactic.

Coping resources, of course, can be derived from many sources (see Zamble and Porporino 1988), and any compendium of resources presented to inmates must obviously be tailored to the specific prison to which they are sentenced. Ethnographic analyses can most meaningfully contribute to orientation program development by identifying the kinds of issues that inmates themselves consider to be important and the contexts in which they become important. With respect to the first of these contributions, our study offers an experiential examination of conventional adaptation tactics that have been devised by inmates in response to practical problems that have been defined by inmates. With respect to the second, our analysis shows that inmates' initial problems of survival give way to problems of boredom during the middle of their sentences and problems of reintegration during the final months (and the inmates change their adaptation tactics accordingly). These subsequent problems of imprisonment, however, are all but irrelevant to new inmates at the beginning of their sentences. While it is reasonable for an orientation program to identify longer-range issues and to encourage inmates to begin thinking about them, a temporal implication of our analysis is that an effective programmatic response to these "prison" and "postprison" problems would ideally take place later in inmates' sentences, during the career phases in which these issues are experienced as problems by inmates.

Most prison sentences are intended as time-limited punishments, through which convicted felons are forcibly removed from the outside world, confined in a correctional institution for a designated amount of time, and then returned to the outside world. Whether the purpose of prison is viewed as rehabilitation, incapacitation, deterrence, or retribution, it follows that the postprison social reintegration of inmates must be a primary correctional goal. Orientation programs and all subsequent prison programs should be directed at preventing inmates from becoming prisonized and encouraging them to retain a continuing identification with the outside world. Our examination of new inmates' social marginality, the ambivalence that results from their marginality, and the ongoing effects of this ambivalence on their prison behavior is directly relevant to these objectives. Restated in terms of our analysis, social reintegration will be advanced by correctional programs that promote inmates' marginality in the prison world and minimize their marginality in the outside world.

We identified (in Chapter 7) those points in the inmate's career where he is most likely to experience ambivalence, and we described the general form and emphasis of his ambivalence at each of these points. This analysis has temporal implications for correctional intervention aimed at social reintegration. Each point of ambivalence can be viewed as a juncture point in an inmate's prison career, at which the outside world and the prison world are pulling at him in opposing directions. At some of these points, such as his initial desire to postpone his sentence versus his desire to proceed with his sentence, he has little or no control over which path he will follow. At other points, such as his midcareer temptation to terminate outside contacts versus his desire to maintain these contacts, he has considerably greater control. It is these latter juncture points, where an inmate does face a real choice of actions, that suggest when correctional programming should encourage one line of action or another.

Using outside contacts as an example, there is strong evidence to support the contention that an inmate's relationship with family and outside friends is the key to successful reintegration (see Johnson 1987; Homer 1979; Cobean and Power 1978; Schafer 1978; Burstein 1977). Our research suggests that there is little need to encourage inmates to maintain outside contacts at the beginning of their sentences, because this is already one of their deepest concerns. At the conclusion of their prison careers, more liberal visiting, telephone, and furlough privileges, such as those available through the Minimum Security Unit at Midwestern, obviously help to reestablish an inmate's ties to the outside world. But such end-of-sentence programs are restorative measures, which are made available after many inmates have already adopted the insiders' tactic of placing considerable social distance between themselves and the outside world. Programs or policies that encouraged inmates to maintain outside ties during the middle of their sentences, when they are most ambivalent about their outside relationships, would discourage inmates from adopting such prison world tactics for dealing with the outside world.

Our analysis of inmates' identity work, presented most directly in Chapter 8, holds additional implications for reintegration programming. The men we studied entered prison with conventional identities and with a desire to preserve their identities during their imprisonment. Faced with the intimidating world of a maximum security prison, however, these men took on identities that were modeled directly on more experienced prisoners, all of whom were "prisonized" to some degree and many of whom were deeply entrenched in criminal lifestyles. That new inmates initially view their prison identities as false does not prevent these identities from affecting their adaptation to the prison world. Moreover, their identity work ultimately comes to center around the question of how their prison identities will affect their reintegration into the outside world. During the middle of their sentences when they experience occasional doubts about whether they will be able to recover their preprison identities, and at the end of their sentences when they struggle with questions of how their prison experience has changed them and how it will affect their lives on the outside, these inmates are actively working on precisely those issues that must be addressed by prison reintegration programs. The challenge for correctional practitioners is how to facilitate and reinforce this identity work in order to encourage inmates' own efforts at social reintegration. Understanding the theoretical principles behind their identity work, a matter we address in the final section of this chapter, is a first step in meeting this challenge.

CULTURAL ADAPTATION AND IDENTITY

The most significant theoretical implication of our research concerns the effects of imprisonment on new inmates' identities. Our analysis indicates that while inmates' identities do change in prison, these changes are as much a result of their own identity work as they are a passive response to imprisonment per se. That is, although inmates are necessarily unsuccessful in their resolve not to change in prison, the identity work they undertake to preserve their prior identities nonetheless inhibits identity change that might otherwise occur. Inmates' tactics—suspending their preprison identities, taking on new prison identities, and subsequently engaging in a dialectic between these identities—suggest an identity transformation model that may have application in other, nonprison, circumstances. In the first part of this section, we briefly review the sociological concept of identity. We then discuss the theoretical issues represented in the identity challenges faced by new inmates and speculate on other situations in which the suspended identity model presented in Chapter 8 might be useful.

Identity

"Identity" is a fundamental concept in social psychology. In its most general expression, identity can be defined simply as the meaning given to the self in a social situation. This meaning, however, involves an interplay of at least three elements: the individual's subjective meaning and presentation of his or her self; the meanings that others attribute to the individual's self; and the characteristics of the social situation, including the social structural and cultural context in which it occurs. Stone (1962, p. 399) observes: "One's identity is established when others place him as a social object by assigning him the same words of identity that he appropriates for himself or announces. It is in the coincidence of placements and announcements that an identity becomes a meaning of the self." Identity is thus both a *product* of social interaction in specific situations and a continuing development *process* that takes place through interaction.

As an interactive process, identity can be viewed as a negotiation between the individual and others, in which the individual presents a meaning of his or her self to others, and others then validate this meaning, fail to validate it, or counter with another meaning (see Blumer 1969; Hadden and Lester 1978). From another angle, the process can also be seen in the attributions that others make toward the individual and the acceptance, rejection, or modification of these attributions by the individual (see Guiot 1977). Implicit in this processual viewpoint is the idea that identities are never static; any identity held by any individual necessarily changes over time.

Interactionist theories of social psychology offer two general models of identity transformation. The model that applies to most identity changes is a gradual process that entails a balance between situational adjustments and commitments (Becker 1960, 1964). Situational adjustments are essentially accommodations that an individual makes to the demands of new situations. While situational adjustments promote both behavioral and identity changes, the individual's commitments to existing statuses and roles inhibit such changes. Because this process is gradual, most people are able to maintain an overall sense of "identity continuity" over time, recognizing changes that have taken place only at certain "turning points" (Strauss 1959) in their biographies. A second model is employed for those identity transformations that are so extensive and occur so rapidly that a sense of identity continuity becomes impossible. Radical identity changes, which are used to describe such phenomena as brainwashing or conversion, are characterized by external change agents, the destruction of old group loyalties and the development of new ones, and the provision of a new perspective for self-evaluation (Strauss 1959).

Identity Transformation in Contextual Shifts

The experiences of the inmates we studied differ from both these models, although they share some characteristics with both models as well. As in cases of brainwashing and conversion, there is an external change agency involved, the inmate does learn a new perspective (an insider's perspective) for evaluating himself and the world around him, and he does develop new group loyalties while his old loyalties are reduced. But, unlike a radical identity transformation, the inmate does not interpret the changes that take place as changes in a *central* identity; the insider's perspective he learns and the new person he becomes in prison are viewed as a false front that he has to present to others, but a front that does not affect who he really is. And while suspending his preprison identity necessarily entails a weakening of his outside loyalties, it does not, in most cases, destroy them. Because he never achieves more than a marginal status in the prison world, the inmate's ambivalence prevents him from fully accepting an insider's perspective and, thus, prevents him from completely severing his loyalties to the outside world. He retains a fundamental, if ambivalent, commitment to his outside world throughout his sentence, and he expects to reestablish his outside relationships (just as he expects to revive his suspended identity) when his sentence is over.

Like a religious convert who later loses his faith, an inmate cannot simply return to his old self. The liminal conditions (V. Turner 1977) of the prison world remove him, for too long, from his accustomed identity bearings in everyday life. He does change in prison, but his attempt to suspend and subsequently revive his preprison identity forestalls more radical identity transformation by allowing him to maintain a general sense of identity continuity for most of his prison career. As in the gradual identity transformation process delineated by Strauss (1959), he recognizes changes in his identity only at periodic turning points, especially during his midcareer doubts about his ability to revive his suspended identity and his self-dialogue at the end of his sentence. Also, like a gradual identity transformation, the extent of his identity change depends on a balance between the situational adjustments he makes in prison and his continuing commitments to the outside world (Becker 1960, 1964). His release identity depends, in other words, on the outcome of the dialectic between his prison identity and his suspended preprison identity.

Neither the radical nor gradual identity transformation model alone provides an adequate explanation of how prison affects new inmates' identities because neither addresses the particular identity circumstances of the inmates we studied. These inmates understand that prison presents them with severe identity challenges, and they actively seek to counter these challenges by suspending their preprison identities and creating and presenting artificial prison identities. These circumstances are both harsh and unusual, but they are not unique. Describing them in broader sociological terms, we can say that the inmates we studied experienced a sudden but temporary shift in the cultural and structural contexts of their everyday lives. Phrased in this manner, inmates' cultural adaptations and identity challenges can be viewed as parallel to those of others who experience sudden contextual shifts, ranging from hostages or prisoners of war to missionaries or international students. From a more global perspective, such contextual shifts are also associated with periods of rapid social change and the realignment of cultural borders, conditions that have become increasingly common in the contemporary world. Thus, other examples of groups who experience contextual shifts include refugees, voluntary immigrants, guest workers, expatriates, and citizens of nations undergoing political revolution.

Sudden changes in cultural or structural context raise a host of important sociological questions. What happens when people leave a familiar culture or social world and become immersed in a different one? How are their experiences constrained by the intention or desire to return to their original culture? How are cultural and situational dissimilarities experienced? What forms of sociological ambivalence are created by these dissimilarities? What problems are perceived, and how are they resolved? What personal changes do individuals make in these circumstances? What identity issues arise and what identity work takes place? There is only a limited body of social science knowledge available to address these questions. On a theoretical level, Zurcher (1977) has argued that rapid social change has led to the emergence of a new basis for self-concept, a flexible meta-self (the "mutable self") through which a person is highly conscious of the various bases of selfhood and is able to select among the physical, social, reflective, and oceanic modes of self-concept to accommodate and actively shape changing social situations. A parallel cognitive flexibility is suggested in Zerubavel's (1991) idea of the "flexible mind." Other theorists have come to more pessimistic conclusions, arguing that sudden or frequent changes in social context lead to the loss of a sense of self or personal responsibility (Lash and Friedman 1992; Lasch 1979, 1984). Gubrium and Holstein (1994) have argued that postmodern discourse necessitates a reconceptualization of the self as something that is fluid, decentered, and subject to situational construction and mediation within diverse local cultures. There is also some empirical evidence available: identity challenges presented by contextual shifts and varieties of identity work used to address these challenges have been documented through ethnographic studies of diverse social worlds, including Warren's (1980; Warren and Ponse 1977) research on identity and community in the gay world, Risman's (1982) work on gender acquisition among transsexuals,

SanGiovanni's (1978) research on role passage among former nuns, and Adler and Adler's (1989, 1991) research on college athletes who experience a sudden rise to fame. It is clear, however, that the relationship between contextual shifts and identity transformation requires more focused sociological examination.

One means of exploring this relationship is through "controlled comparisons" (Deising 1971) of case studies on contextual shifts. In this regard, we have found a number of similarities between the experiences of new inmates and those of international students in the United States, particularly those who intend to return to their home cultures after their studies are completed (Schmid and Jones 1999). Both groups face a new and encompassing social world on a temporary basis. In anticipation of cultural changes, many international students and all first-time inmates had concerns about the effect their experiences would have on their identities. (For inmates, these concerns are a central part of their preprison self-dialogues. For students, they are typically initiated through the comments or warnings of family members.) Both groups report more frequent and longer periods of solitude than they are normally accustomed to, and for both groups at least some of this solitude is devoted to thoughts about personal change. The challenges encountered by both groups result from the need to solve practical problems (albeit very different ones) and from differences in interaction patterns. Both groups employ associational and impression management strategies in response to these challenges. As a result of these strategies, some students and most new inmates come to confront specific concerns about distinguishing between their artificial self-presentations and their authentic identities.

There are also some important differences between the contextual shifts experienced by these groups, particularly regarding the matter of volition: international students *choose* to leave their home cultures for temporary residence in another culture, while inmates are involuntarily imprisoned. This difference directly affects the salience of "older" identities in the new cultural context. While inmates find their preprison identities to be generally inappropriate within their new social world, this is less true for international students. Volition also influences the relative value an individual gives to his or her existing identities and to any "new" identities that emerge with the shift in social context. First-time inmates draw a sharp distinction between their preprison, "authentic" identities and their artificially constructed prison identities, placing little value on the latter. For international students, however, either old or new identity traits (or both) may be valued, and either old or new identities could present problems for the other.

For prison inmates, international students, or others, the impact a contextual shift will have on an individual's life course and identity depends directly on that individual's personal experiences but will also be affected by such contingencies as: length of time in the new context; the perceived permanence of the new context; the degree to which the contextual shift was voluntary or involuntary; the degree of separation between old and new context; the individual's commitment to his or her prior identity; and the amount of group support that exists for the old identity in the new context. Regardless of the specific contingencies in effect, however, there is a strong likelihood that people who are living in a new and temporary context will have to present themselves in ways that are at odds with their prior presentations of self. Because of this, any theoretical understanding of identity issues associated with contextual shifts must logically begin with dramaturgical analyses of impression management.

As the concept is most often used, impression management refers to the presentation of temporary "on-stage" identities in specific, well-delineated, and time-limited situations. Individuals express these situational identities through what Goffman (1959, p. 10) calls a "front," which he defines as "that part of the individual's performance which regularly functions in a general and fixed fashion to define the situation for those who observe the performance." This front is then removed or relaxed for "back-stage" or "off-stage" areas of social life, presumably allowing for more genuine forms of interaction.

Impression management is clearly a useful theoretical idea for examining a wide variety of interactional situations, but the extent to which it represents a general model of human social interaction has long been a matter of theoretical controversy. Almost 40 years ago, the work of Goffman and other dramaturgical theorists such as Gregory Stone (1962) implied that impression management is a common form of everyday interaction, which characterizes large segments of social life. Others, including Herbert Blumer (1969, 1972), and Sheldon Messinger and his colleagues (1962) discounted this idea, asserting instead that most human interaction takes place in exchanges that are far more open and honest than depicted by this theory. Twenty years ago, sociologists such as Jack Douglas and his colleagues (1977, 1980) and John Irwin (1977) hypothesized that the situational identities presented through impression management were becoming an *increasingly* common feature of contemporary interaction. More recently, ethnomethodological and postmodern theorists have challenged not only the idea of an authentic "core" self that exists outside managed situational presentations, but even the dramaturgical idea of an authentic but multiple and performed self that exists between and behind these presentations. In this model, the self exists only as it is constructed and maintained in specific situations (Gubrium and Holstein 1994; Gergen 1991; Lyotard 1984).

Sociological research on inmates and others who experience sudden contextual shifts allow us to pursue this theoretical debate further. Crossing a boundary from a familiar social world to an unfamiliar one almost invariably brings about a greater use of impression management, in part because the likelihood of categorical thinking increases (Zerubavel 1991). Beyond this expectation, some cultures or social worlds are characterized by the routine use of impression management as an everyday interactional form. Majors and Billson (1992), for example, view impression management as part of the ritualized masculinity routinely experienced by black males in American society. In our study, regardless of how commonplace impression management was in their preprison worlds, inmates found themselves forcibly removed from these worlds and exiled to a prison world in which virtually every social interaction is filtered through impression management practices. In this respect, our research provides both an ethnographic depiction of a cultural setting in which interactional patterns are based almost entirely on managed impressions, and documentation of the existential discomfort such patterns can evoke, as manifested in participants' frustrations that they cannot "be themselves" within this world.

Generalizing beyond our study, we would expect that many individuals who have experienced sudden but encompassing shifts in social context will find it necessary to present temporary identities in a greater number of social situations and for longer periods of time. In corresponding fashion, fewer of their interactions with others will be grounded in identities that were established prior to the shift in social context. Because identities are not only created but also sustained and transformed through interactions between the individual and others (Berger 1963), this raises the possibility that individuals' situationally created, temporary identities will receive more consistent social affirmation than their already established identities. In R. Turner's (1978) theoretical framework, these conditions increase the prospect of a "role-person" merger, based on roles performed in the new social context.

Our study of how new inmates experience imprisonment, and the identity work they perform as part of their accommodation to the prison world, is thus perhaps best viewed as a case study on the identity implications of a sudden contextual shift. Although the suspended identity model we presented in Chapter 8 applies specifically to new prison inmates, we would nonetheless expect similar identity transformation processes to occur under similar circumstances: among individuals who desire to preserve their identities despite finding themselves involved in temporary but encompassing social worlds or social situations that subject them to new and disparate identity demands and render their prior identities inappropriate. Contextual shifts that impose these circumstances are an increasingly prevalent feature of contemporary societies, and the experiences of new inmates provide a basis for further theoretical and empirical explorations of the identity work required by these circumstances.

Appendix

Research Methods

Prison is both a hidden social world and a highly restricted one. One of the most difficult steps in sociological research on prisons is gaining unrestrained access to inmates' day-to-day lives within the prison world. The existing prison literature is testimony to the fact that social scientists have nonetheless managed to collect data in prisons with some regularity, but they typically do so under closely negotiated and highly controlled circumstances (Peak 1985; Unnithan 1986; Farkas 1992). Zwerman and Gardner (1986), for example, discuss concerns about possible state intrusion into the research process, by attempting to define the nature of the study or by demanding access to research data. And beyond the obstacles presented by official gatekeepers are those presented by the social world itself. Silberman (1995, p. 4) discusses a number of these, including possible inmate concerns about confidentiality regarding their own prison misconduct, inmate concerns that research findings might be used to justify more restrictive policies, and misunderstandings arising from the separateness of the prison world, where the cultural values and norms of inmates are likely to be very different from those of the researcher.

These formal restrictions and informal impediments favor selective and time-limited methods, such as survey research, which allow the efficient collection of isolated elements of information from large numbers of inmates or staff (see Garabedian 1963; Wheeler 1961). Although these methods have contributed valuable knowledge about prisons, they also suffer from serious limitations, including a tendency to focus on issues of administrative concern (Fleisher 1989). Moreover, the preconceptualized and prestructured nature of survey data collection instruments is not conducive to an understanding of everyday life within prisons, and sometimes profoundly distorts such an understanding (Irwin 1987).

To understand how inmates (or staff) interpret the prison world and act on their interpretations, it is essential for researchers to interact directly with them—to observe and talk with them repeatedly, over an extended

183

period of time and within the natural setting of the prison itself. Participant observation, in one form or another, thus has been the most fruitful approach for the development of sociological knowledge about prisons. Gresham Sykes (1958, p. 136), while expressing reservations about the method's neutrality, nonetheless concluded that participant observation "leads to a far more detailed view of either the captives or captors than is possible by other means." But the kind of access necessary for detailed participant observation is extraordinarily difficult to secure. Our study, however, originated in exactly this kind of access when one of the authors (Jones) was sentenced to Midwestern prison; our access to the prison world thus preceded, and ultimately shaped, our research plan.

Participant observation research in prisons (or in other hidden or highly stratified social worlds) raises the issue of *whose* viewpoints will be represented in the resulting ethnographic analysis and, therefore, the question of the *specific participant observation role* used by the researcher to discover the "subjective meaning-contexts" (Schutz 1967) of social world participants. In the prison world, to be identified to staff and inmates as sociologist, university professor, or student is hardly an assurance of intimate or unbiased information. Jacobs (1977, pp. 215-229) describes the suspicions and hostilities he encountered during the early phases of his study of Stateville prison and the effect these difficulties had on the information he received. Because academic roles may not be fully understood by prison inmates, and because anyone whose role is not clearly defined is automatically suspect, prison researchers often have to assume alternative roles. Jacobs, for example, subsequently came to be viewed in the more acceptable role of prison advocate, although this role also affected both the nature and the amount of information he received. Clemmer (1958) and Fleisher (1989) conducted their observations while performing staff roles, a strategy that provides direct access to both inmates and staff but nonetheless inhibits the acquisition of personal information from inmates. Marquart (1986), on the other hand, worked as a prison guard while conducting his research on guards; although this strategy led to role conflict and other difficulties, it did furnish him with first-hand knowledge of guards' interpretations of the prison world.

Any specific role that is held, assumed, or negotiated by a researcher—sociologist, prison advocate, staff member, and so on—will affect that researcher's access to the prison world. Within any role, the nature of the relationships established with prison world participants will also influence what information the researcher will be allowed to hear and see. No matter how skilled he or she is at establishing field relationships, however, a researcher who is interested in *inmates'* perspectives will be restricted to only a partial view of the inmate social world because of an inability to achieve full-time membership in that world. Even a researcher who performs full-time staff responsibilities or manages to devote an extensive amount of time to research activities cannot fully come to know "what it means to be in prison." Like a prison employee, a researcher has greater control over his or her actions within the prison and retains the ultimate choice of being able to leave the institution at will. In this respect, virtually every participant observer role will be relegated to the status of an "outside observer" of the inmate social world.

Fuller access to the inmate social world requires a stronger and more direct affiliation to that world. Among the most remarkable prison accounts, for example, are those provided by John Irwin (1970), who had served a prison sentence before pursuing a graduate degree and subsequently returning to the prison as a participant observer. Irwin's prior experience as an inmate unquestionably contributed to his ability to provide an insider's perspective on the prison world. In our study, Jones' prison sentence similarly afforded an insider's view. In contrast to Irwin's research, Jones' sociological observation took place *while* he was serving time. This means, on the one hand, that he had a highly limited stock of prison world knowledge when our research began. It also means, on the other hand, that he was in an ideal position to document the process through which new inmates experientially discover the prison world.

Jones' (1995) dual role as inmate and sociologist provides an advantageous viewpoint for sociological analysis of the prison experience, but it also raises certain methodological issues about his ability to examine and document this experiential process. We sought to compensate for the limitations of this role by working together. Our methodology therefore can best be described as an ethnographic study of the prison experience conducted through a research collaboration between an "inside observer" and an "outside observer." In this appendix, we briefly describe our research process, then look at our research collaboration in more detail, and finally, examine the phenomenological parallels between our methodology and our findings.

THE RESEARCH PROCESS

Our research actually began as a graduate sociology course. The authors had known each other as professor and student prior to Jones' imprisonment, and it was a subsequent extension of this relationship that eventually evolved into a research collaboration. Through negotiations with prison officials, Jones was permitted to enroll in a graduate course in field methods. The initial plan for this course was simply for Jones to conduct an observational study on various features of prison life, and for Schmid to supervise the project by correspondence and through biweekly meetings at the prison. It soon became apparent that the scope and significance of this project demanded more attention than was feasible through a directed studies format and that Jones' inmate-researcher role was presenting some formidable methodological difficulties. At Jones' suggestion, we decided to conduct a study together. It was also at this point that we altered the focus of our research, from a general observational study of prison life to an analysis of the experiences of new inmates who were in the process of learning and adapting to the prison world.

Our data collection essentially began before either the graduate course or the formal study were initiated, with a journal that Jones started keeping prior to the beginning of his sentence. His earliest entries were predominantly personal reactions to his own situation, although (as the directed studies course developed) he also included more traditional ethnographic descriptions. Once our collaborative research project was under way, he generally restricted his journal entries to introspective thoughts and expressions and to a chronology of his daily experiences. Using a process similar to the "diary-interview" method described by Zimmerman and Wieder (1977), we used these entries to provide a framework for extended conversations between the researchers. Schmid's notes on these conversations were then used to derive new observational strategies and to identify potential analytic themes.

In addition to journal entries, Jones also prepared fieldnotes on his participation in prison activities, his conversations with individual prisoners and groups of inmates, and his general observations of prison life. This procedure meant that the journal and the fieldnotes contained different kinds of information, and it had the additional advantage of keeping the fieldnotes more objective than they otherwise might have been. Although his general observations incorporated the experiences of hundreds of prisoners, most of the fieldnotes were based on his repeated, often daily, contacts with about 50 inmates as well as on personal relationships established with a smaller number of inmates.

We were able to discuss our research progress through letters, occasional telephone calls, and regular meetings arranged with the cooperation of prison officials. Shortly after the beginning of the study, we settled on a communication routine that proved to be quite efficient. Jones prepared one to three field observations each week (averaging 8-10 handwritten pages) and mailed them to Schmid for annotation and suggestions. Every other week, Schmid would meet with Jones in an office or testing room provided by the prison's education department. At these meetings, we would review the journal entries and observations, plan our research strategy, and piece together our emerging conceptualization of the prison world.

One of the initial steps in ethnographic analysis is the search for recurrent themes in the accumulating body of data (Deising 1971). At an early research meeting, one theme in particular became unmistakable: for first-time inmates, prison was something very different from what they had anticipated. It soon became apparent that these inmates' understandings of the prison world continued to change as they progressed through their sentences. These themes led us to ask more detailed questions about inmates' expectations and changing views of prison; the resulting data, in turn, eventually led to empirical generalizations about how these men begin to prepare themselves for prison and how their prison orientations change through acquired experience. In similar fashion, when we encountered the prison world concept of "partnership" or evidence of inmates using associational or impression management tactics, we would use these thematic discoveries both to guide our data collection efforts and, if verified through further inquiry, as concepts in our developing model.

Our fieldwork continued in this manner for 10 months (the actual term of Jones' sentence, including the "good time" sentence reduction). The accumulating body of fieldnotes included descriptions of specific prison events and interactions, quotations from Jones' fellow inmates, and general observations of the prison world. Jones also continued to record his own prison experiences in his journals throughout this time. Following Jones' release from prison, we formalized the coding system that had emerged in the field and continued to analyze the fieldnotes.

About a year later, with our participant observation analyses as a foundation, we returned to the prison to conduct focused interviews. Using information provided by prison officials, we were able to identify and interview 20 additional first-time, short-term inmates. We decided that Jones should do the actual interviewing, on the assumption that inmates would be more willing to talk freely with someone who had only recently completed his own prison sentence. To retain the methodological advantages of having both "inside" and "outside" observers, Schmid reviewed a tape recording of each interview so that we could continuously refine the interviewing procedures. We then coded and analyzed the interview data, checking these data against our original findings.

Proceeding in that manner, we gradually developed an analytic model of the experiences of new inmates at Midwestern prison. The framework for our model was derived from a general inductive analysis of our data, guided by our three research questions. Any points of uncertainty in this model resulted in specialized analyses, in which we again searched all of our data for evidence on a particular question or concept. When "negative cases" were encountered—cases that did not seem to fit our generalizations—we inspected all of the available evidence about these cases and eliminated, revised, or qualified our generalizations accordingly. For every generalization, we cross-checked the fieldnotes, journal entries, and interview data against one another. Through this process, we repeatedly revised elements of our model until we were confident that it depicted the essential features of new inmates' prison experiences.

THE RESEARCH COLLABORATION

Alfred Schutz (1962) observed that social science constructs are necessarily "second-order constructs"—that is, they are constructs of social actors' own (first-order) constructs about their lives and their world. The fundamental methodological requirement for a phenomenological analysis, therefore, is that researchers must understand the first-order constructs through which people interpret their own social worlds. While there is general agreement that ethnographic methods such as participant observation are necessary to achieve this understanding, there is disagreement about the attributes of the participant observer role through which it can best be accomplished. Our methodology is an attempt to understand inmates' interpretations of their prison experiences and to make sense of them sociologically, through our collaborative effort.

Understanding other peoples' subjective interpretations is necessarily both an imperfect and a quintessentially human process. Meaningful human interaction of any kind is predicated on the human capability to "take the role of the other" (Blumer 1969), and participant observation is simply a special usage of this human capability. Both people's interpretations of their social worlds and the actions they base on these interpretations should be comprehensible to anyone, including researchers, who can take the role of the other. But interpretive processes are cognitively and interactionally complex, and the methodological act of *representing* others' interpretations is correspondingly complex. People not only interpret their worlds; they also reflect back upon their interpretations and, in conjunction with others, regularly reinterpret their worlds and their lives. Their specific interpretations, moreover, are often grounded in specific social contexts, and they can only be understood by others who acquire this contextual knowledge. To complicate matters further, people are fully capable of helping or hindering others, including researchers, who seek to understand their viewpoints (Prus 1996, p. 18).

The primary methodological challenge in any social world analysis, therefore, is to accurately understand and faithfully render the interpretations, or first-order constructs, of members of that social world. To do so requires, above all else, a commitment on the part of the researcher to listen to and be open to the interpretations that people give to their lives. This commitment is evident in Cooley's (1909) insistence on "sympathetic introspection" as the method of choice in social psychology, and it is made explicit in Blumer's (1928, 1972, 1969) and Hughes' (1961, 1971) subsequent elaboration of this approach. As the Chicago School's tradition of urban ethnography developed, increasing methodological emphasis was also placed on the need for researchers to discover these interpretations in the *natural settings* in which they occur. Thus, Anderson's (1923) study *The Hobo*, Cressey's (1968/1932) *The Taxi-Dance Hall*, Zorbaugh's (1983/1929) *The Gold Coast and the Slum*, and other ethnographies of this era established the criterion that researchers must somehow participate directly in the social worlds that they study. The interpersonal complexities of this methodological convention, in turn, led to greater reflection on the nature of the researcher's role (see Adler and Adler 1987; Bruyn 1966; Gold 1958; Hughes 1961) in ethnographic research.

While any attributes of a participant observer's role—from the researcher's personal characteristics to his or her sponsorship within a social world—can affect data collection, the ethnographic literature has placed particular emphasis on the development of fieldwork roles that can effectively combine the "intimate familiarity" (Prus 1996; Lofland 1976) afforded by first-hand participation with the "objectivity" provided by detached observation (see Davis 1973; Hammersley and Atkinson 1983; Schwartz and Jacobs 1979). The further the social world being studied is from the everyday world of the researcher, the more incumbent it is upon the researcher to establish personal relationships with members of that social world in order to achieve cognitive and perhaps experiential familiarity. Conversely, a researcher must sometimes also work at maintaining or enhancing an outsider status in order to "grasp the human situation with wholly fresh or, better yet, stranger's eyes" (Davis 1973, p. 336). This objective becomes especially critical when a sociological researcher is studying an already familiar social world, when some degree of defamiliarization is an essential part of the research process (see Berger and Kellner 1981). Even in novel or hidden social worlds, however, ethnographers have sought to avoid "going native" by periodically withdrawing from the field or by other means.

This intimacy-objectivity balance is directly expressed in Raymond Gold's (1958) often-cited typology of participant observer roles. Within this typology, the "complete participant" role, through which the researcher actively participates in the group being studied but does not reveal the intentions of the research, offers the greatest access to intimate knowledge about the group and the greatest opportunity for introspection. At the same time, the "role pretense" inherent in this strategy can lead to personal difficulties for the researcher and to methodological problems ranging from the awkwardness of secret notetaking to the danger of "going native"—of losing a detached objectivity and seeing the group wholly from the perspective of its members. At the other extreme, the complete observer role, through which the researcher records observations in a manner that does not require direct participation in the group being studied, allows considerable detachment but virtually no access to group members' own interpretations of their social world. Between these extremes, the "participant as observer" role (through which the researcher actively participates in the group as a scientific observer) and the "observer as participant" role (through which the researcher engages in only minimal interaction with group members in an official role as an observer) represent intermediate strategies for balancing intimacy and objectivity. If we look at our methodology through this typology, Jones' research role can be viewed as something like a "complete participant" while Schmid's role was closer to the "observer as participant" or even "complete observer." To a degree, these role classifications are accurate, in the sense that we did consciously attempt to make use of our differing vantage points to balance first-hand observations and experiences with a more detached and sociologically grounded perspective. But Gold's typology does not fit our research roles precisely, in that Jones' observations were not based on the kind of role pretense that Gold describes. He did not play the role of an inmate in order to learn more about the prison world—he *was* an inmate in this world, and this distinction is crucial for the kind of data he was able to collect.

Jones' "complete membership role" (Adler and Adler 1987) thus approximates the ethnomethodological admonition for the researcher to "become the phenomenon" (Mehan and Wood 1975) under study. It also falls within a developing trend of ethnographic research that incorporates the researcher's own experiences and social world memberships (e.g., Kortoba 1983; Zola 1982; Hayano 1979, 1982; Damrell 1977) or that incorporates participants' experiences through collaborative studies (e.g., Taylor and Tewksbury 1995; Cardozo-Freeman 1984; Prus and Sharper 1977). The underlying assertion of these studies is that authentic participation in a social world enables a depth of feeling and introspection which is not attainable through scientific detachment (Ellis 1991). As Krieger (1985, p. 320) argues, "the great danger of doing injustice to the reality of the other does not come about through the use of the self, but through lack of use of a full enough sense of self which, concomitantly, produces a stifled, artificial, limited, and unreal knowledge of others." Nonetheless, just as Gold's typology provides only an approximate classification of Jones' role, so too does the ethnomethodological role prescription, in that we did not actively embrace a subjectivist methodology in which "going native is the solution" (Adler and Adler 1987, p. 28). In fact, a stated objective of our research strategy, and a central component of Schmid's "outside observer" role, was to ensure that our analysis did not rest exclusively or even principally on Jones' personal experiences.

Jones' full-time membership in the prison world enabled us to build our analytic model of how new inmates experience prison around his own prison experiences. When he began his sentence, he had no more knowledge about prison than any other first-time inmate and he was no better prepared to face the ordeal of his sentence. It was in conjunction with his own process of discovery that we were able to document how others defined their situations and acted upon their definitions. At our biweekly prison meetings, we regularly discussed how to convert his experiences and reactions into broader observational strategies and questions to be addressed through conversation with other inmates. We also viewed the interviewers we conducted after Jones had completed his sentence as further assurance that our analytic model would be based generally on the experiences of new inmates at Midwestern Prison. In this manner, we made use of Jones' membership role and the sociological introspection it provided as an experiential guide, but not as the primary empirical basis, for our ongoing analysis.

There were certain tactical limitations associated with Jones' inmate-researcher role, but we could redress most of these through specific fieldwork practices. As a new inmate, he did not have immediate access to the entire prison world, but he was in a position to discover this world through the same means as other new inmates, and to document the discovery process. By shifting our research focus to the discovery process itself and then devising observational strategies to examine how other new inmates learned about the prison world, we were able to ascertain how representative Jones' experiences were. For reasons of personal safety, it was necessary for Jones to conduct field observations largely on a covert basis, although a few inmate associates knew of his research activities. Writing the fieldnotes themselves did not prove to be particularly difficult because prison cells offer some degree of privacy and because Jones was known to be taking college courses, so his writing activities did not seem unusual. At the same time, we were vigilant about not including anything that could be misconstrued as identifying information in the fieldnotes, for reasons of personal safety as well as research confidentiality. A problem that we could do relatively little about was that Jones, like other new inmates, was constrained by the interaction norms that exist in prison, especially those governing interaction between members of different racial or ethnic groups. Although we were able to compensate for this racial selectivity to some extent in our subsequent interviews, we nonetheless acknowledge that Jones' initial observations primarily depicted the experiences of white inmates.

The primary limitation of a complete participant role, according to Gold (1958), is the high risk that the researcher will lose his objectivity by "going native." While Adler and Adler (1987, p. 67) argue that a researcher in a complete membership role intentionally embraces and takes advantage of "native" status, they acknowledge that an extreme manifestation of this role is to relinquish the research objectives entirely. Jones did encounter problems with "observational distance," beginning with his earliest fieldnotes. Because he was a new inmate and because he was reacting directly to everything that was happening to him, he struggled with the quandary of experiencing prison while also observing how others experienced prison, as well as the problem of accurately recording both his own and others' reactions to their experiences. He also found it difficult, at times, to identify the sociological significance of his observations. It was at this point that we agreed to conduct the research together, so that we could combine an insider's and an outsider's perspectives. Our division of labor was such that Jones tended to have the leading role in data collection while Schmid had the dominant role in analysis, although both of us participated in both of these activities throughout the research process. We are certain that this working arrangement resulted in a sociological understanding of the prison experience that is experientially richer and more empirically grounded than either of us could have accomplished alone.

THE RESEARCH-IN-PRISON EXPERIENCE

We have discussed various ways in which Jones' inmate role affected his research role, but his research activities influenced his inmate role as well. In this final section of the appendix, we wish to consider the interplay of these two roles, by examining several parallels between his "insider research" orientation and our analytic model of new inmates' prison orientations. The most significant of these can be grouped into two general categories, concerning the relationship between his research activities and prison adaptation tactics and the additional measure of social marginality imposed on him by virtue of his participant observation research.

Research as Adaptation

Conducting participant observation research through a complete membership role always carries the possibility of role conflict (Adler and Adler 1987). This conflict was minimized for Jones during the early months of his sentence because the research process itself became intertwined with the adaptation tactics used by Jones and other new inmates. The most direct parallel between the research project and a new inmate's early-career adaptation strategy is that both are fundamentally *informa-tion-seeking* processes. New inmates arrive at prison with the understanding that their prison knowledge is inadequate for their needs; they begin expanding their knowledge before their sentences actually begin, and their early survival tactics in prison enable them to acquire information as well as to protect themselves. Jones' research inquiries were simply a more systematic version of the kind of information gathering which all new inmates pursue.

This correspondence of research and inmate roles did not occur simply because Jones was conducting sociological research in prison, however, and it did not hold for his entire sentence. It was not until we refined our research focus, initially to other new inmates and subsequently to the question of how these inmates experience prison, that his inmate and research roles came into alignment, because both of these roles then demanded similar kinds of information. What is prison like? How does it differ from the images of prison formulated by new inmates in advance of their sentences? What does it take to survive in prison? How do you avoid trouble? Who is relatively safe and who is dangerous? What prison job or program makes the most sense? How do you maintain contact with the outside world? These are the kinds of questions that are addressed by every new prison inmate, and they are also the questions that must be addressed, methodically, in a sociological analysis of how new inmates experience prison. By the middle of their sentences, however, inmates no longer perceive much need for new prison information, and they turn their attention instead to the problem of enduring the prison routine. At this point in Jones' sentence, his research and inmate roles became less compatible.

The principal survival (and information-seeking) tactics that inmates use at the beginning of their sentences are territorial caution, impression management, selective interaction with other inmates, and a prison partnership. Jones' research role was congruent with the first three of these because it gave him additional motivation for exploring the prison environment and for interacting with other inmates. His research practices were essentially an extension of the information-seeking practices used by all first-time inmates. His activities differed from other inmates' in that they were more systematic and more reflective: territorial caution, impression management, and selective interaction were both *topics* of his research and the *methods* through which he conducted his research.

The relationship between Jones' research role and the partnership tactic is more complex. A partnership is the single most important tactic in an inmate's strategy. It is itself a first-order construct, in that it exists as a concept in the prison world itself (as opposed to a tactic such as "impression management," which is a second-order sociological concept brought to the analysis because it names and describes observed behaviors). Partnership is also an analytically central concept because we found it to be empirically linked to all other adaptation tactics and, in fact, to every other major concept in our analysis (see Deising 1971). For example, when we examined our data to determine how inmates explored unfamiliar prison locations, we not only found that they practiced territorial caution but also that they often entered new territory together with their partners. Similarly, when we were looking at how inmates managed their outside relationships or their thoughts about the outside world, we found that their ideas about these things were often formulated in conjunction with their partners. There are a number of reasons why a partnership becomes so significant, but the primary one is undoubtedly its function as an *interpretive coalition* for understanding the prison experience. Our collaborative methodology, however, provided Jones with a larger interpretive framework that introduced second-order sociological concepts as well as first-order constructs to this understanding. In effect, our research relationship, reinforced through our regular correspondence and biweekly meetings, became an alternative partnership for Jones. While this relationship did not apparently alter his prison partnership or its interpretive function, it did introduce some reflexive entanglements both to his own prison adaptation and to our analysis.

As inmates move from the preprison to the prison orientation, their views of prison and imprisonment change, and their adaptation strategies change accordingly. The two tactics that dominate their mid-sentence strategies are diversions and a self-imposed thought control about the outside world. Jones' research interests did constitute an intellectual diversion for him, though it was one of inconsistent value during the middle and later months of his sentence. His research activities were not conducive, however, to his own use of thought control as an adaptation tactic. Engaging in participant observation research required him to examine, reflect upon, and write about the contrasts between the outside and prison worlds, even when the cognitive norms of his inmate role suggested that it was unwise to do so. At this point, his research and inmate roles did conflict.

Research as Marginality

The essential characteristic of the inmates we studied was their social marginality, which resulted from their existence on the fringes of both the prison and the outside social worlds and led to a social ambivalence that circumscribed their adaptations to prison throughout their sentences. Included in their adaptations was the development of a dualistic self, through which inmates could express both directions of their ambivalence by "suspending" their preprison identities while interacting with other inmates in terms of an artificial prison identity created through impression management. All of these attributes—marginality, ambivalence, and even a divided self—are also inherent in participant observation research.

Any participant observer role carries with it some degree of social marginality. In the Chicago School's ethnographic tradition, it is considered to be an *inherent* attribute of the role because of both the researcher's need to participate directly in the social world under study and the corresponding need to observe that world with some degree of detachment. Even from an ethnomethodological position, which places considerably less emphasis on detached observation, there is still some degree of marginality associated with a role that requires the researcher both to participate in and also to observe and record a social world. Within the ethnographic literature, marginality is sometimes treated as a desirable attribute that should be cultivated because of the sociological vantage point that it offers (Schwartz and Jacobs 1979; Lofland and Lofland 1995; Freilich 1970). At the same time, it is considered an attribute that must be *managed* because of the stresses that it can induce (Hammersley and Atkinson 1983; Lofland and Lofland 1995). It routinely leads to feelings of ambivalence, and even to a sense of divided self, among fieldworkers. Thus, Jackson (1990) found that anthropological ethnographers typically have ambivalent feelings about their fieldnotes because of the liminal nature of fieldwork, which places the researcher between social worlds and between social roles. Adler and Adler (1987, p. 73), in their discussion of the complete membership role, note that it "signifies a bifurcation of the self" and "exemplifies the ultimate existential dual role."

Regardless of how desirable marginality is as a research attribute, it is clear that the marginality Jones experienced as a first-time, short-term inmate was further exacerbated—at least with respect to the prison world—by his participant observation research. How this affected him varied over time, following the same general pattern we described in our discussion of research as adaptation. During his earliest months in prison, when new inmates are actively working to differentiate themselves from other inmates, the distinctiveness of his research role unquestionably benefitted him. Observing prison life, talking with other inmates, taking fieldnotes, and undertaking other fieldwork activities provided daily evidence that he was indeed different from other inmates. Moreover, this difference was externally validated by our correspondence and biweekly meetings. His research activities *continued* to underscore his marginality, however, through the midcareer prison orientation, when new inmates come to view most other prisoners as "normal" and devote very little time to the self-dialogue through which they conduct the identity work of differentiating themselves from others. While his research role did not render Jones immune to these experiential developments, it did introduce a degree of role conflict and, hence, role detachment. Similarly, in the postprison orientation, when inmates engage in the contrastive work of reestablishing their relationships with the outside world, Jones needed to do this with the additional detachment and reflectiveness of a sociological researcher.

Just as the marginality of the new inmate role results in expressions of ambivalence throughout the prison career, so too did the marginality of Jones' participant observation role. This was most directly evident in the frequency, volume, and level of detail in the fieldnotes. At the beginning of the project, his notetaking was profuse, fueled by the amount of new information before him, the adaptive value of the research, and his commitment to the research role. This rate leveled off over time, as would be expected, but nonetheless resulted in one to three sets of fieldnotes per week. During the middle of his sentence, at a time when the inmate role becomes routinized and most inmates attempt to suppress thoughts about the outside world, there were occasional periods in which the frequency and depth of both the fieldnotes and the journal entries diminished. A good portion of the research meetings during these periods were devoted to discussions about the importance of continuous data collection and the development of structured fieldwork exercises to promote this activity. The need for such encouragement increased substantially again in the final months of Jones' sentence, when the frequency of fieldnotes declined considerably. This decrease may be explained in part by the generally ambivalent relationship between fieldworker and fieldnotes, as expressed in the notion that "as understanding increases, fieldnotes decrease" (Jackson 1990, p. 24). More specifically, however, this is also a phase of the prison experience that is characterized by highly personal forms of reflection. It is significant in this regard that Jones' journal entries increased during these final months, even as his fieldnotes decreased.

Research-imposed marginality does constitute a bifurcation of the self, as suggested in the ethnographic literature. While the dualism of academic versus inmate identities was not as pervasive as that of suspended preprison identity versus prison identity, it was nonetheless a complicating factor in Jones' inmate role. To be not just a "complete participant" but a "complete member" of the prison world, while at the same time observing it, more or less covertly, is to ask for a certain amount of existential trouble. There were times when the research activities—observing prison life, talking with others about research-inspired topics, recording fieldnotes, attending research meetings, and so on—impinged upon the inmate role that Jones would otherwise have been performing. Despite this role conflict, and in part because of it, Jones was able to compile detailed ethnographic fieldnotes on the experiences of new maximum security inmates. There were also times when the inmate role overwhelmed the research role, especially at the beginning of his prison career, because of the intensity of the initial experiences and the fact that the research role was not yet established, and again at the conclusion, when anticipation of the outside world and the continuing prison routine resulted in near-abandonment of the fieldnotes. It was during these times that we relied most heavily on our insider-outsider partnership to keep the research process intact.

References

Adler, P.A., and P. Adler. 1987. "Membership Roles in Field Research." *Qualitative Research Methods, Series 6.* Newbury Park, CA: Sage.

_____. 1989. "The Gloried Self: The Aggrandizement and the Constriction of the Self." *Social Psychology Quarterly* 52: 299-310.

_____. 1991. *Backboards and Blackboards: College Athletes and Role Engulfment.* New York: Columbia University Press.

Akers, R.L., W. Gruninger, and N. Hayner. 1974. "Homosexual and Drug Behavior in Prison: A Test of the Functional and Importation Models of the Inmate System." *Social Problems* 21: 410-422.

_____. 1977. "Time Served, Career Phase and Prisonization: Findings in Five Countries." Pp. 216-226 in *The Sociology of Corrections,* edited by R.G. Leger and J.R. Stratton. New York: John Wiley and Sons.

Allen, F. 1981. *The Decline of the Rehabilitation Ideal.* New Haven, CT: Yale University Press.

Allen, H., and C. Simonsen. 1995. *Corrections in America.* New York: Macmillan.

Anderson, N. 1923. *The Hobo.* Chicago, IL: University of Chicago Press.

Atchley, R.C., and M.P. McCabe. 1968. "Socialization in Correctional Communities: A Replication." *American Sociological Review* 33: 774-785.

Athens, L. 1985. "Character Contests and Violent Criminal Conduct: A Critique." *Sociological Quarterly* 26: 419-431.

Becker, H.S. 1960. "Notes on the Concept of Commitment." *American Journal of Sociology* 66: 32-40.

_____. 1964. "Personal Change in Adult Life." *Sociometry* 27: 40-53.

Berger, P.L. 1963. *Invitation to Sociology: A Humanistic Perspective.* Garden City, NY: Anchor Books/Doubleday.

Berger, P.L., and T. Luckmann. 1966. *The Social Construction of Reality.* Garden City, NY: Doubleday and Company.

Berger, P.L., and H. Kellner. 1981. *Sociology Reinterpreted: An Essay on Method and Vocation.* Garden City, NY: Anchor Books/Doubleday.

Blumer, H. 1928. "Method in Social Psychology." Ph.D. dissertation, University of Chicago.

_____. 1969. *Symbolic Interactionism: Perspective and Method.* Englewood Cliffs, NJ: Prentice-Hall.

_____. 1972. "Action vs. Interaction: Review of Relations in Public by Erving Goffman." *Transaction* 9: 50-53.

Blumstein, A. 1995. "Prisons." Pp. 387-419 in *Crime,* edited by J. Wilson and J. Petersilia. San Francisco, CA: ICS Press.

Bottoms, A., and R. Preston. 1980. *The Coming Penal Crisis: A Criminological and Theological Exploration.* Edinburgh, UK: Scottish Academic Press.

Boulding, K. 1961. *The Image.* Ann Arbor, MI: University of Michigan Press.

Bruyn, S. 1966. *The Human Perspective in Sociology: The Methodology of Participant Observation.* Englewood Cliffs, NJ: Prentice-Hall.

199

Burstein, J. 1977. *Conjugal Visits in Prisons: Psychological and Social Consequences.* Lexington, MA: Lexington Books.

Burton, V., F. Cullen, and L. Travis. 1987. "The Collateral Consequences of a Felony Conviction: A National Study of State Statutes." *Federal Probation* 51: 52-60.

Camp, G., and C. Camp. 1994. *The Corrections Yearbook 1994: Adult Corrections.* South Salem, NY: Criminal Justice Institute.

Cardozo-Freeman, I. 1984. *The Joint: Language and Culture in a Maximum Security Prison.* Springfield, IL: Charles C. Thomas.

Christie, N. 1993. *Crime Control as Industry: Towards Gulags, Western Style?* New York: Routledge.

Clemmer, D. 1958. *The Prison Community.* New York: Holt, Rinehart and Winston.

Cobean, S., and P. Power. 1978. "The Role of the Family in the Rehabilitation of the Offender." *International Journal of Offender Therapy and Comparative Criminology* 22: 29-38.

Cohen, S., and L. Taylor. 1972. *Psychological Survival.* London: Vintage Books.

Collins, R. 1988. *Theoretical Sociology.* San Diego, CA: Harcourt Brace Jovanovich.

Conrad, J. 1981. "Where There's Hope There's Life." Pp. 3-21 in *Justice as Fairness*, edited by D. Fogel and J. Hudson. Cincinnati, OH: C.J. Anderson.

Cooley, C.H. 1909. *Social Organization: A Study of the Larger Mind.* New York: Shocken.

Cordilia, A. 1983. *The Making of an Inmate: Prison as a Way of Life.* Cambridge, MA: Schenkman.

Coser, R. 1966. "Role Distance, Sociological Ambivalence and Traditional Status Systems." *American Journal of Sociology* 72: 173-187.

Cressey, P.G. 1968 [c. 1932]. *The Taxi-Dance Hall: A Sociological Study in Commercialized Recreation and City Life.* New York: Greenwood Press.

Cullen, F., P. Van Voorhis, and J. Sundt. 1996. "Prisons in Crisis: The American Experience." In *Prisons 2000: An International Perspective on the Current State and Future of Imprisonment*, edited by R. Mathews and P. Francis. London: Macmillan.

Currie, E. 1993. *Reckoning: Drugs, the Cities, and the American Future.* New York: Hill and Wang.

Dale, M. 1976. "Barriers to the Rehabilitation of Ex-Offenders." *Crime and Delinquency* 22: 322-337.

Damrell, J. 1977. *Seeking Spiritual Meaning.* Beverly Hills, CA: Sage.

Davidson, T. 1974. *Chicano Prisoners: The Key to San Quentin.* Prospect Heights, IL: Waveland Press.

Davis, F. 1973. "The Martian and the Convert: Ontological Polarities in Social Research." *Urban Life* 2: 333-343.

Deising, P. 1971. *Patterns of Discovery in the Social Sciences.* Chicago, IL: Aldine-Atherton.

Dickey, W. 1989. *From the Bottom Up: Probation and Parole in Milwaukee.* Madison, WI: University of Wisconsin Law School, Continuing Education and Outreach.

DiIulio, J. 1991. *No Escape: The Future of American Corrections.* Scranton, PA: Harper Collins.

Douglas, J.D., P.A. Adler, P. Adler, A. Fontana, C.R. Freeman, and J.A. Kotarba. 1980. *Introduction to the Sociologies of Everyday Life.* Boston: Allyn and Bacon.

Douglas, J.D., and J.M. Johnson. 1977. *Existential Sociology.* Cambridge, UK: Cambridge University Press.

Durham, A. 1994. *Crisis and Reform: Current Issues in American Punishment.* Boston: Little, Brown and Co.

Dyer, J. 1999. *The Perpetual Incarceration Machine: How America Profits From Crime.* Boulder, CO: Westview Press.

Ellis, C. 1991. "Sociological Introspection and Emotional Experience." *Symbolic Interaction* 14: 23-50.

English, K., and M. Mande. 1991. *Community Corrections in Colorado: Why Do Some Clients Succeed and Others Fail?* Denver, CO: Department of Public Safety, Colorado Division of Criminal Justice.

Farkas, M.A. 1992. "The Impact of the Correctional Field Setting on the Research Setting: A Research Chronicle." *Journal of Crime and Justice* 15: 177-184.

Flanagan, T. 1983. "Correlates of Institutional Misconduct Among State Prisoners." *Criminology* 21: 29-39.

Fleisher, M.S. 1989. *Warehousing Violence.* Newbury Park, CA: Sage.

Forer, L. 1994. *A Rage to Punish: The Unintended Consequences of Mandatory Sentencing.* New York: W.W. Norton.

Foucault, M. 1977. *Discipline and Punish: The Birth of the Prison.* New York: Pantheon.

Freilich, M. 1970. *Marginal Natives.* New York: Harper and Row.

Garabedian, P.G. 1963. "Social Roles and Processes of Socialization in the Prison Community." *Social Problems* 11: 139-152.

Garfinkel, H. 1956. "Conditions of Successful Degradation Ceremonies." *American Journal of Sociology* 61: 420-424.

_____. 1967. *Studies in Ethnomethodology.* New York: Free Press.

Garland, D. 1990. *Punishment and Modern Society: A Study in Social Theory.* Chicago, IL: University of Chicago Press.

Gergen, K. 1991. *The Saturated Self: Dilemmas of Identity in Contemporary Life.* New York: Basic Books.

Giallombardo, R. 1966. *Society of Women: A Study of a Women's Prison.* New York: John Wiley and Sons.

Gibson, M.A. 1988. *Accommodation Without Assimilation: Sikh Immigrants in an American High School.* Ithaca, NY: Cornell University Press.

Gillard, D., and A. Beck. 1994. "Prisoners in 1993." *Bureau of Justice Statistics Bulletin.* U.S. Department of Justice (June) II: Washington DC: GPO.

Glaser, B.G., and A.L. Strauss. 1964. "Awareness Contexts and Social Interaction." *American Sociological Review* 29: 269-279.

Glaser, D. 1969. *The Effectiveness of a Prison and Parole System.* New York: Bobbs-Merrill.

Goffman, E. 1959. *The Presentation of Self in Everyday Life.* Garden City, NY: Anchor Books/ Doubleday.

_____. 1961. *Asylums: Essays on the Social Situation of Mental Patients and Other Inmates.* Garden City, NY: Doubleday/Anchor Books.

_____. 1963. *Stigma: Notes on the Management of Spoiled Identity.* Englewood Cliffs, NJ: Prentice-Hall.

_____. 1967. *Interaction Ritual: Essays on Face-to-Face Behavior.* Garden City, NY: Anchor Books.

Gold, R. 1958. Roles in Sociological Field Observations. *Social Forces* 36: 217-223.

Goodstein, L., D.L. MacKenzie, and R.L. Shotland. 1984. "Personal Control and Inmate Adjustment to Prison." *Criminology* 22: 343-369.

Goodstein, L., and J. Hepburn. 1985. *Determinate Sentencing and Imprisonment.* Cincinnati, OH: C.J. Anderson.

Goodstein, L., and K. Wright. 1989. "Inmate Adjustment to Prison." Pp. 229-251 in *The American Prison: Issues in Research and Policy*, edited by L. Goodstein and D. Mackenzie. New York: Plennum.

Gordon, D. 1994. *The Return of the Dangerous Classes: Drug Prohibition and Policy Politics.* New York: W.W. Norton.

Gottfredson, S. 1995. "Fighting Crime at the Expense of College." *Chronicle of Higher Education* (January 20): B1-B2.

Grogger, J. 1989. *Employment and Crime*. Sacramento, CA: Bureau of Criminal Statistics and Special Services.

Gubrium, J.F., and J.A. Holstein. 1994. "Grounding the Postmodern Self." *Sociological Quarterly* 35: 685-703.

Gubrium, J., J. Holstein, and D. Buckholdt. 1994. *Constructing the Life Course*. Dix Hills, NY: General Hall Inc.

Guiot, J. 1977. "Attribution and Identity Construction: Some Comments." *American Sociological Review* 42: 692-704.

Hadden, S.C., and M. Lester. 1978. "Talking Identity: The Production of `Self' in Interaction." *Human Studies* 1: 331-356.

Hammersley, M., and P. Atkinson. 1983. *Ethnography: Principles in Practice*. New York: Tavistock.

Hawkins, G. 1976. *The Prison*. Chicago, IL: University of Chicago Press.

Hayano, D. 1979. "Auto-Ethnography: Paradigms, Problems, and Prospects." *Human Organization* 38: 99-104.

Hayano, D. 1982. *Poker Faces: The Life and Work of Professional Card Players*. Berkeley, CA: University of California Press.

Hayner, N.S., and E. Ash. 1939. "The Prison as Community." *American Sociological Review* 5: 577-583.

Heffernan, E. 1972. *Making It in Prison: The Square, the Cool and the Life*. New York: Wiley-Interscience.

Holt, N., and D. Miller. 1972. *Explorations in Inmate-Family Relationships*. Report 46. Sacramento, CA: California Department of Corrections.

Homer, E. 1979. "Inmate-Family Ties: Desirable But Difficult." *Federal Probation* (March): 47-52.

Hughes, C.E. 1961. "Introduction: The Place of Field Work in the Social Sciences." Pp. v-vix in Fieldwork: An Introduction to the Social Sciences, eEdited by B.H. Junker. Chicago, IL: University of Chicago Press.

———. 1971. *The Sociological Eye*. Chicago, IL: Aldine.

Irwin, J. 1970. *The Felon*. Englewood Cliffs, NJ: Prentice-Hall.

———. 1977. *Scenes*. Beverly Hills, CA.: Sage.

———. 1980. *Prisons in Turmoil*. Boston: Little Brown and Company.

———. 1987. "Reflections on Ethnography." *Journal of Contemporary Ethnography* 16: 41-48.

Irwin, J., and. J. Austin. 1997. *It's About Time: Solving America's Prison Crowding Crisis*. Belmont, CA: Wadsworth.

Irwin, J., and D.R. Cressey. 1962. "Thieves, Convicts and the Inmate Culture." *Social Problems* 10: 142-155.

Jackson, J. 1990. "Deja Entendu: The Liminal Qualities of Anthropological Fieldnotes." *Journal of Contemporary Ethnography* 19: 8-43.

Jacobs, J.B. 1977. *Stateville: The Penitentiary in Mass Society*. Chicago, IL: University of Chicago Press.

Johnson, R. 1987. *Hard Time: Understanding and Reforming the Prison*. Monterey, CA: Brooks/Cole.

Jones, R.S. 1995. "Uncovering the Hidden Social World: Insider Research in Prison." *Journal of Contemporary Criminal Justice* 11: 106-118.

Jones, R.S., and T.J. Schmid. 1989. "Inmates' Conceptions of Prison Sexual Assault." *The Prison Journal* 76: 53-61.

Kalinich, D. 1986. *Power, Stability and Contraband: The Inmate Economy*. Prospect Heights, IL: Waveland Press.

Kortoba, J.A. 1983. *Chronic Pain*. Newbury Park, CA: Sage.

Krieger, S. 1985. "Beyond Subjectivity: The Use of the Self in Social Science." *Qualitative Sociology* 8: 309-324.

Langan, P., C. Perkins, and J. Chaiken. 1994. "Felony Sentences in the U.S., 1990." *Bureau of Justice Statistics Bulletin* (September). Washington, DC: Government Printing Office, September.

Lash, S., and J. Friedman. 1992. *Modernity and Identity.* Oxford, UK: Blackwell.

Lasch, C. 1979. *The Culture of Narcissism: American Life in an Age of Diminishing Expectations.* New York: Norton.

_____. 1984. *The Minimal Self: Psychic Survival in Troubled Times.* New York: Norton.

Lemert, E. 1967. "Role Enactment, Self, and Identity in the Systematic Check Forger." Pp. 119-134 in *Human Deviance, Social Problems and Social Control.* Englewood Cliffs, NJ: Prentice-Hall.

Lenihan, K. 1975. "The Financial Condition of Released Prisoners." *Crime and Delinquency* 21: 226-281.

Lewis, D.J. 1979. "A Social Behaviorist Interpretation of the Median I." *American Journal of Sociology* 84: 261-287.

Lockwood, D. 1980. *Prison Sexual Violence.* New York: Elsevier.

Lofland, J. 1976. *Doing Social Life.* New York: John Wiley.

Lofland, J., and L.H. Lofland. 1995. *Analyzing Social Settings: A Guide to Qualitatice Observation and Analysis.* Belmont, CA: Wadsworth Publishing.

Lyotard, J.F. 1984. *The Postmodern Condition: A Report on Knowledge.* Minneapolis, MN: University of Minnesota Press.

Majors, R., and J.M. Billson. 1992. *Cool Pose: The Dilemmas of Black Manhood in America.* New York: Touchstone Books.

Marquart, J.W. 1986. "Doing Research in Prison: The Strengths and Weaknesses of Full Participation as a Guard." *Justice Quarterly* 3: 15-32.

Mauer, M. 1994. *Americans Behind Bars: The International Use of Incarceration.* Washington, DC: The Sentencing Project.

McCorkel, J. 1998. "Going to the Crackhouse: Critical Space as a Form of Resistance in Total Institutions and Everyday Life." *Symbolic Interaction* 21: 227-252.

Mead, G.H. 1934. *Mind, Self, and Society.* Chicago, IL: University of Chicago Press.

Mehan, J., and H. Wood. 1975. *The Reality of Ethnomethodology.* New York: John Wiley and Sons.

Meisenhelder, T. 1985. "An Essay on Time and the Phenomenology of Imprisonment." *Deviant Behavior* 6: 39-56.

Merton, R.K., and E. Barber. 1976. "Sociological Ambivalence." Pp. 3-31 *Sociological Ambivalence and Other Essays,* edited by R.K. Merton. New York: The Free Press.

Messinger, S.E., H. Sampson, and R.D. Towne. 1962. "Life as Theater: Some Notes on the Dramaturgic Approach to Social Reality." *Sociometry* 25: 98-111.

Morawska, E. 1987. "Sociological Ambivalence: Peasant Immigrant Workers in America, 1880s-1930s." *Qualitative Sociology* 10: 225-250.

Nacci, P., and T. Kane. 1983. "The Incidence of Sex and Sexual Aggression in Federal Prisons." *Federal Probation* 47: 31-36.

Parisi, N. 1982. *Coping With Imprisonment.* Beverly Hills, CA: Sage.

Parker, E., and C. Lanier. 1997. "An Exploration of Self-Concepts among Incarcerated Fathers." Pp. 335-337 in *Correctional Contexts: Contemporary and Classical Readings,* edited by J. Marquardt and J. Sorenson. Los Angeles, CA: Roxbury.

Paulus, P. 1988. *Prison Crowding: A Psychological Perspective.* New York: Springer-Verlag.

Peak, K. 1985. "Correctional Research in Theory and Praxis: Political and Operational Hindrances." *Criminal Justice Review* 10: 21-31.

Pownell, G. 1969. *Employment Problems of Released Offenders.* Washington, DC: U.S. Department of Labor Report.

Prus, R. 1996. *Symbolic Interaction and Ethnographic Research: Intersubjectivity and the Study of Human Lived Experience.* New York: State University of New York Press.

Prus, R., and C.R.D. Sharper. 1977. *Road Hustler: The Career Contingencies of Professional Card and Dice Hustlers.* Lexington, MA: Lexington Books.

Richards, S.C., and R.S. Jones. 1997. "Perceptual Incarceration Machine: Structural Impediments to Post-Release Success." *Journal of Contemporary Criminal Justice* 13: 4-22.

Rieman, J. 1998. *The Rich Get Richer and the Poor Get Prison.* Boston: Allyn and Bacon.

Risman, B.J. 1982. "(Mis)Acquisition of Gender Identity Among Transexuals." *Qualitative Sociology* 5: 312-325.

Room, R. 1976. "Ambivalence as a Sociological Explanation: The Case of Cultural Explanations of Alcohol Problems." *American Sociological Review* 41: 1047-1065.

SanGiovanni, L.F. 1978. *Ex-Nuns: A Study of Emergent Role Passage.* Norwood, NJ: Ablex.

Sawyer, F., J. Reed, and D. Nelson. 1977. *Prison Homicide.* New York: Spectrum.

Schafer, N. 1978. "Prison Visiting: A Background for Change." *Federal Probation* 42: 47-50.

Schechner, R. 1985. *Between Theater and Anthropology.* Philadelphia, PA: University of Pennsylvania Press.

Scheff, T. 1970. "On the Concepts of Identity and Social Relationships." Pp. 193-207 in *Human Nature and Collective Behavior,* edited by T. Shibutani. Englewood Cliffs, NJ: Prentice Hall.

Schmid, T.J., and R.S. Jones. 1990. "Experiential Orientations to the Prison Experience: The Case of First-time, Short-term Inmates." *Perspectives on Social Problems* 2: 189-210.

_____. 1991. "Suspended Identity Dialectic: Identity Transformation in a Maximum Security Prison." *Symbolic Interaction* 14: 415-432.

_____. 1993. "Ambivalent Actions: Prison Adaptation Strategies of First-time, Short-term Inmates." *Journal of Contemporary Ethnography* 21: 439-463.

_____. 1999. "Personal Adaptations to Cultural Change: International Students' Responses to Cultural and Interactional Challenges." *Perspectives on Social Problems* 11: 317-342.

Schutz, A. 1962. *Collected Papers II: The Problem of Social Reality.* The Hague: Martinus Nijhoff.

_____. 1967. *The Phenomenology of the Social World.* Evanston, IL: Northwestern Univesity Press.

Schwartz, B. 1971. "Pre-institutional vs. Situational Influences in a Correctional Community." *Journal of Criminal Law, Criminology, and Police Science* 62: 532-542.

Schwartz, H., and J. Jacobs. 1979. *Qualitative Sociology.* New York: Free Press.

Seymour, J. 1977. "Niches in Prison." Pp. 179-205 in *Living in Prison: The Ecology of Survival,* edited by H. Toch. New York: Free Press.

Shibutani, T. 1955. "Reference Groups as Perspectives." *American Journal of Sociology* 60: 522-529.

Shokeid, M. 1988. *Children of Circumstances: Israeli Emigrants in New York.* Ithica, NY: Cornell University Press.

Silberman, M. 1995. *A World of Violence: Corrections in America.* Belmont, CA: Wadsworth Publishing.

Skolnick, J. 1994. "Wild Pitch: Three Strikes, You're Out and other Bad Calls on Crime." *American Prospect* 18: 30-37.

Smith, R. 1984. "Reported Ex-Offender Employment in American Adult Corrections." *Journal of Offender Counseling, Services and Rehabilitation* 8: 5-13.

Solomon, D.N. 1970. "Role and Self-Conception: Adaptation and Change in Occupations." Pp. 286-300 in *Human Nature and Collective Behavior,* edited by T. Shibutani. Englewood Cliffs, NJ: Prentice Hall.

Stone, G.P. 1962. "Appearance and the Self." Pp. 86-118 in *Human Behavior and Social Processes*, edited by A. Rose. Boston: Houghton Mifflin.

Strauss, A.L. 1959. *Mirrors and Masks: The Search for Identity*. Glencoe, IL: Free Press.

_____. 1978. *Negotiations: Varieties, Contexts, Processes and Social Order*. San Francisco, CA: Jossey-Bass.

Sykes, G. 1958. *The Society of Captives: A Study of a Maximum Security Prison*. Princeton, NJ: Princeton University Press.

Sykes, G., and D. Matza. 1957. "Techniques of Neutralization: A Theory of Delinquency." *American Sociological Review* 22: 664- 670.

Sykes, G., and S. Messinger. 1960. "Inmate Social System." Pp. 5-19 in Theoretical Studies in Social Organization of the Prison, eEdited by R.A. Cloward, D.R. Cressey, G.H. Grosser, R. McCleery, L.E. Ohlin, G.M. Sykes, and S.L. Messinger. New York: Social Science Research Council.

Taylor, J.M., and R. Tewksbury. 1995. "From the Inside Out and Outside In: Team Research in the Correctional Setting." *Journal of Contemporary Criminal Justice* 11: 119-136.

Thomas, C.C. 1975. "Prisonization or Resocialization? A Study of External Factors Associated with the Impact of Imprisonment." *Journal of Research in Crime and Delinquency* 10: 13-21.

Thomas, C.W., and S. Foster. 1973. "The Importation Model Perspective on Inmate Social Order." *Sociological Quarterly* 16: 226-34.

Thomas, C.W. 1977. "Theoretical Perspectives on Prisonization: A Comparison of the Importation and Deprivation Models." *Journal of Criminal Law and Criminology* 68: 135-145.

Thomas, J. 1999. "Communicating Punishment: Cultural Meaning in Dreadful Enclaves." Unpublished manuscript, Department of Sociology, Northern Illinois University, DeKalb, IL.

Thomas, W.I. 1931. *The Unadjusted Girl*. Boston: Little, Brown and Co.

Tittle, C. 1969. "Inmate Organization: Sex Differentiation and the Influence of Criminal Subcultures." *American Sociological Review* 34: 492-505.

Tittle, C.R., and D.P. Tittle. 1964. "Social Organization of Prisoners: An Empirical Test." *Social Forces* 43: 216-221.

Toch, H. 1977. *Living in Prison: The Ecology of Survival*. New York: Free Press.

_____. 1982. "Studying and Reducing Stress." Pp. 25-44 in *The Pains of Imprisonment*, edited by R. Johnson and H. Toch. Beverly Hills, CA: Sage.

Tropin, L. 1977. Testimony before the U.S. House Judiciary Subcommittee on Crime, September 27. Washington, DC.

Turner, R.H. 1978. "The Role and the Person." *American Journal of Sociology* 84: 1-23.

Turner, V. 1977. *The Ritual Process: Structure and Anti- Structure*. Ithaca, NY: Cornell University Press.

Ungar, S. 1984. "Self-Mockery: An Alternative Form of Self- Presentation." *Symbolic Interaction* 7: 121-133.

Unnithan, P. 1986. "Research in a Correctional Setting: Constraints and Biases." *Journal of Criminal Justice* 14: 401-412.

Unruh, D. 1980. "The Nature of Social Worlds." *Pacific Sociological Review* 23: 271-296.

Walker, N. 1983. "Side-effects of Incarceration." *British Journal of Criminology* 23: 61-71.

Warren, C.A. 1980. "Destigmatization of Identity: From Deviance to Charismatic." *Qualitative Sociology* 3: 59-72.

Warren, C.A., and B. Ponse. 1977. "The Existential Self in the Gay World." Pp. 273-289 in *Existential Sociology*, edited by J.D. Douglas and J.M. Johnson. Cambridge, UK: Cambridge University Press.

Weigert, A.J. 1986. "The Social Production of Identity: Metatheoretical Foundations." *Sociological Quarterly* 27: 165-183.

Welch, R. 1990. "Private Prison–Profitable and Growing." *Corrections Compendium* 15: 1, 5-8, 16.

Wellford, C. 1967. "Factors Associated With Adoption of the Inmate Code." *Journal of Criminal Law, Criminology and Police Science* 58: 197-203.

Wheeler, S. 1961. "Socialization in Correctional Communities." *American Sociological Review* 26: 697-712.

Wieder, D.L. 1988. *Language and Social Reality.* Lanham, MD: University Press of America.

Williams, V., and M. Fish. 1974. *Convicts, Codes, and Contraband.* Cambridge, MA: Ballinger Publishing.

Wormith, S. 1984. "The Controversy over the Effects of Long-term Incarceration." *Canadian Journal of Criminology* 26: 423-435.

Zamble, E., and F. Porporino. 1988. *Coping, Behavior and Adaptation in Prison Inmates.* New York: Springer-Verlag.

Zerubavel, E. 1991. *The Fine Line: Making Distinctions in Everyday Life.* New York: Free Press.

_____. 1997. *Social Mindscapes: An Invitation to Cognitive Sociology.* Cambridge, MA: Harvard University Press.

Zimbardo, P. 1994. *Transforming California's Prisons into Expensive Old Age Homes For Felons: Enormous Hidden Costs and Consequences for California Taxpayers.* San Francisco, CA: Center on Juvenile and Criminal Justice, November.

Zimmerman, D., and D.L. Wieder. 1977. "The Diary: Diary-Interview Method." *Urban Life* 5: 479-498.

Zimring, F., and G. Hawkins. 1995. *Incapacitation: Penal Confinement and the Restraint of Crime.* New York: Oxford.

_____. 1991. *The Scale of Imprisonment.* Chicago, IL: University of Chicago Press.

Zola, I.C. 1982. *Missing Pieces: A Chronicle of Living With a Disability.* Philadelphia, PA: Temple University Press.

Zorbaugh, H.W. 1983 [c. 1976]. *The Gold Coast and the Slum: A Sociological Study of Chicago's Near North Side.* Chicago, IL: University of Chicago Press.

Zurcher, L.A. 1977. *The Mutable Self.* Beverly Hills, CA: Sage.

Zwerman, G., and G. Gardner. 1986. "Obstacles to Research in a State Prison." *Qualitative Sociology* 9: 293-300.

Index